THE MANY DEATHS OF MARY DOBIE

THE MANY DEATHS OF MARY DOBIE

**MURDER, POLITICS AND REVENGE
IN NINETEENTH-CENTURY NEW ZEALAND**

DAVID HASTINGS

AUCKLAND
UNIVERSITY
PRESS

First published 2015

Auckland University Press
University of Auckland
Private Bag 92019
Auckland 1142
New Zealand
www.press.auckland.ac.nz

© David Hastings, 2015

ISBN 978 1 86940 837 4

Publication is kindly assisted by

A catalogue record for this book is available from
the National Library of New Zealand

This book is copyright. Apart from fair dealing for the purpose
of private study, research, criticism or review, as permitted under
the Copyright Act, no part may be reproduced by any process
without prior permission of the publisher. The moral rights of
the author have been asserted.

Cover photograph: Mary Dobie in 1879. *Family album*
Cover design: Kalee Jackson

Printed in China by 1010 Printing International Ltd

CONTENTS

1. TOMB WITH NO EPITAPH — 1
2. DAUGHTERS OF EMPIRE — 8
3. THE GRAND TOUR — 24
4. ON MEASURED GROUND — 44
5. THE FATAL DAY — 63
6. BREAKING NEWS — 79
7. THE MANY DEATHS — 95
8. SON OF A DIVIDED WORLD — 112
9. THE LAST BURNING QUESTION — 127
10. MAY GOD HAVE MERCY ON YOUR SOUL — 146
11. FOOD FOR THE BIRDS OF HEAVEN — 158
12. POLITICS AND REVENGE — 167
13. IN MEMORIAM — 181

NOTES — 193
BIBLIOGRAPHY — 214
ACKNOWLEDGEMENTS — 221
INDEX — 223

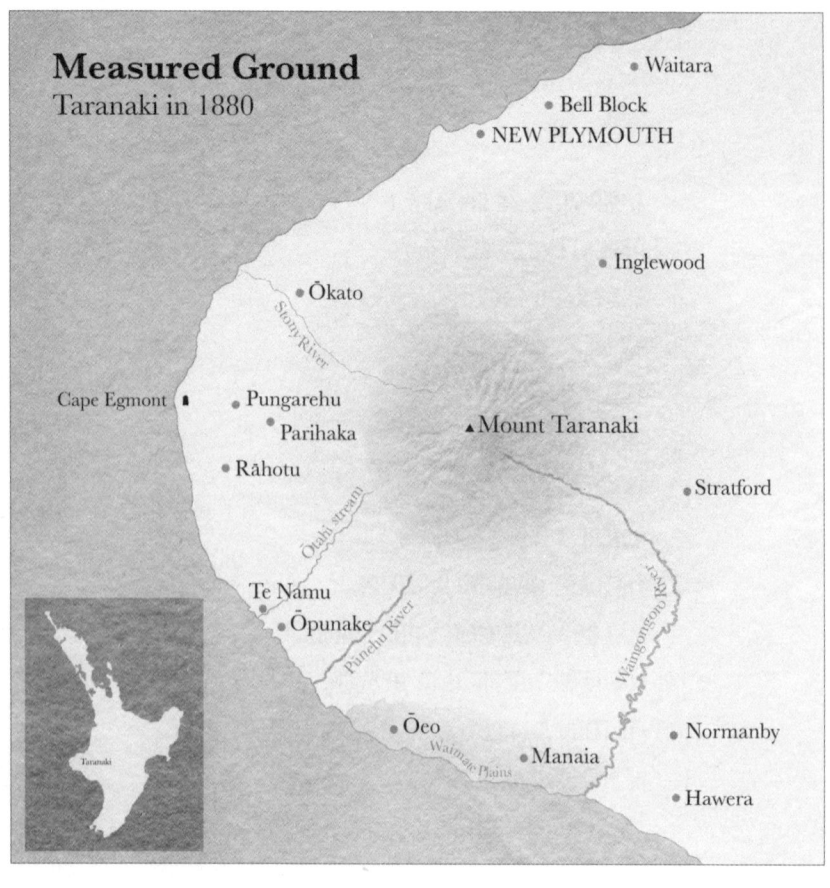

Measured ground: Lands in Taranaki were confiscated after the wars of the early 1860s. By the late 1870s the surveyors were moving in to prepare the land south of the Stony River for sale. MICAELA LOWIS

1.

TOMB WITH NO EPITAPH

After lunch on the last day of her life Mary Dobie went for a walk along the road leading north from the small settlement of Ōpunake on the Taranaki coast. It was late spring in 1880 and she was staying at the well-fortified redoubt in the town with her sister Bertha, the wife of an Armed Constabulary officer. Mary, who was an accomplished artist, stopped briefly to buy a pencil, apparently intending to do some sketching near Te Namu Pā about 2 kilometres away. She was more than just a dabbler; examples of her work from New Zealand and the Pacific Islands appeared in the London *Graphic* magazine, renowned for the quality of its illustrations.[1] To the west of Te Namu were spectacular views of the ocean and, on a clear day, the landward aspect was dominated by the majestic mountain that the Māori called Taranaki and the Pākehā Egmont. It was an ideal place for an artist, said the local paper, 'one of the most beautiful spots in the district, and of an evening, and when the sun is setting, the scene is a most magnificent one'.[2] Mary was making the most of these natural splendours because she was about to return to England with her mother after three years living and travelling in New Zealand and the South Pacific.

The road she walked that day was as rich in history as the scenery was beautiful. One of the best tales told on the coast was about a local chief, Wiremu Kingi Matakātea, who had won fame at Te Namu Pā in 1833 when he led 150 Taranaki defenders as they fought off an attack by a superior force of 800 from the Waikato during the musket wars.[3] Then, in 1834, the pā was put to the torch by British troops trying to rescue Betty Guard, an Englishwoman who had been held by the Taranaki and Ngāti Ruanui tribes since her ship, the *Harriet*, had been wrecked five months previously.[4] Thirty years later Matakātea and Eruети – who was known as the famous prophet Te Whiti-o-Rongomai by the time of Mary's visit – helped to rescue and protect the survivors of another shipwreck, the *Lord Worsley*. The 600-tonne steamer with 60 people on board hit rocks and sank in the bay beneath the famous pā.[5]

Despite the beauty of the landscape there were signs of desolation everywhere. As Mary walked along the road she passed the ruins of an old flax mill which had thrived briefly ten years before. And the dwellings at Matakātea's settlement were now deserted, a reminder that she was on contested ground claimed by the first inhabitants and the new settlers.

The coast was frequently stormy but on the last day of Mary's life there was a gentle southwesterly breeze, with mostly clear skies and a flat sea. She gathered a bunch of flowers as she went and the last people to see her alive, other than her killer, recalled a young woman in a blue dress, wearing a hat and making her way along the road accompanied by a spaniel and a retriever.[6] The dogs belonged to her brother-in-law, Major Forster Goring, who was stationed in Taranaki on account of tensions over the disputed land. The great walls of the redoubt – perched, like Te Namu Pā, on a clifftop overlooking a bay – testified to fears that those tensions might explode into deadly violence. But Mary had never allowed conventions or stuffy Victorian customs to inhibit her and she wasn't about to be corralled behind high, defensive walls on account of some fear that might be more imagined than real. In the few weeks of her visit, she had freely walked around the countryside sketching and chatting to people from all walks of life: Māori and Pākehā, soldiers and civilians.

Her plan on that springtime day was to be back at the redoubt in time for a game of tennis with Bertha. But the sisters never did play. The appointed time came and went with no sign of Mary. At first Bertha was not too worried. She thought her sister must have lost her way in the dense flax that covered the land between the road and the sea or, perhaps, had slipped on the rocks near the beach and sprained an ankle.[7] Three Armed Constabulary (AC) men went to look for her in the late afternoon. By the time darkness was falling and there was still no sign of Mary, the search party was expanded to include every available man. They called out to her, lit fires along the coast and, with flaming torches held high, retraced her footsteps along the road.

After a few hours one of the searchers found Mary's body lying in dense flax about fifteen paces from the road near a cluster of stones. Forster, as the senior officer in the redoubt, was summoned to view the horrifying scene by torchlight.

He described his sister-in-law lying partly on her left side under a flax bush with one arm across her throat as if to guard against a blow. Her face was covered in blood and her throat was cut so deeply that her head was almost severed.[8]

Everyone in small-town Ōpunake heard the news that night and by the following afternoon, when the evening papers came out, the rest of New Zealand knew about it too. The tone of the coverage was set by the headlines: 'Dreadful murder at Opunake', said the *Taranaki Herald*, 'Shocking outrage', was how the *Evening Post* in Wellington put it and other papers called the murder 'horrible', 'diabolical' and 'brutal'.

As with all big, breaking news stories journalists hastened to gather and publish as much information as they could. In the rush, it was disorganised with many papers running two, three or even four versions of the story simultaneously.

Readers were confronted with a mass of information, much of it contradictory. For instance, there was no certainty about the time the body was found. Some said 9.30 p.m., others 10.30. The scene of the crime was another source of confusion. Some said the body was 100 yards from the road, others 40. The *Evening Post* was even more confused. It said the crime had been committed south of Ōpunake when every other paper except the Auckland *Star* reported correctly that Te Namu was to the north.[9] The *Star* had it both ways, in one story saying north and in another saying south.[10] And how old was Mary? One paper said 22 and another 26. Her correct age was 29; she was just a few weeks from her thirtieth birthday.

But if getting the basic facts right was a difficult task on that first day, it was as nothing compared to the deeper questions: who had committed this atrocious crime and why? A number of answers were to be given in the coming days and Mary was to have many deaths in print and in the popular imagination as people struggled to explain and understand what had happened. Many Pākehā feared it was an act of political terrorism in response to the state's determination to take the land of the tribes in the region. Conversely, many Māori thought it would be the cue for the state to use force against them. Rape was another motive that was reported with the certainty of fact even before the results of the post-mortem examination were known. Or was it robbery or maybe just the inexplicable act of an uncivilised savage? Then again, it might have been simply a crime of drunkenness. And who had done the deed? A gang was to blame, said one theory. Someone acting alone said another. A Pākehā was the killer, but no, maybe it was a Māori. One school of thought even blamed Mary because she had put herself in harm's way by strolling unescorted along a lonely road.

Mary was buried in the AC cemetery outside the redoubt, which is the last resting place of about fourteen people from the old days. No one knows the exact number because the graves of between six and ten Irishmen who served with the AC are unmarked.[11] Of the four marked graves, Mary's stands out because of an elegant tombstone dedicated to her memory by the soldiers of the constabulary. It was fashioned from a gleaming block of white marble and surmounted by a cross decorated with a wreath of thorns. At nearly 3 metres tall it was far grander than the other three modest gravestones in the little cemetery and a wrought-iron fence was built around it as an extra barrier to protect her memory. But the grave marker carries no moving epitaph to give a sense of who Mary was or why her life was memorialised in such an emphatic way. The two inscriptions on the tomb are confined to basic information. The main one merely gives the span of her days and the names of her parents; her father had been a major in the Madras Army and her mother's name was Ellen. The secondary one says it was the non-commissioned officers and men of the AC who erected the gravestone.

It is puzzling that the men who went to such lengths to commemorate Mary's life could not think of something more to say. It may be that they were simple, pragmatic people not given to expressing deep emotions or ideas and so confined themselves to the safety of specific facts and details. But soldiers frequently wrote or selected epitaphs to put on the graves of comrades who had fallen in battle.[12] A number were to be seen at the Mission Cemetery in Tauranga when the Dobie sisters visited there in the autumn of 1879. 'A man greatly esteemed and deeply regretted by his comrades', read the inscription on the tomb of a soldier killed at Te Ranga in June 1864. 'Time like an ever rolling stream, bears all its sons away', reads another, marking the last resting place of a man who fell at the battle of Gate Pā in March of that same year. Yet another was distinguished for the black humour in its message to the living: 'As you are now, so once was I. As I am now, so you must be. Prepare for death and follow me.'

Of these three epitaphs only the first is original. The second is a quotation from the hymn 'O God our help in ages past' and the third is a standard inscription that can be traced back to a headstone in Ayrshire, Scotland, and perhaps beyond.[13] Even though they are not original, the quotations were most probably chosen to somehow reflect the personalities of the men buried beneath the ground. Yet when it came to Mary words failed the soldiers. They could think of nothing to say, not even an apt quotation. Perhaps it was because her death was so far outside their experience and expectations. They understood that a man would be killed in battle but the brutal murder of a woman was something else. Instead of poetry and fine words, the symbolism of the tombstone left a message to posterity: the wreath of thorns spoke of great suffering and the prominence of the memorial was a reminder of how deeply her death had affected the community.

But memorials are not just inscribed in stone. People leave traces of their thoughts and existence in all sorts of places: letters, diaries, newspapers, official documents, court records, sketches and photographs. Some of these are deliberate and considered, sometimes they are preserved accidentally. Often they are filtered through the eyes of other people and reshaped or distorted by the prejudices and ideas of those who report them and pass them down through the generations. Sometimes they provide evidence of things that their authors did not intend to say. From a multitude of fragments and sources like these Mary Dobie's story emerges. Reports of the murder and the many versions of her death played out across a troubled political and social landscape and the effects lingered long after the story had faded from the headlines.

2.

DAUGHTERS OF EMPIRE

Mary Dobie came to New Zealand as a first-class passenger on the *May Queen* in 1877 with her mother Ellen and older sister Bertha. Nine days into the voyage, when the ship was near Madeira in the Atlantic Ocean, she did something that captured the essence of her character. It was the calmest night since leaving London and the moon appeared for the first time, a bright waxing crescent rising ahead of the ship above the dark ocean. As it was obscured by the sails Mary went to the forecastle to get an uninterrupted view of the glorious sight. To landlubbers this may seem a natural and unremarkable thing to do but the forecastle was the crew's area and passengers were not supposed to cross the boundary that separated them from the men who worked the ship. This was written in the regulations but, more importantly, it was a rule enforced by the crew themselves who jealously guarded their rights and would happily disabuse or even humiliate anyone who thought they could go where they pleased – especially those from first class or women intruding uninvited into a masculine space.[1] Interlopers were usually thrown out or required to pay a fine in alcohol or cash.

Although Mary should have been doubly excluded she was allowed to stay. 'I found myself surrounded by sailors who clamoured for my foot – a big Irishman got it and chalked the X (a little custom gone through when a Passenger goes into the forecastle for the first time),' she wrote in the diary of the voyage she kept with her sister.[2] The intrusion cost her nothing other than the chalk mark and after the initiation ceremony the sailors joined her to admire the view even though, for them, it must have been commonplace. 'It was most lovely,' Mary wrote, describing the reflection of the moonlight on the water as being like a pathway leading the ship onwards.

That Mary was able to turn what might have been an embarrassing episode into an enjoyable celebration of nature with the most unlikely company shows a combination of self-confidence, good humour and a lively disregard for written rules and unwritten conventions. Those who knew her well thought courage was the quality that best defined her. The *Graphic* magazine said she had an enterprising disposition and was entirely without fear. 'She was a bold rider, an expert skater and lawn tennis player – in short she was proficient in all the athletic amusements in which modern young ladies delight.'[3] The About Town columnist for the Auckland *Observer* said she was clever, intellectual, highly educated and, above all, unconventional. Anything that a woman could do, she did and did well. 'It is of women like her that the heroines of history are made,' said the columnist. 'Fear had no place in her composition, in fact the poor girl was daring and courageous to a fault.'[4]

The unconventional Mary did not fit the Victorian ideal of middle-class womanhood as gentle, nurturing, innately weaker than men and in need of protection.[5] But she was by no means unique in her own family, which was notable for its strong, independent-minded women. On the night of Mary's adventure in the forecastle, Bertha tackled the problem of the obscured moon at the other end of the ship's hierarchy; she approached the captain and asked him to change course so everyone could share the view. He did her bidding. 'Lovely old man,' Bertha remarked, having got her way. 'I am not a shy person,' she said in her unpublished memoirs written nearly 30 years later. 'I am always far too much interested in what is going on . . . shyness is only a virulent form of self-consciousness.'[6]

The sisters took after their mother Ellen who, on another voyage years before, famously dealt with a drunken captain by decanting all his liquor into the sea.[7] They owed their self-confidence partly to their upbringing and the example of their strong mother but their social ease was greatly reinforced by their secure place in the world. The British Empire was at its zenith and the Dobie sisters came from an imperial family which was well connected to the political and literary establishment in England. Empire building was the family's stock in trade. Their father was a major in the Madras Army, and their paternal grandfather had been a naval officer who fought the French and pirates in the Indian Ocean for eighteen years before retiring to Essex.[8]

On their mother's side Mary and Bertha came from an even more distinguished naval lineage. Their maternal great-grandfather was Commodore William Locker. When he commanded the *Lowestoffe* in the late eighteenth century his second lieutenant was a youth of just eighteen called Horatio Nelson. Locker and Nelson, who would go on to win fame as the hero of the Battle of Trafalgar, remained friends for life.[9] The Dobies' grandfather Edward Hawke Locker was also with the navy but as civil secretary to the fleet in the Mediterranean during the Napoleonic Wars.[10] It was in this capacity that he was given the job of taking the ceasefire documents to the island of Elba where Napoleon had just gone into exile. After the formalities they chatted for a while and Napoleon explained that he had real trouble with the English language; although he could read it well enough he found it difficult to follow when spoken. 'When you speak to each other I am soon bewildered,' he said, 'your words are all confusion and discord to my ear.' He shook his head and said, *'Ma foi, c'est une langue barbare.'*[11]

When Mary and Bertha were growing up, the family was more noted for its literary and political connections. One of their uncles, Arthur Locker, was a well-travelled man who had been to Australia for the gold rushes, then became a novelist and finally editor of the *Graphic*, a weekly news and cultural magazine published in London.[12] It had a social reform agenda at the same time as it gave great prominence to imperial affairs and royal occasions. The magazine also serialised fiction, most famously Thomas Hardy's *Tess of the d'Urbervilles*. But the *Graphic* was best known for its illustrations which were renowned as being of a very high artistic standard, and many of the top illustrators and artists in nineteenth-century Britain had their work published in its pages. Mary was in good company when Uncle Arthur reproduced some of her sketches from New Zealand and the South Pacific.

Their other uncle was a poet. Frederick Locker – who took the maiden name of his second wife to become Frederick Locker-Lampson – was close friends with the poet laureate Alfred Lord Tennyson, and their families were linked when his daughter Eleanor married Tennyson's son Lionel.[13] Bertha recalled Uncle Frederick taking her to meet Tennyson and hear him read one of his poems, 'Gareth and Lynette', before it was published. They talked about an allusion in the poem to the Written Stone of Gelt, a landmark near the village of Irthington in Cumberland where the Dobies lived. They met again when the Dobies were among the nine bridesmaids at the Locker-Lampson wedding and the great man mused on writing a poem about them, but he never did.[14]

 In old age Bertha liked to remind people of how well connected the family was. 'Tennyson was a great pal of mine,' she said shortly before she died in the 1930s, and commented on his sense of humour. 'I found Tennyson very kind – the dear old man.' She also mentioned the poet Robert Browning. And her family was connected politically as well. 'I used to go a great deal to the House of Commons and often saw Disraeli and Gladstone. I met Disraeli at dinner when I was only a girl.'[15]

Bertha and Mary may have defied oppressive Victorian social conventions but they did not question their heritage which was bound up with the fine words of poets as well as the heroics of their military ancestors. To the end of her life Bertha remained an ardent royalist and imperialist and was fond of quoting Tennyson's poem 'To the Queen', written in 1851 just after he was made poet laureate: 'May children of our children say, "She wrought the people lasting good".'[16] And when the South African war broke out she helped to organise a patriotic meeting to raise money for the New Zealand troops marching off to fight.[17]

With their family history and their connections, the Dobie sisters grew up with the world as their stage and they played their roles with unselfconscious assurance. The one big disadvantage they encountered was the death of their father. Herbert Main Dobie was a major in the 30th Madras infantry when he died of fever in Burma in 1854, leaving his widow to care for six children.[18] Bertha was seven years old at the time and Mary three.

It was on the voyage home from Burma that the newly widowed Ellen displayed the mettle of the Dobie women by depriving the drunken captain of his alcohol.[19] She was in charge of a small party of eight: three of her own children – presumably the three youngest including Mary – three children of a friend and two servants. They were the only passengers on the *Elizabeth* as it carried a cargo of teak from Moulmein to Greenock in Scotland. It soon became apparent that the captain was an alcoholic and Ellen extracted a promise from him that he would lay off the grog, a promise which was broken after a mere fortnight.

When he sobered up after this breach of faith, Ellen confronted the remorseful man and forced him to renew his pledge of sobriety, only this time she took a hostage: the keys to his liquor cabinet. At the first opportunity, she ensured there would be no backsliding by tossing all of his alcohol into the Indian Ocean. Their adventures were by no means over though. It took six months to reach their destination and in that time they faced down a mutiny, survived a storm in which a man was lost overboard and picked up four survivors of a ship that had sunk in the Atlantic.

On returning from Burma, Ellen settled in the village of Irthington, near Carlisle in Cumberland, where she brought up her six children, three boys and three girls. As the girls grew up they tended to follow the Locker side in artistic and literary pursuits. Bertha was a writer whose pen dominated the diary kept on the *May Queen* and who would later write journalism and short stories in New Zealand. Literary ability ran in the family and it may have been stimulated in Bertha by the stories her mother told to delight the children. One of their favourites was about a man convicted of murder after a fellow he had been drinking with vanished. The sting in the tail was that years later the victim reappeared; he had been press-ganged into the navy.[20] Mary was the artistic one. She was adept at sketches and small paintings that captured the family's adventures at home and abroad.

Mary, Bertha and their elder sister, named Ellen after their mother, spent time living with relatives while they were educated. The 1861 census in Britain lists fourteen-year-old Bertha and seventeen-year-old Ellen as scholars in the house of their aunt, Mary Dixon, in Carlisle.[21] And Mary, at the age of 21, moved to London to live with Uncle Arthur, editor of the *Graphic*, and study at the Female School of Art in the Bloomsbury district.[22] The school was founded in 1842 to prepare middle-class women to earn an independent living as graphic artists rather than teaching them art merely as a social accomplishment.[23] By going there Mary showed she was serious about a career and her family connections certainly helped. Unlike her younger sisters, Ellen remained in England, marrying a cotton manufacturer in 1865 when she was 21.[24]

The boys in the family were more in the Dobie mould: one was a doctor and the other an army officer in India, like his father. Another brother, Herbert, had a mix of the Lockers' artistic temperament and the Dobies' pragmatic skills.[25]

By training he was an engineer and spent a few years at sea, but he was a man of multiple talents: a fine cabinetmaker, a keen amateur botanist and a technological front-runner; he was among the first people in New Zealand to adopt the bicycle and the typewriter. Like Bertha he was a writer, and penned a string of unpublished novels – reports of the number vary from nine to sixteen – before finally achieving enduring success when he combined his literary and botanical interests to produce the book *New Zealand Ferns*, which went through at least five editions and was the standard work on the subject until the mid-twentieth century.

One other point of difference about Herbert was that he called himself Dobbie rather than Dobie. When the family went to India, as the story goes, they discovered that the word 'dobie' meant a low-caste laundryman in Hindi so they temporarily changed their name. Everyone changed back to Dobie afterwards except Herbert. However, deeper research into the family background shows they were originally from Scotland and were called Dobbie in the seventeenth century but by the latter part of the eighteenth century, when they were established in England, Dobie was the more usual spelling.[26]

Herbert Dobbie had migrated to New Zealand in 1875, where he took a job with the railways in Auckland, and he was the reason Ellen and her two daughters made the voyage on the *May Queen*. They were not migrating but planning a long leisurely holiday with their brother on the other side of the world. The timing of the trip was decided by Herbert's betrothal to Charlotte Gilfillan. He met Charlotte shortly after his arrival when he presented a letter of introduction to her father. He was 23 and she was just fourteen when she answered the door and called out 'Pa, here's a man'. She must have made an impression on him; she was a pretty girl with startling blue eyes, dressed in white and wearing her hair in ringlets. Two years later they were engaged to be married.[27]

It is a measure of the Dobies' comfortable circumstances that they could afford the luxury of a first-class trip to the southern hemisphere. But they had no intention of being idle. As befitting a family who saw the whole world as their stage they planned to explore as much of New Zealand and the South Pacific as they could in two or three years. Their adventures on the three-month voyage to New Zealand were meticulously chronicled in a diary kept by the sisters, giving a lively portrayal of who they were and how they saw themselves as well as the daily details of living at sea.

The Dobies quickly became leading lights in the ship's social life. They danced on deck with the captain and passengers, they organised reading parties in which the guests would take turns to read out loud to each other and played parlour games including cards and variations on charades and hide and seek.[28] They were also leaders in the craft movement on board, especially needlework, and their cabin became a repository of knowledge and equipment for everyone, including the second- and third-class passengers. 'They borrow crewels from us & Mary has drawn them one or two patterns for the work,' wrote Bertha. The cabin was also the setting for a formal 'at home', during which the Dobies served tea and played poker.[29]

It is not hard to see why they were such social successes. They were bright, imaginative, energetic and curious, qualities all sweetened by their sense of humour. They took pride in their physical prowess and could not help but boast they were immune to seasickness in contrast to their travelling companions. 'Not so many to breakfast,' Bertha wrote early in the voyage before most people had found their sea legs. 'Fellow passengers feeling very ill. We sympathised fully with them and I'm afraid they hated us for being so horrid and well.'[30]

They loved to burn off energy by going for long walks around the deck, one Sunday imagining they were on land and walking to church through the countryside.[31] And when life was quiet they longed for a storm to liven things up.[32] Eventually they got one and while some of the others succumbed again to seasickness, the Dobie sisters made the most of the excitement on deck. 'Lovely waves, beyond description,' said Bertha. 'Mary & I sitting on the deck in the afternoon, watching the waves. One came over the poop and drenched us thoroughly, I rather liked it.'[33]

Bertha's comment was typical of the humour that runs through the diary in words and pictures. The tone was set at the start of the voyage when Henry Dixon, a close friend or cousin who had come to see them off, met with disaster as he was leaving the ship. 'Instead of stepping into the boat he preferred the water,' wrote Bertha, and Mary caught the moment in a sketch (Fig. 15).[34] Henry did not see the funny side.

The sisters could laugh at themselves as well as at other people. Much of their humour had a slapstick quality derived from the splashing, spilling and tumbling caused by the lurching vessel. Both had a dose of it one day; Bertha when the ship rolled at breakfast and emptied her cup of tea on her sleeve, to the great delight of her friends. Mary's turn came that night when her swinging cot collapsed as she was drifting off to sleep. 'Suddenly, crack, crash, bang and down [came] her cot on its head, her heels up in the air and head very low,' wrote Bertha. 'Not a scream was heard only laughter.'[35]

Bertha and Mary's original plan was to write the diary jointly and refer to themselves in the third person. But Mary became less and less interested in the writing, and when they had been at sea for about a month, Bertha declared she would now write in the first person because 'lazy Mary never seems to write in this tho' I always leave spaces for her'.[36] Mary responded with two words: 'Miss Braggart'. She preferred to express herself in pictures, and her drawings contain the same eye for the pratfall as some of the entries written by Bertha. One of her better efforts was of 'the Catastrophe' that occurred when the ship lurched during tea, tipping the three Dobie women and two other passengers backwards out of their seats (Fig. 16).[37] The closest thing to a sour note in the diary was Mary's reaction to the other passengers getting the wrong idea when she became ill, because of the heat and the awful food. 'She is thinking how soon she can leave the table,' wrote Mary in the third person, 'without people thinking she is sea sick.'[38]

The sisters had a similar sense of humour but Mary was more sensitive to other people than Bertha. Bold Bertha brushed off shyness and self-consciousness but Mary worried about what people thought and had occasional pangs of homesickness. Just two days into the voyage she wrote: 'Want to go home no-ow'.[39] A few days later – when Bertha commented how time was flying and how there was so much to do working, reading, playing games, singing, tidying the cabin and tramping the deck – Mary agreed it was a pleasant life and she was enjoying it thoroughly 'but all the same I want to be in England now-w-w'.[40] And although Mary shared Bertha's yearning for a great storm, she worried about the risk to the crew. She expressed her concerns in typically flippant style through a jokey disclaimer which began in the third person and then switched to the first. 'Mary does not wish for a storm except that it would be a fine sight and an event in one's life,' she said. 'Still, I should not like the poor sailors to suffer or the Mates ... how dreadful if any of them were washed overboard.'[41]

Mary's sensitivity was reflected in her love of animals as well, especially dogs and horses which often featured in her artwork. She made a great fuss of a dog on the ship, a black retriever called Bob whom she jokingly promoted to officer.[42] 'Always ready for a game on deck if not too hot,' she wrote of Bob, 'hide and seek behind the skylights, very fond of nuts which he tried to stop when thrown, before they rolled overboard, and always cracked before we could get up to him.'[43]

But for all their differences in personality, the sisters shared a real curiosity about how the sailing ship worked and this led them increasingly to cross the invisible social boundary that was supposed to separate the crew from the passengers. Mary's invasion of the forecastle on that moonlit night was the first of many breaches. Just a few weeks later she was discussing the technical details of the sails, of which she appeared to have plenty of theoretical knowledge but was anxious to see how they worked in practice. 'The sailors have had very little trouble with the sails, tho' we have been a month at sea the fore & aft sails, the skysail & Royals are the only ones that have been touched & they not too often,' she wrote showing easy familiarity with the jargon of the rigging. 'I want to have a change & see the big ones stowed & the others reefed or something exciting. I daresay we shall have plenty of it before the voyage is over.'[44] And she observed how sea shanties – such as 'Whisky for my Johnny' – helped the crew to work as a team. 'The sailors sing lovely songs when they pull at a heavy rope, one sings a solo, just a line or two, then they all sing a line or two together & pull.'

Mary and Bertha peppered the first mate Mr Longmuir with questions about the workings of the ship. They wanted to know why everything was done and to understand what they could about navigation. They were keen stargazers and Longmuir did everything he could to help the sisters, showing them the charts and the ship's log even though it was strictly against the rules and, as Mary said, the skipper would have had a fit if he had known about it. But Longmuir went further. About six weeks after Mary first visited the forecastle, when they had passed through the tropics, he took them forward again to fulfil their wish of watching the crew at close quarters as they took down the light mainsail and replaced it with a heavy-duty sail better suited to the stormy Southern Ocean.[45]

The sisters even assisted with some of the crew's chores. On a couple of days they helped to chip old paint off the ironwork on the poop deck, a task which left Bertha's arm aching so much that she could not go on. In words and pictures they also related how they helped to haul in the logline, which was used to measure the speed of the ship and the distance it travelled.[46] Daily they recorded this information, as well as the latitude and longitude, in their diary.

Perhaps the Dobie sisters' fascination with all things nautical came from an awareness of their family's connections with the sea. But their interest was not simply technical curiosity; they got to know the officers and sailors themselves in a way that would have been officially frowned upon. For instance, Bertha wrote one day about her concern for the helmsman Wishart who had been ill and had to leave the wheel: 'We take an interest in him, he is such a nice looking and mannered man, he is working his passage out.'[47] Wishart was one of the reasons Mary was not so keen to experience a great storm. 'Poor Wishart,' she wrote, 'he would get so wet & cold & illy'.[48]

Whenever she could, Bertha chatted to the helmsmen, sometimes flirtatiously, a point captured in a painting by Mary (Fig. 17). But she had to be careful and would only do so when the captain and officers were out of earshot. The sisters were fortunate that their position as first-class passengers allowed them to get away with thumbing their noses at rules that were written for the express purpose of keeping single women away from the men on the ship. Had they been in steerage their conduct might well have resulted in scandal, official censure and punishment when the *May Queen* reached its destination.[49]

A paradox in the sisters' attitude was that despite their strong interest in crossing the social boundary into the exotic world of the sailors they had no desire to make friends with the second- or third-class passengers, even though they had much in common. Most of the women on the ship shared an interest in needlework but the exchange of ideas and patterns was done through John Tattersall, a first-class passenger who orchestrated the social life at sea and acted as go-between. 'We don't see much of them but Mr Tattersall is a sort of link between the saloon and the main deck. He is so much with them and brings their work to shew us and takes ours to shew them,' wrote Bertha.[50] This stand-offish attitude was reinforced when the Dobies held their 'at home' which was stage-managed like a red-carpet event, with the ordinary people gathering to admire the privileged guests in their improvised finery. 'The Captain, Mates, stewards & some 2nd & 3rd class people assembled to see them come out of their cabins when ready & Mr Tattersall announced them in ours.'[51]

Bertha's reference to the other passengers as second- and third-class *people* may not have been intentional disparagement but it certainly suggests that she thought the status of their tickets reflected their value as lesser human beings. The class barrier, it seems, was of a different quality to the boundary that separated the Dobie sisters and the crew. Perhaps they could see nothing of interest on the other side of this particular divide or perhaps they wanted to reinforce the division to preserve their position at the top of the ship's hierarchy. On the other hand, the crew were fascinating and there was a certain wicked delight in being able to ignore the rules and satisfy their curiosity without in any way endangering their privileged position. This glimpse of class attitudes is an important check on the impression given in the rest of the diary of a couple of easy-going young women who did not stand too much on ceremony.

The antipodean descendants of the family came to regard Bertha as haughty and a snob.[52] It is not hard to see why from comments made in her memoirs, which lay heavy stress on how she maintained her social status even though she had to work hard for her living on an orange orchard in Whangārei. 'One thing I may safely promise you, and that is we shall not become bourgeois, or what would be still worse genteel,' she wrote.[53] She always insisted on dressing for dinner, would not use her dining room as a sitting room, nor would she use a tea cosy, nor would she call a 'table napkin' a 'serviette' or 'stays' 'corsets' and she would not say 'I beg your pardon' instead of 'what'.[54] She sealed her reputation in New Zealand when she wrote an article for a London paper on colonial life. The Auckland *Star*'s London correspondent quoted a passage: 'If one were to be exclusive and only willing to consort with people of one's own standing, one would lead a sorry lonely life, losing much pleasure and acquaintance of many from whom one can derive benefit and enjoyment, though they may not be "people of extraction",' she wrote. This was taking 'too high a standpoint' the *Star* correspondent commented drily.[55]

Despite Bertha's social pretensions, the Dobies really were middle class though quite different from the people below decks, and even their fellow first-class passengers, who were coming to New Zealand to make a new life. They may not have been rich, but they were comfortable, well-connected people on a combined family visit and grand tour of New Zealand and the South Pacific. The friends they made in New Zealand were likewise middle class and from the ruling establishment. But, as on the voyage out, the sisters were always curious, adventurous and keen to cross social boundaries to encounter and learn about people from other cultures, whom they found exotic and fascinating.

3.

THE GRAND TOUR

When the *May Queen* dropped anchor in the Waitematā Harbour early one morning in January 1878, Bertha Dobie declared it to be one of the finest and loveliest harbours in the world. After nothing but sea and sky for three months, it was strange to gaze on a green countryside dotted with houses and to hear birds singing in a wooded bank as the ship passed near the shore.[1] The sisters looked eagerly for their brother but he did not come at first because, from land, he mistook the *May Queen* for another vessel. Boat after boat came out to the ship with people greeting other passengers but no Herbert so Mary and Bertha sent a note ashore. At last, as they were leaning over the stern, they spied him coming towards them in a small rowing boat. 'I can't describe our meeting or the delight of it,' wrote Bertha.[2]

Everything had been organised for their arrival. A friend of Herbert's came out in a larger rowing boat to take them to the wharf where they found a cab waiting to drive them to their new home in Parnell, named May Cottage in honour of the ship. Herbert had already been living there for six weeks and had done everything he could to make it comfortable for his mother and sisters. It was one storey and made of timber, with verandas at the front and back and four bedrooms as well as a drawing room and a dining room (Fig. 18). Herbert was an accomplished cabinetmaker and most of the furniture – beds, tables, a chest of drawers, a bookcase, picture frames and curtain rails – was produced by the skill of his hands.

Outside was an abundant but neglected flower garden with a profusion of geraniums, verbenas and jasmines, and arum lilies running wild. The vegetable patch was in better shape; Herbert had planted plenty of cabbages, lettuces and marrows. At the back of the house the ground was sloping and covered with peach trees and fig trees. From there the family enjoyed a view of the harbour and Rangitoto Island, the dormant volcano that guards the seaward approaches to Auckland.[3]

It was not long before the Dobie women had added their own personal touches to Herbert's basic furnishings. The drawing room had reminders of their imperial connections, with Indian rugs, tiger skins and bear skins on the floor. They also had a couple of Algerian rugs, one used to cover a sofa and the other on Bertha's sewing machine which doubled as a book table. Adding to the furnishings were bookcases they brought out from England and a piano. 'It's so lovely to be in one's own house and to pick flowers in one's own garden again,' wrote Bertha.[4]

The homeliness of the cottage was matched by the warmth of their welcome. The first of many social engagements was a garden party given by Bishop William Cowie, head of the Anglican Church in Auckland. Within two weeks they were receiving 'millions' of visitors and enjoying afternoon tea-parties every day. Prominent among those who enjoyed the hospitality at May Cottage was Herbert's betrothed, Charlotte Gilfillan, who had just turned eighteen. Mary and Bertha approved wholeheartedly of their sister-in-law-to-be and immediately began using her pet name, Tottie. 'She is very small with wee hands & feet, decidedly pretty & rosy & merry looking with dark brown curling hair,' wrote Bertha.[5]

After so long at sea they missed the sounds of the ship, the water rushing by, the bells, the sailors stamping and the officers yelling out orders. Instead their ears were assailed with the shrill summer music of cicadas. They found it hard to believe they were hearing the song of insects and it reminded them constantly that they were in unfamiliar territory where northern hemisphere assumptions were turned upside down. Even the poetry did not fit, wrote Bertha, quoting some lines from her beloved Tennyson: 'For now the noonday quiet holds the hill: the grasshopper is silent in the grass'.[6]

The strangeness of it all was no bad thing for the Dobie sisters whose curiosity was so easily piqued and they soon settled into New Zealand life with its own interesting quirks and customs to explore. As befitted their solid middle-class status they employed a maid but still worked hard at housekeeping themselves, drawing water, cooking, cleaning, gardening and negotiating with the numerous hawkers and tradesmen who came to the house. They thought the wild-looking men in straw hats who rode up to the gate must have been bushmen but they turned out to be butchers and grocers taking orders door-to-door.

May Cottage was where the Dobie sisters recorded their first encounters with Māori people and their language. Among the hawkers were Māori selling mushrooms and peaches which they carried in flax baskets, kete. It was the first Māori word mentioned in the *May Queen* diary – albeit rendered as 'kets'. The Dobies were just as curious on land about their new neighbours as they had been at sea about the sailors. The last few pages of the diary are sprinkled with Māori words and observations about Māori people after Bertha went on a business trip to Riverhead with Herbert.[7] They spent some time at a settlement and Bertha dined in a whare. The hosts spoke hardly any English and the guest hardly any Māori but she put her few words to good use, the greeting 'tēnā koe' (which she rendered as tenekoe) and the expression of approval 'ka pai' (rendered as kappa).

Back in Auckland, the Dobies were making their mark in the upper echelons of colonial society. Ellen the matriarch was distinguished for her unostentatious charities, said the *New Zealand Herald*.[8] Mary and Bertha's friends included the children of men who occupied some of the key positions in the colonial church and state. Among them were Martin Lush, son of the Reverend Vicesimus Lush who was a leading figure in the Anglican Church. The favourite pastimes of this elite group included tennis, music and amateur theatricals.[9] Mary and Bertha soon joined the tennis club, which was just a few minutes' walk from May Cottage, and Mary took a leading role in an amateur production of Richard Brinsley Sheridan's *The Rivals* at the Choral Hall to raise money for the Ladies' Benevolent Society.

The performers were all members of what the Auckland *Star* called the 'upper ten' of Auckland society. The play is a complicated comedy of manners at the heart of which is a love affair between an army captain and a wealthy teenage heiress, Lydia Languish, who wants to elope. Mary, perhaps because of her obvious willingness to challenge social conventions, was chosen to play Lydia (Fig. 20). Martin Lush played Bob Acres, a close friend of the captain. Reviewers at Auckland's two daily papers agreed that the bright young things had pulled it off. 'One of the most remarkable and successful amateur performances ever known in Auckland,' said the *Star*.[10] But for all her artistic ability Mary was no actress, and she struggled playing a romantic and capricious character ten years her junior. The *Herald* reviewer said she was unsuited to light comedy and her delivery was mechanical and forced.[11] Her sense of comic timing, which was one of her great strengths on a sketchpad, deserted her on the stage.

Much as they enjoyed the social life it was not enough for the Dobie sisters who aimed to pack their southern sojourn with as much adventure as they could fit in. Herbert and Tottie were not due to be married until early 1880 which gave Mary and Bertha plenty of time for their South Pacific grand tour. Their travels would include a trip to Samoa and Fiji but before that they went to see the Pink and White Terraces of Lake Rotomahana. The terraces were justifiably renowned for their unique beauty and tourists came from all over the world to visit them. One veteran wrote he had been just about everywhere from the Himalayas to Niagara Falls but he had never seen anything to compare to the terraces for their delicate beauty, chaste design and sublime detail of construction.[12] The terraces were the focus of a tourism boom which lasted from the 1870s until they were destroyed in the eruption of Mount Tarawera in 1886. Sightseers would travel down from Auckland and stay at one of a number of hotels in Ōhinemutu on the shores of Lake Rotorua and Te Wairoa on Lake Tarawera before hiring rowers and guides from the Tūhourangi and Te Arawa tribes to take them to see the marvellous sights.[13]

Penny-pinching tourists were not always happy about having to pay for the privilege of seeing what was then regarded as one of the natural wonders of the world. 'Because negotiating with Māori was the only way to see the Pink and White Terraces and other thermal sights, the question of charges becomes for many tourists the point of tension at which cross-cultural contact is sharpened,' observes Lydia Wevers in her book on travel writing in nineteenth-century New Zealand.[14] These tensions over money were brought into focus when the famous artist and travel writer Constance Gordon Cumming refused to pay a fee for the right to paint watercolours of the terraces in 1877, two years before the Dobies' visit. Traditional owners of the land put up notices setting the fee at £5 and they argued, among other things, that Cumming would make a fortune from selling her work and they were entitled to a financial gain as well. Cumming imperiously dismissed the fee as extortion. 'I was determined not to pay the money, both from a natural aversion to being done, and also because such a precedent would have settled the question, to the detriment of all future sketchers,' she wrote.[15]

Despite the obvious similarities between the Dobie sisters and Cumming, the former had a very different approach to the must-see attractions of the Pink and White Terraces. Instead of following the well-beaten tourist path to the hotels of Ōhinemutu, the Dobies travelled by ship to Ōpōtiki in the Bay of Plenty and from there made their way overland by horseback and upriver by canoe. The trip – including the time they spent in Ōpōtiki – occupied the month of March 1879 and it was thoroughly documented in words and pictures by the sisters, just as they had done on the *May Queen*.

Mary began a diary-sketchbook in Auckland when she and her mother set out to link up with Bertha who had been staying with friends in Tauranga. Bertha was waiting on the wharf to greet them, and they went to church on Sunday and afterwards, in Mary's words, 'to sigh and drop another bitter tear' at the Mission Cemetery where the soldiers who had fallen at the battles of Gate Pā and Te Ranga sixteen years before were buried.[16] Mary did not mention the name of the man for whom she wept, but from the plaques in the cemetery the most likely candidate is Thomas H. Dixon, of the AC. He died in 1870 and may have been connected to Aunt Mary with whom Bertha had stayed in 1861 and to Henry Dixon who fell in the water when saying farewell to the sisters in London.

While at the cemetery Mary was most struck by an epitaph on the grave of another soldier, Private Laurence Manion of the 68th Durham Light Infantry, who died of the shocking wounds he suffered at the battle of Te Ranga.

> My Race I have run, my time I have spent
> In soldiering from home I went
> In India and New Zealand beneath a burning sky
> Far from my beloved parents there to die.[17]

Manion was certainly not the person she mourned but there was something about his epitaph that was special to her. Perhaps it was that the words, unlike so many of the others, were truly original. But the inscription also mentioned India where her father had also died far from home under a burning sky.

The day after their emotional visit to the cemetery, the Dobie women travelled by steamer to Ōpōtiki. On the voyage the sisters suffered an uncharacteristic bout of seasickness before recovering to join the captain on the bridge as he navigated across the dangerous bar at their destination. This was more their style; Mary was exhilarated. 'Such a rolling & thunder the rollers breaking on the bar – and bumping & shivering the steamer being just able to scrape over the sand,' she wrote.[18] The ship took them up the Waioeka River to Ōpōtiki which consisted of a small church, a large hotel, some stores and a cluster of houses. On the wharf, wearing a broad-brimmed sun hat and waiting to greet them, was Forster Goring, who would be their host and guide on the expedition (Fig. 22).

It is not known how the family met Goring but it may have been through their social circle in Auckland. He would have been a natural member of the 'upper ten'. His father was clerk of the Executive Council – a position of real importance in the colony – and he was linked to the Anglo-Irish aristocracy; his maternal grandfather was Viscount Avonmore of Bellisle, Tipperary.[19] Another possible connection was Thomas Dixon, the man buried in the Mission Cemetery. Like Dixon, Goring was in the AC, the little army set up by the colonial state when imperial troops were withdrawn from New Zealand in the late 1860s.

Goring's nickname was 'the boy' because he had volunteered for the colonial militia as a sixteen-year-old in 1863, just before the British Army invaded the Waikato. At first he was told to go home to his mother but he was so insistent that they took him on and his career had followed the course of the military conflict between Māori and Pākehā in the two decades since.[20] He took part in most of the major engagements of the Waikato invasion and later distinguished himself against the great Ngā Ruahine warrior Tītokowaru in 1868. When Tītokowaru's men defeated the AC at the battle of Te Ngutu-o-te-manu, Goring helped bring a wounded officer out from behind the lines. And at the battle of Moturoa – when the AC again were well beaten and forced to retreat – he was in command of the rear-guard and the last one out of the bush.[21] By the time he was waiting on the dock for the Dobies he was a major but he looked much younger than his 33 years. Despite his perilous adventures in war and his heavy responsibilities it was easy to see why the nickname stuck.

A combination of his duties and the rain delayed the start of the trip for three days: Goring had to take his men for rifle practice and until that was done he was going nowhere. While they waited the Dobies made themselves comfortable in Castle Goring, as they called the major's cosy cottage, and acquainted themselves with the horses that would carry them on their week-long trek to see the Pink and White Terraces.[22] They set out on a Saturday morning with six people in the party: the three Dobie women, their host, two constabulary men with a baggage horse and Goring's dogs Snipe and Rowdy. They reached Whakatāne in the late afternoon and spent the night there before heading to Te Teko.

At Te Teko they camped out after dining on fresh-water crayfish and about midnight a party of Māori came to take them to the Hot Lakes by canoe. They reached the White Terraces around 6 a.m. 'Splendid sight, rather like a glacier but very steaming & all round are cauldrons boiling hard,' wrote Bertha.[23] Every step of the terraces had formed hot baths of opal-tinted water, some deep enough to swim in. 'We clambered up it, the water at the bottom is cold but as one ascends gets hotter until it is too boiling for one to walk even on the edges of the basins where the water is only trickling over.'

They spent the day enjoying the terraces and bathing in the hot pools. In the evening Bertha used the geothermal steam to cook a meal of curried wild duck and after dinner everyone went back to bathe by the moonlight in the Pink Terraces. Everyone, that is, except Bertha and Major Goring who together strolled over to the White Terraces. In the morning they were up at five o'clock and ready to retrace their journey, by canoe and horseback, to Castle Goring. The sisters' record of their adventure, 'Diary of a trip to the Hot Lakes', has the same sense of fun and adventure as the *May Queen* diary. Mary's sketches show how they imagined themselves as performers in a travelling circus and she captured with good humour the obstacles and disasters they had to overcome: fording rivers, getting bogged and the packhorse bolting with their baggage (Fig. 24).

The excursion would not have been possible without help from the many Māori people they encountered on the way, whether it was through providing food and shelter, transport in the canoe or helping them cross rivers and recovering the bolted horse or rescuing them from the mud (Fig. 25). There was no mention of any money changing hands and none of the unseemly squabbling that had marred Cumming's visit to Ōhinemutu two years previously. This may well have been because Goring had settled accounts in advance. But it is worth noting that the diary is full of sketches of the journey but there are none of the terraces themselves. Perhaps Mary also decided that £5 was too much but unlike Cumming she respected the right to levy the charge.

The sisters marvelled at how well Goring got on with Māori people. He spoke their language, fluently it seemed, although to Bertha and Mary it sounded like English did to Napoleon, all confusion and discord or, as they put it, so much jabbering. 'He seems to know everyone on the way,' wrote Bertha and she cited an example of how highly he was regarded.[24] The road from Whakatāne to Te Teko was being built by Māori under contract to the government but wisely they would allow no one to use it until they had received payment in full. Forster was an exception to the rule and so the Dobie women became the first white women to travel along the new road, an achievement they recorded with pride. They always enjoyed the role of pathfinders, being the first white women, or among the first, to go places, and meet people.

Mary and Bertha were as interested in the Māori people as they were in the *May Queen*'s crew and everyone else they met on their travels, with Bertha writing about their encounters and Mary expressing herself, as always, in her sketchbook. She produced a series of studies at Whakatāne, including one of the chief Apanui who was said to be 100 years old (Fig. 26). Goring noticed how she liked the Māori and said she would not treat them as inferiors, a point reinforced by her apparent respect for their right to charge artists at the Hot Lakes.[25] But a thread of racism appeared in the sisters' diary when they were joined at Whakatāne by a settler, Captain Swindley. 'Capt. Swindley told us many tales about the "niggers" as he calls them (which they hate),' commented Bertha.[26] It was the only instance in all the writings of the Dobie sisters that the term appeared and Bertha seemed at pains to distance herself from it by inserting the inverted commas and then adding how hateful it was to the Māori people with whom they had such friendly relations. But there was no explicit censure of Swindley; they continued to enjoy his company and did not seem to notice his attitude carried over into the tales he told about Māori in the old days. These were related as simple horror stories designed to thrill, with the all-important social and political context left out.

One of Swindley's stories was about how the missionary Carl Völkner had been hanged and decapitated in 1865 and a chief had eaten his eyes.[27] He took the Dobies to the place where it happened and he also introduced them to Erueti Tamaitoha, the last cannibal in the area.[28] Mary drew a sketch of Tamaitoha and Swindley added a note describing how he had killed a settler on the beach, impaled his head on a stake, cut off a leg and took it away to eat (Fig. 27). Another settler described how he had fled to a small island off Whakatāne ten years previously when the feared guerrilla leader Te Kooti Arikirangi came on a raid.[29]

As children, the sisters had always enjoyed a good murder tale and the ones told by the settlers had much in common with those they had heard at their mother's knee: scary, enthralling but not really threatening given that the bloodshed had happened so long ago.[30] The storytellers saw no need to explain that Te Kooti had once been an ally of the Pākehā and had taken up arms after becoming the victim of land stealing and false imprisonment.[31] And the crucial missing detail in the Völkner story was that he was killed for, among other things, the well-founded suspicion that he had been spying on Te Whakatōhea during a time of war.[32] These omissions suggest that the storytellers regarded these social and political details as no longer relevant. The disputes that had led to bloodshed between Māori and Pākehā in the 1860s had long since been settled in favour of the Pākehā. What remained were the stories, entertaining even if horrifying. But armed with knowledge of Swindley's attitude to their Māori guides and travelling companions, the Dobies surely did not miss the condescending tone in the note that he added to Mary's sketch of Tamaitoha: 'He is now my best friend & chum also landlord renting me 11,000 acres, called the Waimana – has 5 wives keeps them all in order – his word is his bond. A most wonderful thing in a Māori – his great failing RUM.'[33]

One important theme in the Hot Lakes diary is not obvious at first but unmistakeable on close reading: the mutual and growing affection between Bertha and Forster. The diary implies there was some sort of understanding, perhaps unspoken, before they arrived in Ōpōtiki. Mary gave it away with her sketch and the exclamation mark at the end of her entry describing their arrival: 'came to houses little church – big hotel – stores – wharf & Major Goring!'[34] She subtly reinforced the point at every opportunity afterwards. In each sketch of the party riding on their excursion, Bertha and Forster were together; whenever they went for walks in the rain, it was Bertha and Forster side by side; and on boating excursions Bertha and Forster were a team and likewise when they went fishing and shooting.[35] Then there was Mary's sketch of their steamer departing at the end of the trip, where Forster is shown rowing down the river after them as though he could not bear to let a certain someone out of his sight (Fig. 30).

Bertha never said anything directly and never referred to Forster by his first name; at her most intimate it was just 'Major G'. But she did take great delight when she made a curry and he ate four helpings. And on the evening the couple went to the White Terraces together, Bertha said it was because she and Major G thought the hot baths 'too weakening'.[36] But there was surely a more compelling reason. They were away for such a long time that a search party was sent out to find them. Bertha brushed it off saying they were never lost. 'As it was now dark we sat down in the fern till the moon rose to help us back... we could have found the road alone.'[37]

There were plenty of good reasons why Bertha was attracted to Forster. He had distinguished himself in his chosen career and he was popular among the settlers and businessmen of Ōpōtiki as well as the Māori. Everyone liked him; he had their respect as an efficient military officer and a genial fellow citizen.[38] His link to the Anglo-Irish aristocracy would not have hurt his chances with Bertha either. He was, as she would have put it, a person of 'extraction' and soon they were engaged to be married. The proposal may have come on that moonlit night on the White Terraces, and the wedding date was set for the middle of 1880, a few months after Herbert and Tottie were due to tie the knot.

Ellen Dobie, who had come to see her son married in New Zealand, was now preparing for two family weddings. But the new couple would have to endure a long separation before the nuptials. Mary and Bertha, with their brother Herbert, were about to embark on a month-long trip to Samoa and Fiji. They departed in July 1879 and were having such a good time that when the month was up they sent Herbert back on his own while they stayed on until after Christmas, enjoying many adventures as they explored the islands and got to know the local people in their typically curious and bold style. As usual, the sisters combined to record their travels and adventures in a diary-sketchbook, which Bertha reworked and published in the *New Zealand Graphic* twelve years after Mary's death.[39]

They travelled first to Samoa where they spent a fortnight and then on to Fiji where they spent five months on the islands of Ovalau, Viti Levu, Vanua Levu and the Yasawas. They sailed on open boats and paddled up rivers in canoes. They rode through the rapids and crossed fords. They trekked through the bush, once taking five days to cover about 100 kilometres. And wherever they could, they climbed the hills to admire the spectacular views. While Mary and Herbert reached the highest spot on Ovalau, their guide had stopped long before the summit, insisting that Mary was likely to fall and break her neck. On her return Mary told Bertha about the adventure saying at times it had seemed that turning back was only a little more impossible than going forward. But, having heard the story, Bertha thought it was worth the risk. 'They were rewarded by a glorious view of the whole of Ovalau encircled by calm water of the deepest blue, the reef outside it, and beyond the ocean studded with islands and reefs as far as they could see.'[40]

A highlight of their time in Fiji was exploring the caves of the Yasawa Islands. They approached the first one through a dark, narrow passage and were amazed when it opened into a lofty cavern with great arches and a pool of clear water.[41] In moments the Fijian men accompanying them were jumping and diving into the water with a great yelling and hallooing (Fig. 32). As they had on the Bay of Plenty trip, the sisters saw themselves as pioneers and whenever it seemed appropriate they would note they were the first or among the first white women to visit a particular place. For instance, later that day they climbed about 700 metres to the island's upper caves. 'No white woman had ever been there,' wrote Bertha proudly, 'and only one white man.'[42] She recalled how they were relieved by the coolness of the caves after the hot climb and inspired by what they saw, a great space like a cathedral with pillars of stalactites and stalagmites in pure white as though they were marble.

For their adventures they dressed accordingly: none of the finery that they showed off as first-class passengers on the voyage out, but an outfit of their own design. 'M and I had each made a stout dungaree petticoat and a loose blouse bodice of thin cotton stuff, also of dark blue, which we wore with a plain leather belt,' wrote Bertha. 'A big reed hat, a bit of soft white muslin at our throats instead of collars, rough tan gloves and stout boots completed our travelling dress, and a very serviceable one we found it.'[43] Their baggage consisted of a black bag and two bundles wrapped in a waterproof sheet. Inside were a few clothes, a mat, a mosquito screen and a rug as well as their writing and sketching material. 'We found them very useful, as they kept our things dry, and did to sleep on when camping out,' said Bertha, and added that they felt like soldiers on a campaign.[44]

As always, these two soldiers were fascinated by the interesting people they met and their customs. Despite observing that women occupied a lowly status in the local culture, they made friends with chiefs, women, sailors from various navies, government officials, planters and missionaries. They were honoured in Samoa by a Siva, a dance which is performed stationary, sometimes sitting down, but relies on graceful coordinated movements of the arms. And they tried everything including kava and salukas, cigarettes made of Fijian tobacco rolled in a leaf.[45] Mary learned how to play the Fijian nose flute and Bertha how to make mats, Pacific-style.[46] One of their most satisfying achievements was when a Samoan friend taught them how to swim, their lessons taking place in a secluded pool which was approached through an avenue of palm trees.[47]

A significant feature of their South Pacific tour is the way their adventures were ad-libbed. They set out with just one introduction – to a missionary – and yet they co-opted the whole of the British imperial administration of the islands as well as the civilian population and a good proportion of the traditional hierarchy to do their bidding and enable them to go wherever they wanted. They were bold and adventurous, just as they had been on the voyage to New Zealand, and showed the same ability to bend people to their will. A small but telling example of how others went out of their way for the Dobies happened one day when Bertha dropped her hat overboard while they were steaming from Levuka to Viti Levu in a small boat. The skipper, like his opposite number on the *May Queen*, was only too happy to oblige her. He turned around and one of the crewmen dived overboard to retrieve the hat which was an essential garment on a hot tropical day when there was no shade on deck.[48]

Although they started out knowing only a humble missionary, they were soon invited to stay at Government House as special guests of Sir Arthur Gordon, whose next posting was to be New Zealand. The house had French windows opening on to deep verandas and was surrounded by lush gardens, which had something to make the sisters especially happy: a tennis court.[49] They had the run of the place between their adventures and attended great dinner parties and the annual meeting between the chiefs and the governor.[50] When they departed just after Christmas 1879 they were loaded down with gifts from all their new friends, including about 300 metres of tapa cloth, six dozen pineapples, mats, bowls, pottery, spears, bananas and a parrot. Sir Arthur gave them something very special, a log of fragrant sandalwood.[51]

Bertha and Mary were back in Auckland in plenty of time for Herbert and Tottie's marriage at the end of January. In some quarters they were hailed for their courage and originality, for instance Uncle Arthur's magazine the *Graphic*, which said: 'These young ladies, for the pleasure of climbing and sketching, rambled as fearlessly about these islands as if they had been in their Cumberland home, without meeting with the slightest molestation or annoyance, though constantly at the mercy of the natives.'[52] Bertha was proud of their travels, writing that it 'seemed odd' they should have been 'perfectly safe with no white man near us, in a country which three years ago was at war, and its people cannibals'.[53] But they were not quite as original as they thought. Constance Gordon Cumming who preceded the Dobies to Gordon's hospitality in Fiji as well as to the Pink and White Terraces, never worried about her safety either. She said she had ten years' travelling and working by herself 'among brown and yellow races of every hue' and had 'always done so fearlessly, being convinced that among these people a white woman leads a charmed life'.[54]

However, such fearlessness was not necessarily admired and the Dobie sisters, especially Mary, were the subject of gossip in Auckland because of their readiness to go where few European or Pākehā women were prepared to tread. The busybodies were scandalised by the thought of the sisters venturing deep into the Pacific by themselves and malicious tongues were well exercised on the topic.[55] One woman was particularly harsh on Mary when she mistakenly assumed she had spent Christmas 1878 at a Māori settlement in the Bay of Islands with only another young woman as a chaperone.[56] 'My only wonder was (and I know the natives well) that they escaped them with impunity,' she wrote. 'Young English ladies should not, under any circumstances, be allowed to wander into Māori settlements and kaingas sketching, talking, and laughing with natives.'[57]

Even if the gossips had their facts wrong, they offered a good guide to where the social boundaries lay. Their chatter was like the yapping of little watchdogs, alerting society to danger when someone stepped over an imagined line. That line, delineating gender and ethnicity, was implicit in Bertha's comments about how safe they felt in Fiji despite having no white men to look after them. And yet she and Mary made light of the gossips. 'From people's surprise at our safety one would think we had been amongst ferocious savages instead of the kindly peaceable Samoans and Fijians,' wrote Bertha, and hoped that other women would soon be following their example.[58] The critics were not finished, though, and would bite back when they heard the news of Mary's murder.

But that was in the future. For the time being, the Dobie sisters were far too busy to worry about the naysayers; they returned to Auckland in January 1880 for what was shaping up to be one of the most momentous years in the family's history. Herbert and Tottie were married at the end of the month in St Mary's Church in Parnell by Bishop Cowie. Next in line were Bertha and Forster. While the sisters were away Forster's circumstances had changed dramatically. He was transferred from his cosy cottage in the Bay of Plenty to Taranaki where tensions between Māori and Pākehā had resurfaced as the government moved to seize land it had nominally confiscated in the 1860s after the wars.

Forster took leave so the wedding went ahead as scheduled in June, a few days after Mary had appeared as Lydia Languish in *The Rivals*.[59] It was a brilliant winter's day, chilly and crisp. Bertha had still not adjusted to the inverted seasons after two and a half years in New Zealand and like the cicadas of her first summer, having June in winter disrupted her literary sensibilities; the poetry she knew did not quite fit the occasion. It would be 'inappropriate for a New Zealand swain to exclaim with Burns: "O my Love's like a red, red rose / That's newly sprung in June",' she wrote.[60] But, as always, she made the most of it. 'One associates June so entirely with roses and all that is delightful of early summer that I was quite glad to be married in it, despite the difference of latitude.'

Bertha's wedding was the moment when the various characters in the family began to go their separate ways. She went to Taranaki to live in camp with Forster. Herbert remained in town, not just for his career with the railways but because the Auckland Institute and Museum was mounting an exhibition of his impressive collection of ferns, and his book, *New Zealand Ferns*, was about to be published for the first time.[61] Mary helped with the illustrations in the first volume of what would become the standard work on the subject, eventually going through five editions and remaining in print until the 1960s.[62] For Mary and her mother Ellen, the South Pacific grand tour was coming to an end. They had one last trip to complete, a visit to Wellington and then on to Taranaki to say farewell to the Gorings before catching a ship back to England and their home in Irthington.

4.

ON MEASURED GROUND

Shortly after Forster took up his new job in the winter of 1879 the settlers of Taranaki were tipped into a state of fear, almost panic, by a Māori campaign opposing government plans to survey, seize and sell land nominally confiscated after the wars of the 1860s. The opposition had begun the year before with the harassment of surveyors who had started to measure out the ground, but now it had taken a new turn with bands of protesters ploughing settler farms to assert their mana whenua or trusteeship of the land.[1] The campaign was orchestrated by the prophets Te Whiti-o-Rongomai and Tohu Kākahi from their base at Parihaka in the shadow of Mount Taranaki. The prophets insisted their protest was peaceful but the settlers feared the ploughing was the prelude to bloodshed. They felt they were surrounded by 'fanatical natives', claiming that Te Whiti had promised his people they would be put in possession of settler land by some miraculous means.[2]

Mary and Bertha visited Te Whiti in the spring of 1880 and found him to be a gracious and friendly host rather than a fanatic. But in 1879 the fear he inspired in settler hearts cut across all levels of society; it was felt by prominent citizens as keenly as by the working poor. It found expression in private letters and diaries as well as public statements. For instance, Henry Richmond, a leader of settler society, described 'considerable excitement' when the ploughing protest began. 'We all feel that in dealing with fanaticism it is most difficult to predict what will be the result of forcible opposition but all agree that the stronger we can shew ourselves to be, the better the hope of a peaceful solution.'[3] At the other end of the social scale, Charles Taylor, a joiner who travelled the roads looking for work, expressed similar feelings when a party of 20 or 30 Māori rode up on horseback in the bush one day, talking loudly and staring at him. 'If I say I was not afraid, it would be a falsehood,' he wrote. 'I was at their mercy they could easily kill me if it was only for my swag, for there are many mysterious murders happen here.'[4] It was not just murder that he dreaded, but an uprising along the lines of the Indian Mutiny which had shaken British supremacy on the subcontinent two decades previously.

Fear gave wings to rumour and affected how Pākehā interpreted the evidence of their eyes and ears. One story doing the rounds said a family had been murdered at Bayley's farm near Parihaka.[5] A week later there was talk of a mysterious ship landing weapons for an uprising.[6] These rumours were scotched before anyone could act on them but one AC sentry was so jumpy that he opened fire one night when he heard the sound of rustling in the bush. The noise was made by a pig which paid the ultimate price for human folly. The embarrassed soldier survived to claim self-defence with the unlikely story that he had been told warriors would disguise themselves as pigs to mount a surprise attack.[7] Another sentry, Thomas Hughson, nearly made the same mistake when a man on horseback loomed out of the darkness but failed to respond to his challenge until he threatened to fire. The man was a Catholic priest who was annoyed at being bailed up. 'How dare you speak like that to the Holy Father,' he said, breaking his almost-fatal silence. 'You could easily have been more holey,' responded Hughson, perhaps embellishing the story for the entertainment of his descendants. 'How was I to know you were not a Maori getting near enough to pick me off?'[8]

Private disquiet became noisily public in the first week of June when the Premier Sir George Grey came to Taranaki at the invitation of the settlers to hear their concerns. Forster led the guard of honour when Grey landed on a beach at New Plymouth where he was greeted by the city leaders and a cheering crowd who were pinning their hopes on a strong government response to the ploughmen.[9] This was the prelude to several days of meetings, deputations and debate but they had their work cut out to persuade Grey that anything at all needed to be done.[10] He and his advisers were unconvinced there was a threat and thought the ploughmen could be dealt with under civil law. His attitude only increased the nervousness of the Pākehā population in a week when more and more newspaper reports told of the settlers' properties falling under the blade of the protesting plough.[11]

Grey had some support from around the country with correspondents and editorial writers suggesting the threat was being greatly exaggerated and exploited for political purposes.[12]

They had a point. The leading spokesman for the settlers was Taranaki politician and former premier Harry Atkinson who had been defeated ignominiously in a parliamentary vote two years before. Ever since, he had been conducting a relentless opposition to the government of his successor.[13] Now, while disavowing any political motives, he poured on the pressure, demanding that the hesitant premier do something immediately. 'There is one of two things – either the Government must undertake the defence of the Province, or we must,' he said when a deputation of worried citizens met Grey. 'We are not prepared to leave our wives and families in exposed positions.'[14]

The sustained and emotive way he pressured Grey showed how Atkinson was taking advantage of the tensions to win political points. Grey was embarrassed and looked ineffectual whereas Atkinson's aggressive certainty won applause from his constituents. But although he used and even exaggerated the fear, he did not create it; it was not the artifice of a master politician, it was real. The one to express it most forcefully was not Atkinson but T. Wilson of Urenui who said settlers were afraid that at any moment they might be turned out of the homes they had occupied for years and their wives and families might be murdered in their beds. They were without protection or arms and felt utterly at the mercy of the natives. He claimed to speak for everyone and judging by the applause he received from the deputation he was right.[15]

By the end of the week the government had been browbeaten into increasing its response to the protest. Reinforcements of 200 men were assigned to the AC and an offer was made to arm volunteer companies.[16] The task of organising the volunteers went to Major Charles Stapp whose first efforts at recruitment became farcical when a New Plymouth company quit over a public squabble about uniforms.[17] From this evident lack of commitment, it may seem that settler worries were more imagined than real but the dispute took place in the relative safety of New Plymouth. Among the out-settlers – people such as the Wilsons of Urenui – the attitude was very different and a sure indication of the depth of their anxiety. Before the second week of June had passed Stapp had signed up 849 men who were ready to fight. Thirteen units had been formed in Carlyle, Inglewood, Ōpunake, Ōkato, Bell Block, Urenui and Waitara.[18]

The decision to reinforce the state's military presence in Taranaki was backed by an order to arrest the ploughmen. When the order went out it was directed to Major Forster Goring. From that time until his marriage in mid-1880 he was at the forefront of efforts to frustrate the protest.[19] While the Dobie sisters were enjoying the privileges of empire on their South Pacific excursion, Forster was engaged in the dirty work of colonisation. William Skinner – one of the surveyors engaged in measuring the land – witnessed the ploughmen defying the government and recorded the first arrests in his diary. Thirty-four one day, seventeen on another and 27 more a few weeks later. The last lot were given fourteen months' jail with hard labour in a Dunedin prison, far from home.[20] During the months of July and August 1880, 181 ploughmen were arrested.[21] Hundreds more were to follow in the next two years before the government, tired of the obstruction, would mount an armed raid on Parihaka in November 1881 and arrest the two leaders of the peaceful resistance movement.

In the meantime Forster was put in charge of an AC road party. Between late January and March 1880 he guarded the men who made about 20 kilometres (13 miles) of road, cleared large areas of flax and scrub along the roadsides and at bridges, and moved

1500 cubic yards of earth to build embankments and drainage ditches.[22] The settlers regarded the roads as essential to the resolution of the 'native difficulty' as they called it.[23] The work had a military purpose; the roads would make troop movements easier and it was necessary to clear the scrub to deprive cover for any ambush attempt. But it was also about preparing the land for settlement: surveying, measuring and subdividing.

The leaders at Parihaka spoke of measured ground too but it was not the work of Pākehā surveyors they had in mind, nor the authority of Pākehā law.[24] The point was made most clearly by Tohu in March 1880 at the regular monthly meeting held at Parihaka. 'Formerly, the ground was measured and we are now living upon it,' he said. 'It was not given for two people to stand on. The measurement was settled by former generations and no man shall take it from us.'[25]

After his marriage Forster was stationed at Cape Egmont where he was in charge of the company guarding the men erecting the lighthouse that stands there to this day. It was at the cape that he and Bertha made their first home and where they hosted the farewell visit of Mary and Ellen in the spring of 1880. There was a small stone redoubt next to the lighthouse site but the main camp was about 200 metres away, protected by 'substantial palisading'.[26] It was anything but homely though the Dobie sisters, used to sailing the oceans on small boats and tramping through dense tropical bush for days on end, took it in their stride. 'When we married in 1880 we led a nomad camp life,' Bertha wrote in her memoir. 'No shops to tempt one, cheap rations and soldier servants.'[27]

Although the Dobie women prided themselves on breezing through every hardship, they stayed for only a short time at Egmont before Forster changed places with the officer in charge of the Ōpunake camp, about 18 kilometres to the south. The public reason given at the time was to make the women more comfortable but perhaps the idea was really to look after Ellen rather than her hardy daughters.[28] Ōpunake was the main European base on the coast between the Stony and Waingongoro rivers and it was much larger and more sophisticated than the camp at Egmont. It had a substantial redoubt, with comfortable officers' quarters and a small port which handled most of the supplies that were brought in for the soldiers, surveyors, government officials and settlers who were putting a distinctly European stamp on the surrounding land.

Everything known about Mary's time in Taranaki fits the portrait of the lively, curious, unconventional and energetic woman in the *May Queen* diary and on the excursions to the Hot Lakes and the South Pacific islands. She filled in her time going for long walks with her brother-in-law's two dogs, sketching and meeting interesting people.[29] Her happy ability to cross social boundaries made her a popular figure with the soldiers, just as she had been with the crew of the ship and everyone she met in Fiji and Samoa; she often played tennis with the men on a grass court they had made outside the walls of the redoubt. 'She was very fond of the camp,' wrote Thomas Hughson, 'and used to join in games of lawn tenis [sic] with us frequently.'[30] The same applied to Māori. 'She was in the habit of chatting with the natives, she rather liked them,' Forster recalled. 'She had nothing of treating them as inferiors.'[31]

Among the many people Mary met during her stay in Taranaki was the prophet Te Whiti. Every month he hosted a great hui, or meeting, which could last for days. The purpose was cultural and spiritual as well as political.[32] Parihaka was a pan-tribal settlement and the hui were well attended by Māori from all over the Taranaki district and as far away as the Waikato and Wairarapa.[33] About 1200 people usually gathered although sometimes the figures quoted were as high as 3000.[34] Given that the Māori population of the district at the time was about 3000 the numbers show how deeply Te Whiti's message resonated.[35] Often there were scores of Pākehā there too, enjoying the generous hospitality. The *Taranaki Herald* reported that the feast in November 1880 included 40 boilers of tea, 1800 kete of bread and an abundant supply of pork and fish.[36]

A sketch in the *Illustrated London News* expressed the mood of the crowd in a way that statistics never could. It showed a traffic jam on the road to Parihaka with people crammed into a cart and a bullock dray, or riding horses or simply walking along the road. They are young and old – one figure in the foreground appears to be an old woman wrapped in a cloak and supporting herself with a stick. At the right of the picture are a mother and child. Next to them are a man and a woman on horseback who appear to be more prosperous than the others. But no matter what their mode of transport or their relative wealth or their age, all are rushing eagerly towards the same destination (Fig. 75).

An estimated 1300 people attended the hui in November 1880 and amid the throng hurrying along the road were Bertha Goring and Mary Dobie. About 5 kilometres from the settlement they began to pass through Parihaka's cultivations: fields of potatoes, maize, wheat and tobacco all neatly fenced off to protect them from the large numbers of cattle, horses and pigs grazing the countryside.[37] Parihaka itself was made up of about 250 whare about 7 metres long, 5 metres wide and 3 or 4 metres high with roofs supported by central ridge poles. The interiors were comfortably supplied with blankets and pillows and there was plenty of food; the people all looked well nourished.[38] In a letter written a few days after her visit, Mary described it as the 'principal Maori stronghold', an enormous native town of imposing character, with regular streets of houses. Her artist's eye took in the background of partially cleared bush set against the snow-clad peak of Mount Taranaki which loomed over everything.[39]

She and Bertha were given an enthusiastic reception as they entered the township. 'The native women and children were immensely excited when they saw the Pākehā Wahine (English woman),' she wrote, 'they crowded round me, grinning, jabbering, and shaking hands . . . It was a most picturesque sight, such gay colours, fine looking men and pretty girls.' She was just as excited as they were and, typically, felt some pride at being an almost-pioneer again; only one or two white women had been there before. If the sisters were as much a novelty to Parihaka as Parihaka was to the sisters, one sight was familiar: men and boys playing a game of cricket. 'The bats and wickets were home-made,' wrote Mary, 'but they played just like white men, chucking up the ball when a man was out.'

After the game they followed the crowd to the centre of town for the main event, Te Whiti's speech to his people. 'The natives squatted around with upturned, eager faces, listening intently,' she wrote. 'Te Whiti is a very clever looking man, with a fine head and brow. He gesticulated with his arm raised, and his blanket folded around him. It really was a fine sight, the crowds of natives all listening, babies tumbling about, the women staring at us.'

Mary did not mention the great feast with its copious amounts of tea and servings of pork and fish but it made a lasting impression on Bertha who recalled sitting between

Te Whiti and Tohu, as though she were the guest of honour. 'I was presented with a jar of honey and touched it with my fingers to signify acceptance. This is the Maori custom. They were kind to me,' she told an interviewer shortly before she died in 1936.[40] The hospitality was all the more generous given the close relationship the two women had with a military officer who had been steadily working against the interests of the community for eighteen months.

As she did wherever she went, Mary spent some time sketching and, with hindsight, the three pictures she produced on that day became the most important work of her all-too-brief career as a graphic artist. Uncle Arthur's magazine used them in November 1881 to illustrate its coverage of the Armed Constabulary invading Parihaka to arrest its leaders and disperse the people living there. The first was a sketch looking down on the village from an elevated position (Fig. 41). The second was a profile of Te Whiti with his eyes closed as though in contemplation or prayer and the third was Te Whiti addressing his people, wrapped in his blanket and with a raised arm, just as Mary described him in her accompanying letter (Figs 42, 43).

But the sketch of Te Whiti and his people was not made during his speech, it was posed later on. And there is a story behind the drawing of the village as well, both testaments to the persuasive powers and determination of a Dobie woman. When Mary first asked to be allowed up a hill to sketch Parihaka she was firmly rebuffed. 'The prophet said this was impossible,' according to a story circulating in the Taranaki papers, 'the hill was tapu to the pakeha, and no white man or woman had ever set foot on its summit.'[41] But Mary persisted and, so the story goes, managed to persuade Te Whiti to relent. After the many occasions when she had been 'nearly the first' or 'one of the first' this time she was simply the first, no qualification necessary. The result was the picture captioned 'Parihaka, the principal Maori stronghold' that appeared in the *Graphic*. Te Whiti then went further and obligingly gathered some of his people together to pose for her.[42]

Mary's pictures capture some of the social and political realities of the time but there are contradictions between what she drew and what she wrote. For instance, her description of Parihaka as being 'enormous' hardly corresponds with the drawing of a settlement that could fairly be described as a village, a town at most. Indeed, the image fits most estimates of Parihaka's population at the time of between 1200 and 1500 people. On the other hand she may have been speaking in relative terms because she had never before seen such a large concentration of Māori people. In this sense, then, she was right; Parihaka was the largest Māori settlement at the time.

Less convincing is her description of Parihaka as a stronghold which could mean only that it had some military significance. She may have chosen that word because she was used to hearing it referred to as a 'pā', which generally meant a stockade or fortified place.[43] And yet her eyes should have told her it was nothing of the kind and, as a military observer was to write a month later, there was no sign of fortification although the neighbouring country was rough and partly bush-covered making it ideal for irregular warfare.[44] It did not take a trained soldier's eye to see this and the sketch Mary drew accords with other descriptions of Parihaka and other images, notably photographs. There were no fortifications of any kind, none of the palisades, trench systems or bunkers of the modern pā described by James Belich as the central, innovative feature of Māori resistance to the imperial army in the 1860s.[45]

As well as wrongly characterising it as a stronghold, Mary misses the deep social and political problems of Māori society. For instance, all of the people she described seemed happy, healthy and energetic, yet a government agent, Robert Parris, who was there at the same time, saw something different; an overcrowded town where tuberculosis was a great scourge causing more than average mortality, especially among the children.[46] Nor were the people as united in their outlook as she seemed to think. Her sketch shows them gathered at Te Whiti's feet giving him their rapt attention but the political stand-off with the government had created stresses within Māori society. Some prominent chiefs threw in their lot with the government and others went first one way and then the other.

Hone Pīhama, a Ngāti Ruanui chief from Ōeo, about 15 kilometres south of Ōpunake, was the most prominent of those who had accepted the government's authority and has often been vilified for his 'passive, if not servile, attitude to the Pākehā', says Ngāti Ruanui historian Tony Sole. 'To be fair to him, he had fought, but then opted for another means of survival of his people,' writes Sole. 'Perhaps realising that in the long run he could never survive by force, he seems to have opted for coexistence.'[47] Pīhama's reward came in the form of respect from the settlers and a 1214-hectare (3000-acre) land grant near the towns of Ōeo and Pātea.[48] His choice created tensions within his own family. His wife took his government salary to Parihaka and one of his daughters was steadfast in her loyalty to the prophet.[49] To Te Whiti, Pīhama was one of those who had erred.[50]

By contrast with Pīhama, Wiremu Kingi Matakātea went over to join the Parihaka protest. He had given valuable assistance to the Pākehā not just when they were in distress – as they were when the *Lord Worsley* sank – but in aiding their progress by allowing a trading post at Ōpunake. The government left him alone at first but later he suffered the fate of so many loyal Māori and his land was confiscated too.[51] Although the government returned the land they never confirmed his possession of it so no one could have been surprised when he switched sides and moved his 400 people from their dwellings near Te Namu to Parihaka. He joined the ploughmen and was duly arrested and exiled to the South Island.[52]

Mary's published account also omitted any mention of a telling moment at the end of Te Whiti's speech, one that went to the heart of the political dispute between him and the government. As soon as he finished speaking the government agent Robert Parris – who had been sent to explain a Royal Commission's decision on the land question – began to address the people but Te Whiti stopped him. He had little time for Parris because he was merely the messenger. 'Your speech will be the words of your superior, not your own,' he was quoted as saying in the *Taranaki Herald*. 'Let your superior come and speak for himself. Where is he? Let him come.'[53] These words show the dispute was more than just a material question about who had the right to possess what land; in its fullest sense it was about who had the authority to decide the question and under what rules. The all-encompassing stand-off was over political power, law and custom as well as property. The Royal Commission's recommendation to resolve the problem by setting aside reserves for the Māori population would cut no ice with Te Whiti because it was not their decision to make.

As Sole points out, Te Whiti was asserting article two of the Treaty of Waitangi which, in its Māori text, guaranteed tino rangatiratanga – or chieftainship – which meant full control over the land as well as its possession.[54] If the government of the day had taken any notice of the Treaty they would have asserted article one under which the chiefs who signed it ceded sovereignty in the English text or kawanatanga – governorship – in the Māori text. The dispute, from the government's point of view at least, had nothing to do with the Treaty, which had been declared a nullity by Chief Justice James Prendergast in 1877. But this could not disguise the profound contradiction that separated the two sides. The government was not prepared to recognise Te Whiti's chieftainship as an equal authority and Te Whiti would not recognise the government as superior.

Tohu's comments about the 'measured ground' show how important it was to the Parihaka leaders that the question should be settled according to the customs of their people. Confiscation was possible under these customs – raupatu they called it – but it had to be done as soon as land was conquered.[55] The government, however, had waited for more than ten years to claim the land that it had formally confiscated in the 1860s.[56] By this time the people living between the Waingongoro River in the south and the Stony River to the north had come to assume that the confiscation was meaningless.[57] In asserting his chiefly authority, or tino rangatiratanga, Te Whiti made it very clear that any resolution should be decided in accordance with Māori custom and not Pākehā law. 'Why did not you occupy [the land] at the time of your conquest?' he said to a pair of government emissaries in 1879. 'According to Māori custom you should have done so. I am now in occupation: and even if the land had been taken, I, according to the same custom, having been allowed to reoccupy the land, have not lost my rights of ownership.'[58]

Te Whiti was an enigma to many Pākehā. He appeared to be at once a hard-headed political leader and activist and also a prophet steeped in the Old Testament as well as his native culture. The mixture of his uncompromising political stand and his eloquent but difficult-to-follow speeches and prophecies confounded the Pākehā mind. For them his pacifism was especially hard to grasp and this helped to create wildly contradictory characterisations of him. Some recognised him as a genuine pacifist, others thought that, although he was a pacifist, he would not be able to control his followers who, in the end, would resort to warfare.[59] Still others, men like the Native Minister John Bryce and many of the settlers who badgered the premier in June 1879, thought he was a dangerous fanatic whose peaceful protest would inevitably transform into bloody conflict.[60]

Mary's sketch of Te Whiti addressing his followers shows where she stood in this spectrum of contradictory opinion. It is reminiscent of the Sermon on the Mount with the central figure appearing as a prophet of peace. She must have heard the gossip and theories that he was really a bloodthirsty savage biding his time and yet something had persuaded her otherwise. Maybe it was his demeanour or maybe she was influenced by what she heard at Parihaka that day when he made a fatalistic speech full of scriptural references but clear in its pacifism. 'This day (or time) is quite altered from former days,' the *Taranaki Herald* reported him as saying. 'All old things shall pass away. War shall cease, and shall no longer create disunion in the world.'[61]

If that seems unequivocal, there were occasions when commentators divined the opposite in his words. For example, the speeches at the hui in March 1880, when Te Whiti and Tohu spoke of measured ground, were interpreted by several papers as being 'significant for war'.[62] There were many reasons why the newspapers could portray Te Whiti simultaneously as

FIGS 1 & 2: Mary Dobie and her sister Bertha in 1879, the year before Mary was murdered. *Family album*

FIG. 3: On the fatal day Mary passed near Te Namu Pā, a place as rich in history as the scenery was beautiful. *Rigby Allan, image reproduced by permission of the Allan family, PH2011-0484, PA*

FIG. 4: The tomb with no epitaph pictured in 1929. *PHO2014-0360*

FIG. 5: Bertha, Mary and their mother Ellen on the *May Queen* in 1877. *Mary Dobie, courtesy Drake Brockman family*

FIGS 6 & 7: Uncle Arthur Locker, editor of the *Graphic*, and Uncle Frederick Locker-Lampson, the poet. *Family album*

FIGS 8 & 9: Mary's cousin Eleanor Locker who married Lionel Tennyson, son of the poet laureate. *Family album*

FIG. 10: The Dobie family in Irthington, near Carlisle, about 1860. Standing are daughter Ellen, holding the baby; her husband, John Slater; and Bertha; Stanley poses on one knee. Seated are Mary; Ellen, the matriarch; Herbert; and Hugh, the youngest. *Family album*

FIG. 11: Herbert in 1875, the year he migrated to New Zealand. *Family album*

FIG. 12: Portrait of the artist as a young woman. *Family album*

FIGS 13 & 14: Examples of Mary's work in England. A family picnic at Talkin Tarn park near Irthington and the beach at Sheerness in Kent where Mary stayed the year before she came to New Zealand. *Family album*

FIG. 15: Henry Dixon steps out. *Mary Dobie, from* The Voyage of the May Queen, *courtesy Drake Brockman family*

FIG. 16: The catastrophe. *Mary Dobie, from* The Voyage of the May Queen, *courtesy Drake Brockman family*

a pacifist and bloodthirsty fanatic. His oratory was difficult to translate says the historian Hazel Riseborough in *Days of Darkness* and the task was beyond the competence of most, if not all, of the interpreters who often lacked integrity, had their own axes to grind and were beholden to their political masters.[63]

Another factor that influenced how the settlers saw Te Whiti and interpreted his words was their emotional state, so forcefully expressed during public meetings when Grey came to New Plymouth in 1879. They did not get much sympathy at the time either from the government or the *New Zealand Herald* which pointed out that Māori were no longer able to mount a conventional war as they had done in the 1860s. They were generally believed to be a dying race, a belief reinforced by statistics which showed five times as many Pākehā as Māori in Taranaki and eleven times as many across the whole country.[64] The settlers have not gained much sympathy in posterity either with historians making the point that by 1880 the scaremongering had a hollow ring and the hysteria it provoked made it easier to justify the later use of force.[65]

The settlers' fears certainly were used for political purposes and they were irrational but this does not mean they were not genuine. The cool logic of the census figures does not explain what really frightened them, which was not so much a resumption of open war as envisaged by the *Herald*, but of being murdered in their beds as Wilson, the anxious Urenui settler, told Grey. He was referring to something that in twenty-first-century military parlance would be called 'asymmetrical war' in which one side, knowing it cannot win a set-piece battle, conducts small-scale campaigns which are sometimes defined as guerrilla tactics and sometimes terrorism.

Within living memory there had been plenty of examples of this kind of warfare. William Seffern, editor of the *Taranaki Herald*, recalled a series of massacres and murders in the 1860s which would have encouraged feelings of insecurity among the settlers: Te Kooti's attack on Poverty Bay which left 50 or more people dead and, closer to home, the killing at White Cliffs of the Reverend John Whiteley and six settlers including a woman and two children, not to mention the fate of the Reverend Carl Völkner.[66] Memories of these killings would surely have played on the minds of settlers and nullified the logic of population numbers. Added to that was the presence of Tītokowaru, who had returned to the Waimate Plains; though he joined the pacifist ploughmen his fearsome reputation lived on.[67]

One man became the focus of settler unease. Not Te Whiti but Hiroki of Ngā Rauru and Waikato descent who had killed a surveyor south of the Waingongoro River in September 1878 and escaped to find sanctuary at Parihaka. The reason for the killing was not clear. One version had the motive as personal, a dispute over a dog and a pig. Another said it was a political killing; Hiroki was protesting against the confiscation of land.[68] To the Pākehā it bore an uncomfortable resemblance to the killing of three settlers caught felling timber on Ngā Ruahine land in 1868 which were the opening shots of Tītokowaru's war.[69] Like the people of Parihaka, Ngā Ruahine were resisting the alienation of their land but they did it by fighting. Under Tītokowaru they inflicted heavy defeats on the colonial forces at Te Ngutu-o-te-manu and Moturoa and burned some settler houses.[70]

The Dobies probably would have known about Tītokowaru's campaign because Forster had fought with distinction at the two losing engagements. They knew about Hiroki too. He was the settlers' bogeyman, a lightning rod for all their anxieties, representing their worst nightmare, an example of someone who could commit a stealthy murder with impunity. His sanctuary at Parihaka suggested to Pākehā that Te Whiti was not only insincere about pacificism but was condoning and protecting what they feared most. Hiroki was at Parihaka when Mary visited and she expressed the feelings of many when she wrote: 'I saw . . . Hiroki, the murderer, and he looked such.'[71]

With the bloody recent history and so much uncertainty in the air, it would be reasonable to expect that the settlers might be careful about going out alone and that folk of the two races would be wary about mingling. But by the time of Mary's visit the anxiety that had been so obvious in the winter of 1879 had faded. Major Stapp, who at first had such success in raising his volunteer corps, was now having trouble persuading the men to stay on. His official letterbook for the months of May to September 1880 is full of correspondence about units disbanding because of lack of interest.[72]

The absence of tension was reflected out on the roads where, despite the worries of joiner Charles Taylor, Pākehā usually travelled with confidence that they would not be molested. There was Mary, of course, who explored the countryside on foot and a farmer's wife who regularly walked to Ōpunake with a baby wrapped in a shawl and carrying a kete of butter to sell or barter.[73] It was not just that the two peoples left each other alone, there was plenty of cordial mixing between Pākehā and Māori. An itinerant labourer, Thomas Blanchett, received nothing but kindness from people he met in the bush. Once when he was lost, two old Māori fed him: 'They had had dinner but pointed to a saucepan with some cooked mashed potatoes, and as I was a bit ravenous I quickly dug my fingers into it and appeased my hunger. I found them absolutely lovely.'⁷⁴ Next day a young woman gave him a lift to the beach on a bullock dray, also fed him and then directed him to his destination.⁷⁵

Although surface tensions had eased, Blanchett's encounter with the woman revealed that there was still deep Māori animosity towards one section of Pākehā society, the soldiers. 'I was just about to thank her again for the lift when she asked me if I was a soldier,' he wrote. 'I said no I am going to my brother at the soldier's camp . . . Although she spoke very broken English she was able to say "I kill the Soldier", really meaning that every soldier was their enemy.'⁷⁶ Constable Thomas Hughson would have understood the point; his contacts with Māori at the time had none of the goodwill described by Blanchett. 'The Maories was very sulky with us all,' he said, referring to the period in mid-1880 which he spent working on the roads with a rifle by his side.⁷⁷

So although the great fear had subsided considerably by the time of the Dobies' visit, it still festered beneath a veneer of calm, and Mary's mother could not help but worry about her adventurous daughter. 'I am now here going about and doing all sorts of things,' Mary wrote a few days after visiting Te Whiti, 'but my mother says I'm too daring, and if I go on something will happen to me.'⁷⁸

5.

THE FATAL DAY

Mary woke on the last day of her life in Ōpunake, a few kilometres from Parihaka but in a different world. Unlike Te Whiti's village, the settlement on the coast fully deserved the description of stronghold. Its most outstanding feature was the redoubt built on a spectacular 30-metre cliff at the southern end of Ōpunake Bay. To the south the ground sloped away to a depression, an old watercourse where the soldiers had planted a kitchen garden. They had also cleared some ground and made the tennis court where Mary and Bertha often played. The redoubt was first established in the 1860s to supply the British Army which was campaigning in Taranaki at the time. By 1880 its massive earth walls enclosed a barrack room, a storeroom, quarters for the officers and an open area for tents.[1] It even had a library and a band. On the landward side was a deep trench which made the walls seem higher than their 4 metres. Entry was by two heavy gates, one on the north side and the other on the south. Within the walls was room enough for 100 men but the constabulary boasted that the redoubt could be held by a handful from a bulletproof, loopholed blockhouse on one of the corners.[2]

Differences between the two settlements went much deeper than military engineering. Quite apart from the obvious political tensions, the economic and social lives of the two places had little in common. Parihaka was a rural settlement, dependent on its extensive cultivations and dedicated to Māori customs and a Māori way of life. Ōpunake was a military base, a port, a trading post, a service town and social melting pot. Apart from the soldiers, its most important industry in the early days was flax, harvested, milled and turned into rope for export. At the time of the Dobies' visit it had two general stores, Martin Coffey's and Emanuel Bayley's, and all manner of useful tradesmen from butchers to builders and any others needed to keep the horse-drawn economy operating smoothly including saddlers, bridle makers, blacksmiths and wheelwrights.[3]

It also had a brewery and two hotels, the Empire and the Telegraph which was run by the Middleton brothers. The hotels did a roaring trade especially with the soldiers. Thomas Hughson said the men dreaded doing guard duty on pay day because the guard tent would be overflowing with their drunken comrades and there would be no room for those on duty to sit down.[4] According to one story Forster played an unintended but critical role in the establishment of the Telegraph Hotel and the larger township. While stationed at Ōpunake as a young officer in the 1860s he noticed that many Māori came to the redoubt to trade, so Forster suggested to Matakātea that they should build a store. Matakātea agreed and offered the land, probably not expecting the Pākehā to take a square mile and build a hotel first, albeit one with a general store attached.[5]

Despite the hiccup at the beginning, Forster's vision was realised and by 1880 Ōpunake was thriving. People – Māori and Pākehā – came from all over the district to buy the goods and services they needed as well as to sell their produce. Hone Pīhama, for instance, sold supplies including potatoes and horse feed to William Skinner the surveyor.[6] And one of his people, Tuhiata or Tuhi as he was better known, followed the chief's example by selling produce to the hotels and the redoubt. His family cultivated potatoes and maize and raised pigs for slaughter on their land near the mouth of the Pūnehu River, about 6 kilometres to the south. Tuhi also had a sideline in selling horses to the AC. He followed Pīhama's example in politics as well. Although, like most of his people, he sometimes attended the monthly meetings at Parihaka he refused to join the ploughmen. One reason he gave was an overwhelming dread of being imprisoned.[7] Another was that his parents would not allow him to go, perhaps because he was too important to the family enterprise which was enmeshed in the Pākehā economy.[8]

Ōpunake was no metropolis but it must have seemed like a welcome oasis for Bertha who had not yet spent enough time in military camps to become used to them. Mary loved it but as much for its natural beauty as anything else. On the morning of Thursday, 25 November 1880 she wrote a letter full of high spirits and enthusiasm for the lovely scenery to her brother Herbert who was in Auckland preparing for the publication of his book *New Zealand Ferns*.[9] Her plan that afternoon was to walk towards Te Namu Pā and possibly do some sketching one last time before she set out on the return voyage to England. To walk there and back would probably take an hour or an hour and a half, maybe a little longer if she stopped to sketch. On returning she had a date with Bertha for a game of tennis. There would be plenty of time with summer coming and the days growing longer; the sun would not go down until after 7 p.m. While Mary was making her plans for an easy-going day, Forster was grappling with the cares and duties of being a minor cog in an obscure part of the great British imperial machine. He left the women about 8.30 a.m. to head for Ōeo on official business.[10]

The main task at the redoubt in the morning was to unload a government steamer which was anchored in the bay. This was a difficult job requiring plenty of strength and stamina. There was no wharf so the AC men rowed out in surf boats to bring the cargo and passengers ashore. At the best of times this was a challenging job but the bay's exposure to strong westerlies sometimes meant it was all but impossible. The men often had to strip to the waist and wade into the shallows to pull the boats ashore through the pounding surf.[11] It had been a day like that when Thomas Hughson arrived as part of an AC contingent in March 1880. The boats ran aground and the soldiers carried all the people and the cargo ashore on their backs.[12] When they made it to the beach the task was only half done; they still had to carry the cargo up a winding path cut into the cliff at the southern end of the bay.[13]

As a reward for a hard morning's work, the team would be given the rest of the day off and, on the last day of Mary's life, most of them headed to the Middletons' Telegraph Hotel. For all the advantages Ōpunake had over a place like the Egmont camp, life was so dull that the AC band was considered the brightest thing about it. The little library did not do much to alleviate the boredom either because the books were mostly serious novels, sermons and uplifting literature. A much greater attraction was the pub. The town's hotels were the centres of the social melting pot; people from all over the district, settlers and soldiers, Māori and Pākehā, women and men, came to Ōpunake to mingle in the pubs as well as to conduct their business. In its own way, Ōpunake was as open and welcoming as Parihaka although Te Whiti would not have approved of the alcohol which he regarded as a scourge of his people and had tried to exclude from the areas under his authority.[14]

Temperance was the last thing on the minds of those who crowded into the Telegraph Hotel on this springtime morning. Harry Middleton, who was on duty at the time, said there were 'a great many people in'.[15] As well as the soldiers the customers included Rona Matiu, an Ōpunake man who epitomised Te Whiti's reasons for opposing alcohol; he spent part of the morning on the beach drinking beer and the rest of the day in the pub doing likewise. Also in the pub were Tuhi and his friend William Eyes, a settler who lived near him at Pūnehu.[16]

By midday patrons were spilling into the street and showing the effects of drink. Tuhi was in the thick of the fun and games although, as he told Middleton, he was supposed to be riding to Te Namu to catch a horse which had broken free and which he planned to sell so he could settle his debts.[17] Whatever his economic value to his family, he appeared to be in poor financial shape. He was raggedly dressed and in debt all over town; he owed storekeeper Emanuel Bayley 17s 6d for a coat and Middleton one or two pounds for drinks and tobacco. At one point he was play-wrestling in the street and later he took off his jacket and reluctantly performed a haka in the tap room after being egged on by other drinkers. A couple of times during the morning he broke away from his companions and went to Martin Coffey's store to try to buy a pair of moleskin trousers on credit. His own were so torn and ragged that he wore a pair of tweeds underneath them to camouflage the holes left by the tears. Coffey would not do a deal with him because his credit was so bad.

After lunch Mary came out for her walk. She wore a blue serge dress and a hat and was accompanied by her brother-in-law's two black dogs, one a cocker spaniel, probably Snipe who had been on the trip to the Hot Lakes, and the other a retriever, barely more than a puppy. Her first stop was Coffey's store where she bought a carpenter's pencil for twopence, paying with a sixpenny piece and taking a threepenny piece and two halfpennies in change. She asked Coffey to sharpen it but, perhaps being particular about how she wanted the job done, changed her mind, borrowed his knife and did it herself. Then she headed up the road.[18]

At least three people saw her as she left the store and began her walk; an off-duty constable Dennis Connor and Tuhi from Pūnehu were on the veranda of the hotel at the time and the settler William Eyes was outside Coffey's.[19] It was a beautiful day with a light southwest breeze and clouds scudding across the sky. As Mary and the two dogs strolled along, she picked a bunch of wild flowers. The road was straight for most of the way and the seaward side was thickly covered with flax, some of it taller than a man, but there were gaps through which a walker might snatch glimpses of the sea.[20] Te Namu itself was regarded as one of the most beautiful spots in the area and the *Taranaki Herald* had no doubts about why Mary would want to go to there. 'For an artist, this spot would have more than usual charms,' it said, 'and no doubt wishing to see the place again for the last time she was attracted thither'.²¹

Along the way Mary passed the ruins of an old flax mill which had thrived briefly during the early 1870s and remained as a reminder of Pākehā interest in the natural resources of the land. Te Namu Pā itself was also deserted now that Matakātea's people had gone to Parihaka. It was a sign of how dramatically times had changed since Matakātea and Te Whiti had played a leading role in helping the survivors of the *Lord Worsley*. In those days the chiefs were very much in charge and the negotiations and decisions over what happened to the wreck and its survivors were conducted by their rules. But now the government had taken control of the coastal area and was vigorously staking its claim to the hinterland as well, insisting that the question of ownership and occupation should be decided by the state according to Pākehā law.

Harry Middleton said the road was so straight it was possible to see someone nearly all the way to Te Namu from the hotel.²² But he was surely exaggerating. At a distance of nearly 2 kilometres a figure would be like a speck of dust to the naked eye, if visible at all. And even if some sharp-eyed observer could see Mary, the road veered inland and dipped into a gully carved out by the Ōtahi Stream before it passed on the landward side of the pā. On the high ground just beyond the stream was a cluster of stones which was the best place to view and sketch the mountain if the weather was clear, as it was on Mary's last day. Eyes saw her pass the post office and Connor said he watched her from outside the hotel until she had gone about 800 yards.²³

Apart from her killer, the only others to see her alive that afternoon were two men on horseback cantering north along the road. One was a soldier, Constable McGrath, and the other was Walter Stannard, a horse-breaker from Hawera who had been hired by a settler to catch a stray horse. In the three years he had spent in New Zealand, Stannard had worked at various places and various jobs before settling down. He had been married just a week and unlike Tuhi, the other horse-catcher in town that day, remained focused on the job, resisting any temptation of taking refreshment at the pub. McGrath and Stannard recalled seeing the woman in the blue dress with the two dogs as they hurried by, although they differed slightly on where they saw her. Stannard thought they passed her when she was about a mile (1600 metres) from Ōpunake whereas McGrath thought she was much closer to town at the time, just 40 metres north of the telegraph office.[24]

The road that Mary trod seems lonely by twenty-first century standards, but around the time of the monthly meetings at Parihaka it could be the busiest highway in the province as hundreds of people came and went. On the afternoon of Mary's last day at least ten people passed along it, some of them more than once. Going north at first were Stannard, McGrath and Tuhi who had managed to pull himself away from the pub in the early afternoon and was riding quickly up the road on his black horse.[25] Coming south were Thomas Reilly, a labourer on his way to Ōpunake for provisions, and a group of six, led by Hone Pīhama, on their way home to Ōeo from the November meeting at Parihaka where Mary had been so impressed with Te Whiti. They were divided between two buggies and three horses strung out along the road; the buggies setting the pace at a trot and the horses cantering some distance behind.

Reilly was going home with his shopping in the late afternoon when he passed Stannard heading south to Ōpunake, leading his captured horse which had no bridle. He described the horse as 'restive'.²⁶ By this time, Pīhama and his party had already arrived in town where they were joined by Tuhi who, unlike Stannard, had failed in his objective and was returning to the pub. Middleton recalled an influx of about a dozen Māori including Tuhi and Pīhama's party.²⁷ Later Stannard and John Stevenson, the man who had hired him to catch the horse, came in for a meal and once again the hotel was crowded. Business was booming for the Middleton brothers.

Amid the comings and goings of the bar the two horse-catchers stood out, though for different reasons. Patrons could not help but notice Tuhi, who was in an 'excitable' mood according to Middleton, and, over a beer with the Ōeo party, resumed his campaign for a new pair of moleskins. 'Give me a pair of trousers, you see that mine are broken,' he said to Pīhama, holding up his leg and showing his torn moleskins.²⁸ Pīhama, who described Tuhi as 'one of my people', refused but Tuhi kept nagging him and followed him to Coffey's store where he asked the question again and again. But, as it had been from Coffey in the morning, the answer was no, and Pīhama's party resumed their journey home to Ōeo after just one or two drinks.

Tuhi lingered and made Harry Middleton the new target of his campaign for a pair trousers, only now he had raised his sights and wanted a bottle of brandy as well and to borrow a bridle because his own was broken. Middleton also refused the request for trousers but gave him the brandy and told him to go to the stables where the groom would lend him a bridle. Even though Tuhi had failed to catch his horse and therefore would have no money, Middleton was intending to take some pigs from him as a trade. In the stables Tuhi showed the effects of a long day at the pub when he pulled the brandy bottle from his pocket and it slipped through his fingers and smashed on the floor. With the overconfidence and distorted judgement of a drunken man he returned to Middleton, asking him to replace the shattered bottle. This time his host was not so generous even though he later said he did not think Tuhi was drunk at the time.

Stannard, the other horse-catcher, was quiet and well behaved by contrast; he drew attention to himself not because of anything he said or did but because his clothes were smeared with blood when he came in for dinner. At first the other drinkers did not read anything into it. He was, after all, a horse-breaker who might well spill blood at his work. But that was before they heard about the disappearance of Mary Dobie.

Bertha had expected Mary back for her game of tennis by mid- to late afternoon. When Mary failed to appear Bertha and her mother were naturally anxious. Their first thought was that she must have tried to make her way down to the beach and become lost in the flax, or perhaps she had slipped on rocks and sprained her ankle.[29] With Forster away in Ōeo, Bertha turned to Sergeant Arthur McKeon and asked him to send someone to look for her sister.[30] McKeon, if anything, was more worried than the two women and about 4.30 p.m. he sent three men instead of one. William Wilson went south in case Mary had changed her destination without telling anyone. Joseph Tosland went north along the beach to search among the rocks. Mounted Constable Handed followed Mary's footsteps along the road where, near Te Namu, he encountered Stannard in his bloodstained clothes taking his captured horse to Ōpunake.[31]

Goring's two dogs suddenly appeared from the flax bushes and Handed cooeed for Mary about 5 p.m. but there was no response.[32] The appearance of the dogs and the silence that greeted the searcher's call transformed the mood from a general sense of disquiet into alarm. Dusk was coming and now the best that anyone could hope for was that Mary had met with a serious accident and needed rescuing before she was enveloped in darkness. The worst? That remained unspoken for the time being.

Word of Mary's disappearance had spread quickly through the camp and the village so when McKeon decided to expand the search at about 6 p.m. he had plenty of volunteers.[33] As Mary had last been seen heading north he concentrated all his efforts on the main road. The search party trudged up both sides in the last hour of daylight and when the sun set they bolstered their efforts with fire and noise: bonfires lit along the coastline and a bugler sending out regular calls in the hope of guiding Mary home to safety.[34] But still there was no response and the searchers, lighting their way on the moonless night with torches made from flax, uncovered no clue to what had become of her.

Forster returned from Ōeo about 8.30 p.m. and on hearing the disturbing news went out immediately to join the search party.[35] They had found nothing and were spreading ever deeper into the flax bushes along the seaward side of the road near Te Namu where eventually they found her. By one account it was the combination of a trail of blood and the dogs that led them to Mary but the truth was not so sophisticated.[36] The flax torches did not give up enough light to pick out bloodstains in the dark and the dogs had long since retired to the comfort of the officers' quarters.

It was Constable Wilson who made the discovery. And it was luck rather than good management that brought him to Mary's body. 'I searched about,' he said, 'and eventually came upon the deceased, Miss Dobie'.[37] He was looking for her on the high ground just beyond the Ōtahi Stream and had drifted about 30 metres from the road, past the cluster of stones and over the rise of a small hill, when his torch caught the reflection of something white in the flax.[38] It was Mary lying partly concealed in a bush. Most of her torso was obscured but her legs were visible and her blue dress was above her knees, leaving the white of her underclothes exposed to catch the light of the searching torch. 'She's here,' cried Wilson at the top of his voice and all the others hurried over to him.[39]

Forster was among them. 'I saw her lying under a flax bush with her left arm over her throat as if to protect it,' he said. 'She was lying partly on her back and partly on [her] left side.' He added the gory details in a series of short, sharp stabs: 'Her knees bent, her face covered with blood, her legs were exposed as far as her knees. Her throat was cut. She had a collar on her neck and a silk handkerchief – these were saturated with blood.'[40] In most respects his description accorded with that of other eyewitnesses, but perhaps because of the shock, he confused the left and right arms. Everyone else said the left arm was stretched out and the right was in what could be interpreted as a defensive position.[41]

The search party sent for a stretcher and by the time it arrived the body was stiff and cold, set in its grotesque posture.[42] A melancholy procession headed towards Ōpunake as they took Mary's body back along the dark road with only the pale light of the flax torches to guide the way. Judging by the distance it must have taken about an hour from the time the body was found and this may explain the discrepancies in early news reports which put the discovery at either 9.30 or 10.30 p.m. Once at the redoubt, they took the body to a tent and laid it on a table where Sergeant William Ebbett and his wife Mary Ann took charge. Checking the top pocket of Mary's dress, they found it empty, and then left the body to await a full examination by the doctor in the morning.[43]

Some of the drinkers at the Telegraph Hotel had been too preoccupied with their own pleasures and interests to take much notice of the bugle calling outside. Tuhi's campaign for new trousers, a bridle and more alcohol saw him come and go during the evening. As well as visiting the stable and Coffey's store with Pīhama he went to Emanuel Bayley's place in the vain hope of buying some alcohol on credit and, finally, back to Coffey's where he bought a box of matches. Meanwhile Stannard seems to have spent most of the time explaining himself to Stevenson; the horse he brought back to Ōpunake did not belong to his employer. And then there was the blood on his clothes. His story was that it came from his own horse which had fallen and cut its nose while in pursuit of the stray.[44]

News from the outside eventually penetrated the public bar and when Stannard told Stevenson that he had passed a woman on the road near Te Namu that afternoon they decided to join the search. In the company of another man they set off but they had just reached the telegraph office when Tuhi rode up and told them Mary had been found dead with her throat cut.[45] The effect on Stannard was instant and startling. He was 'much excited' said Stevenson and drew his knife, swearing that no one would attack him with that in his hand. 'He also said if he had a good horse he would catch the murderer wherever he might be.'[46]

But Stannard would never be the hunter; he was already the hunted himself. The manner of Mary's death gave significance to the conspicuous bloodstains on his clothes. Word of the incriminating evidence spread as fast as the news that Mary's body had been found and everyone in town was on the lookout for the Hawera horse-catcher. It was Constable Wilson who spotted the prime suspect first. He came upon the three men shortly after they had heard the news from Tuhi and asked Stannard to accompany him to the redoubt.[47] Sergeant McKeon did not waste any time. He could hardly have missed the bloodstains but he noticed something else that justified the accusing finger: there were traces of flax on Stannard's boots.[48] The stains, the flax and the certain knowledge that this man had been in the right place at the right time added up to enough evidence to arrest him on suspicion of murder.[49]

As soon as Mary's death was confirmed the news began to spread beyond the boundaries of the small settlement on the Taranaki coast. The first message was carried out by an orderly who rode north through the darkness for Pungarehu where the commanding officer, Lieutenant Colonel John Roberts, was staying. The night had been pitch black since sunset but about midnight the moon in the last quarter rose to cast a guiding light for the messenger on his grim mission. Captain Stuart Newall recalled him arriving about two o'clock in the morning 'bearing the horrible intelligence that Miss Dobie, sister of Mrs Goring had been murdered last evening while taking a walk this side of Ōpunake'.[50] Colonel Roberts immediately saddled his horse and rode south. He was followed from Pungarehu by the army medical officer Dr Langer Carey, who would perform an autopsy on the body in the morning.

That night the news also reached the Egmont camp where Thomas Hughson was based. He recorded that one of the men was woken at about midnight and sent to Ōpunake, presumably because he was under suspicion, too, having passed the scene about the time the deed was done.[51] All day the Pungarehu garrison was starved of news and desperate to hear more. 'Up till 4PM today we know nothing more than that the poor victim's head is nearly cut off and that a man . . . has been arrested on suspicion,' wrote Newall in his diary that evening. The routine of surveying and road making went on as normal but there was only one thing on everyone's mind. 'I am suffering from headache; and have not been able to dismiss poor Miss Dobie and her mother & sister from my mind all day', said Newall.[52]

The family were crushed when they got word of Mary's death.[53] When Roberts returned from Ōpunake he told Newall that Bertha and Forster did not have the heart to tell Ellen her daughter was the victim of a bloody murder so they told her she had been fatally gored by a bull.[54] They were being kind to be cruel because they must have known that sooner or later Ellen would discover she had been misled. The story was the first of many deaths ascribed to Mary and it was unique in a couple of ways; it was obviously not true and it remained private. All the many other versions of how Mary died were loudly canvassed in public and it was hard to tell whether they were true, untrue or partly true. The public were so impatient for information they could not wait for the police investigation or for the law to take its stately course; they wanted to know with an urgency that would not be restrained for a single moment. Who had done this terrible thing, how did it happen and why? Burning questions all, but the last one was the deepest and hardest to answer.

Even more than answers the folk of Ōpunake wanted justice served, by which they meant revenge. Whoever had done this thing, and for whatever motive, he would pay with his life. Such was the intensity of feeling that no one paused to await a dispassionate and objective weighing of the evidence. Each new fact or opinion that appeared in the newspapers or was picked up in the porous network of national gossip was seized upon to advance one theory or to knock down another. The guiding principle was not the cool, bright light of logic but a hot, red flame which burned with prejudice, fear and anger.

6.

BREAKING NEWS

By dawn everyone in Ōpunake had heard the news and many could not resist the macabre urge to visit the scene of the crime. All morning, crowds retraced Mary's steps along the road where they found a trail of blood, invisible by torchlight the night before but all too clear in the morning. It began on the side of the metal road and led through the flax and the toe toe, past the cluster of stones and over the hill to the place where the body was found. The bloodstains were faint at first but the further from the road the darker they became. Thirty metres along the trail there was a pool of dried blood the size of a saucer. A few metres further on the grass was flattened, suggesting that Mary had been dragged the last few steps of the way to her temporary grave.[1] The sight proved too much for some of those who had come to gaze and gawp. 'Strong "rough and ready" men were seen crying like children,' reported the *Taranaki Herald*, 'and at the same time vowing unutterable vengeance on the murderer.'[2]

The mixture of shock and lust for revenge was echoed again and again as news of Mary's death spread across the land. It reached William Skinner in New Plymouth early on Friday morning. 'It is a most dreadful occurrence and one on which hanging seems too good for the perpetrator,' he wrote in his diary.[3] By Friday evening few, if anyone in the country, remained unaware of Mary's fate. Diabolical, dreadful and brutal were the words favoured by the headline writers.[4] Every newspaper tried as best it could to report on the mood of its particular community. In the town where Mary had made her home for the past three years, her death was the only topic of conversation. 'Probably very few events could have caused the painful feeling manifested in Auckland yesterday when the news was received of the murder of Miss Dobie,' said the *New Zealand Herald*. 'The young lady was widely known in Auckland, and few were more highly esteemed for amiable disposition and high talent.'[5] The About Town columnist for the *Observer* seemed to be suggesting a good proportion of the city was teetering on the edge of a nervous breakdown: 'When the news first came, strong men turned faint and white, and expressions of pain and sorrow were on every lip,' he wrote. 'About three in the afternoon I met a gentleman, who knew the lady well, hurrying home. He was so much upset as to be quite unable to converse, and stayed in the house ill for two days afterwards.'[6]

Mary's host on her Fiji trip, Sir Arthur Gordon, had just arrived in New Zealand to take over as governor. He was preoccupied with the political stand-off over Parihaka but one of his first official statements was to offer his condolences for the young woman he had farewelled on the waterfront of Levuka ten months ago. 'His Excellency . . . was greatly shocked and grieved,' said a report published by most papers. 'He greatly admired the talent, refinement, and enthusiasm of these young ladies, more particularly the ability of the lamented victim of this atrocious outrage.'[7] For some people the news – and the shock – took weeks or months to hit home. Far out on Norfolk Island the Reverend Vicesimus Lush heard of Mary's death when he received copies of the *Thames Star* ten days later. He wrote that his son Martin – who played in *The Rivals* with Mary – was 'greatly shocked at the dreadful deed'.[8] And it was not until the end of January 1881, nearly two months after the murder, that the Tennyson family in Britain heard about it and were similarly shocked. 'No further news from New Zealand . . . there do not appear to be any horrid details about poor Mary,' wrote Lionel Tennyson to his father, the poet laureate.[9]

Though communications in those days were much slower than in the twenty-first century the wheels of justice whirred much faster. Representatives of the justice system did not waste any time in seeking the answers to the burning questions. The day after Mary's death a coroner arrived to hold an immediate inquest, starting even before the police investigation was complete. He was to hear from 39 witnesses on the Saturday and Monday. Also called to Ōpunake were civilian detectives to take over from the AC who were soldiers rather than investigators. Led by Superintendent William James from Whanganui, the civilian police would run the inquiry and prepare the evidence to go before the coroner. But it would be Friday afternoon before the first detective arrived and in the meantime the AC men did what they could.

In the coming days there would be all kinds of theories published as the papers rushed each update and fresh snippet of information into print. Breaking news could not wait for confirmation and many reports, and the conclusions drawn from them, were contradictory, exaggerated or plain wrong. Opinion and rumour shot ahead of the painstaking business of gathering evidence and were repeatedly confounded as new facts were drip-fed to the inquest. Many theories, advanced confidently and stridently on one day, had to be abandoned on the next. The private writings of men such as William Skinner, Thomas Hughson and Stuart Newall show the public were following every development with intense interest.[10]

Most at first jumped to what seemed the obvious conclusion that Mary had been raped and then killed. No one said the word 'rape' but there was no mistaking the meaning of the euphemisms they employed in its stead. 'Later intelligence is that the unfortunate young lady was outraged before death,' reported the Auckland *Star* on the day after the body was found.[11] Other reports – which frequently referred to her as a girl even though she was 29 – said she had been 'ravished' or 'ill-treated' or, at least, the killer had made the attempt.[12] 'The object of the murderer appears to have been to violate her chastity, but failing in his object he seems to have slaughtered the poor girl. It is a most revolting affair,' said the *Manawatu Herald*.[13] Those who believed it was a sex crime emphasised that Mary's clothing was in disarray.[14]

The most powerful statement of revulsion came from the *New Zealand Times* in Wellington on the Saturday morning after the murder. Fired by the hot flame of anger, the paper said the crime would cause a thrill of horror to vibrate through the heart of every man and woman in New Zealand.[15] 'No crime has caused so intense a feeling of horror as this probable attempt at outrage, and murder of Miss Dobie.' The killer was 'a fiend in human shape' and a 'very monster of iniquity'. He was one of those men in this world so degraded and embrutalised that the human imagination could scarcely fathom the depth of their cruelty, wickedness and baseness. 'Someone must be brought to justice and hanged for the foul murder. The blood of the innocent victim calls out aloud to the God of Justice for vengeance upon her murderer.' The hysterical tone reflected accurately the anger and desire for vengeance in the community as expressed by the strong men of Ōpunake, the citizens on the streets of Auckland and, ironically, by Stannard, the accused man, when he first heard the news from Tuhi.

Even those whose better nature made them call for a calm and rational response to the crime could not resist the emotional power of the event. 'It is not our intention to inflict upon our readers any of those wild and hysterical outbursts which some journals seem to consider indispensable on such occasions,' said the *Evening Post* in a sanctimonious commentary on the *Times*.[16] 'In truth all those antiquated and inflated references to "the God of justice," and "a damned deed," and "calling aloud for vengeance on the murderer," and so forth, approach much too nearly to the ludicrous to be in good taste under circumstances so painful.' But the upwelling of anger in the community proved too much even for the self-righteous *Post*. Halfway through the editorial, the writer seemed to undergo a personality change, flipping from a rational attempt to calm the storm to a flight of hysteria as wild as the one he had been criticising. 'It is hard to conceive a crime more atrocious in all its circumstances, and the public mind will not be at rest until it has been clearly proved that such horrors are not to be perpetrated in our midst with impunity,' said the paper introducing an argument in favour of the death penalty.

Before the identity of the killer was known, the paper compared him to Ned Kelly the Australian bushranger who had been executed two weeks previously for the murder of a policeman. Both, said the *Post*, were 'noxious vermin, scourges of the human race, and, in the interest of humanity, ought to be extirpated with all possible despatch'. The paper expected opposition to the death penalty as had happened in Melbourne, where thousands of Kelly's sympathisers had glorified him as a hero and protested violently at his 'well deserved execution'. Such people were weak-minded, according to the *Post*, but they could do infinite harm by allowing the deeds of people like Kelly and Dobie's killer to go comparatively unpunished. Sympathy for Kelly in the Australian colony of Victoria had cost many lives and encouraged many to emulate his deeds. Men should understand, said the *Post*, that if they don't want to be hanged they should not commit murder. 'We urge, therefore, that no exertion, trouble or expense should be spared to discover, capture, and convict the murderer of Miss Dobie, and that, when convicted, nothing should be allowed to save him from his well-deserved fate: he should be put to an ignominious death, without pity and without compunction.'

Mixed with these outpourings of vengeful anger was a paradoxical note, a sense of relief that the crime appeared to be motivated by sex rather than politics. The former produced an eruption of righteous anger but the latter would have provoked an even more powerful and uncontrollable emotion: fear. Although their anxieties had eased from the extremes of mid-1879 when the Parihaka ploughmen began their protests, the settlers could never free themselves from the worry that colonisation's steadily increasing pressure over the land would eventually result in a violent response.

The arrest of Stannard the Pākehā was therefore greeted eagerly as a sure sign the settlers had nothing to fear even though there was plenty to be angry about. If Stannard was the guilty man the possibility of political motives could be ruled out and therefore the crime was an isolated incident unlikely to be the first in a series of random killings that could lead to a general uprising or the start of a terror campaign. 'It is very satisfactory . . . to think that the atrocious deed has not been committed by the Māoris, nor anyone connected with the settlement,' said the *Taranaki Herald* referring to Parihaka, 'as the suspicion points to a man whose character has never been of the best, and who, from information to hand, we find has blood upon his clothes'.[17] In Auckland, the *New Zealand Herald* agreed even as it acknowledged the widespread expectation of some event which would be equivalent in Māori notions to a declaration of war. However, it said that if the Māori wanted to kill someone in protest against the occupation of their land – in referring to 'their land' inadvertently conceding their rights – they would have chosen a man, perhaps a surveyor, a constable or a government official. 'The idea that the murder of Miss Dobie is consequent upon our political position with regard to the natives is, we think, out of the question,' said the *Herald* in its editorial on Saturday morning.[18]

To reinforce their conviction that this was not a political murder, the press set out to discover as much as they could about the accused. The *Taranaki Herald* had said his character was not the best and now papers in almost every town where he had lived in New Zealand added scraps of information to flesh out a picture of this fiend in human form, this monster of iniquity, this noxious vermin and scourge of the human race. Within a day of his arrest the results of their enquiries began to appear in print and although the worst of it was hardly flattering, nothing suggested he was capable of committing a crime as brutal as the murder of Mary Dobie. One report said he had been wanted for horse stealing in Auckland three years earlier and that he had been sued for two or three pounds in Palmerston North and left town threatening to commit suicide when he lost the case.[19]

Yet these reports turned out to be wrong; either cases of mistaken identity or perhaps rumours fertilised by the wishful thinking of a populace that did not want to consider, much less confront, an alternative explanation for Mary's death. But the more people heard about Stannard, the harder it became to bat away doubts. Running simultaneously with the weak stories about his bad character were reports suggesting he was a decent fellow. Two men went to the offices of the *Star* in Auckland to say they knew him well and that he was the most unlikely person to commit such a crime. Nearly all the settlers in the Hawera and Normanby area, where Stannard lived, believed in his innocence, they said.[20]

There were many reports along these lines. Stannard had arrived in Lyttelton as the mate of a ship and, after working around the country for about two years, had settled in Hawera in late 1879 where he worked as a billiard marker at one of the hotels – keeping scores and helping to run the billiard room. He had also worked as a clerk for a butchery before reverting to his preferred career of horse-breaker.[21] In Palmerston North, where he allegedly had financial troubles, he was remembered as 'a young man rather handsome, and of a quiet disposition' who had acted as bailiff.[22] In the late 1870s he had worked in Napier as a horse-breaker and people who knew him there said he was quiet, sober and exceedingly well educated, not the sort of man to carry out a brutal crime.[23] He received a vote of confidence from Auckland as well where he had been a popular worker at the Manukau mills.[24]

Doubts about Stannard's guilt were bolstered by reports that he was newly married and alternative explanations for the blood on his clothes.[25] He claimed the blood came from his horse which fell and cut its nose while chasing the stray colt on the fatal day.[26] But other explanations were volunteered on his behalf as well. Some early reports said the blood came from the stray rather than Stannard's own horse. Then a Press Association story said the wife of a storekeeper had wiped blood off him even before he had departed for Ōpunake that morning. Another said he had been covered in blood when he intervened in a fight at Hawera between two drunken men who were bleeding profusely.[27]

The statements in favour of Stannard were heavy counterweights to the evidence against him and they induced doubt in the minds of those who had been certain of his guilt the day before. But they were not regarded as conclusive by everyone. The arresting officer, Sergeant McKeon, remained convinced that he had the right man in custody. The different explanations of how Stannard came to have blood on him could well be made-up stories and therefore a sign of guilt. And it did not necessarily follow that he was innocent just because so many people believed in him strongly. But on Friday morning, out of sight of the public and press, the investigation made two big breaks that were to change everything.

The first came from Dr Carey's post-mortem examination of the body. Carey arrived in Ōpunake at 7.30 a.m. from Pungarehu. He went straight to the redoubt and was shown into the bell tent where the stretcher-bearers had laid Mary to rest on a table the night before. He ordered the body be moved to the library where, surrounded by volumes of moralistic literature, he did his grisly but necessary work. Before starting the autopsy he watched as Mary Ann Ebbett again searched the dress, this time checking all the pockets. She found the carpenter's pencil that Mary had bought from Coffey the day before, a handkerchief and a piece of India rubber. 'I put the articles on the table,' she said. 'I was too nervous to notice anything. I saw blood on the dress, down the bosom of it.'[28] Ebbett didn't find any money but Mary still wore a gold ring with jewels on her right hand and a bone bracelet on her left arm.[29] When Ebbett had finished, Carey checked the pockets for bloodstains. He was trying to establish whether robbery was the motive and the killer, with blood on his hands, had rifled the clothing in search of cash. But although other parts of the dress were heavily stained there was no sign of blood in the pockets.

Having satisfied himself on this point Carey moved to the autopsy proper. 'The body was lying on the left side on the table – the left arm stretched out – the right arm bent over the chest,' he said. 'Both legs were drawn up. The right knee bent over the left leg and the lower part of the right leg twisted over the left.'[30] He observed six cuts probably made by a knife. Four on the right side of the neck, one on the left and one on the middle finger of the right hand. One wound extended across the throat from right to left and was so deep it severed everything down to the vertebral column. This was the fatal injury; the killer had stabbed first and then drawn the knife across. 'The depth was three inches,' said Carey, 'my forefinger went right in.' The largest of the other cuts was about 3 centimetres long on the right side. One cut had gone through Mary's collar which was lying open and saturated with blood.

Once he had established the facts, Carey drew his conclusions. He said the killer must have stood in front of Mary and inflicted the cuts by drawing his weapon, probably a knife, from right to left. Mary would have been able to run away after receiving one or more of the smaller wounds but not after the deep slash across her throat. After that she would have been incapable of moving. He could not say which cut came first. 'The wounds had the appearance of having been given in a death struggle, they were not all given with the same force.' From the state of the body he estimated the time of death at between 2 and 4 p.m. on Thursday, the very time that Mary was on her walk.

None of these horrifying details would have been unexpected given what had already been reported. But what Carey concluded next was to have a profound influence on the way people reacted to the crime. 'I examined every part of the body,' he said. 'I am positive no attempt at violation had been made. The underclothing was intact.'[31] He never wavered from this conclusion.[32] When challenged he reiterated the point even more emphatically. Not only was there no sign of rape but no sign of any attempt at rape, 'not even by the appearance of the clothes'.[33] Carey's firm view must have come as a shock to those who wanted to believe the motive was rape because the alternative did not bear thinking about. And, in any case, the widely reported disarray of her clothes surely suggested a sexual impetus for the crime.

Those who had seen the body in the flax bush the night before must have found Carey's conclusion especially surprising. They thought the state of her clothes indicated at least an attempt at rape even though they did not spell it out in so many words. William Wilson said the clothes were more disarranged above the kneecap than could be explained by Mary falling down.[34] Tosland was more specific. 'The head was towards the road,' he said. 'The dress was up above the knee showing the thigh – you could see the top of the stocking & the naked flesh.'[35] It seemed to him the dress had been 'drawn up' in a deliberate act by the killer rather than something incidental to the concealment of the body. On the other hand his observation that the head was towards the road – coupled with the evidence of the grass nearby being flattened – suggested the killer dragged Mary by her feet causing the dress to ride up. Goring, at least, could see the logic of this point. 'The dress was not torn so far as I could see,' he said. 'I think the fact of the body being dragged might cause the dress to drag up.'[36]

News of the autopsy result broke on Saturday, just as the voices of support for Stannard were gaining traction in the papers. 'Body not violated,' reported the Auckland *Star* on Saturday afternoon and immediately began floating an alternative theory. If there was no rape, and the Pākehā Stannard was not the killer, then the nightmare of a political murder perpetrated by angry Māori was back on the agenda with all its frightening implications.[37]

The second big break was made about the same time as Carey was examining the body. A team of constables, including Wilson and Tosland, returned to search the scene of the crime in daylight. They followed the trail of blood to the place where they had found Mary the night before.[38] It was not long before Constable John Hickey spotted her hat in a toe toe bush near where the grass had been flattened.[39] Then Tosland found a pair of old moleskin trousers bundled up in the flax. They were streaked with blood as though the wearer had brushed against the bloodstained plants at the crime scene before discarding

FIG. 17: Flirting on the high seas. *Mary Dobie, from* The Voyage of the May Queen, *courtesy Drake Brockman family*

FIG. 18: May Cottage, Herbert's home, painted by Mary in February 1878. She added a numbered caption: 1. Mother's room 2. Drawing room 3. Front door 4. Dining room or work shop 5. Herbert's room.

FIG. 19: Mary and Bertha approved wholeheartedly of Tottie, their brother Herbert's fiancée. *Family album*

FIG. 20: Mary as Lydia Languish in *The Rivals*. Unfortunately her sense of comic timing deserted her on stage. *Family album*

FIG. 21: 'The boy', Forster Goring as a dashing young officer. *PA2-2507 ATL*

FIG. 22: Mary's view of Ōpōtiki with the big hotel, small church and Major Goring standing on the wharf ready to escort them to the Pink and White Terraces. *'Trip to the Hot Lakes', courtesy Babette Tregent*

FIG. 23: The major and his friend relaxing at Castle Goring in Ōpōtiki. *'Trip to the Hot Lakes', courtesy Babette Tregent*

FIG. 24: 'The Circus', off to see the Pink and White Terraces with the unmistakeable shape of Mount Edgecumbe / Pūtauaki in the background. *'Trip to the Hot Lakes', courtesy Babette Tregent*

FIG. 25: The trip would not have been possible without all the help received from the many Māori people they encountered on the way. *'Trip to the Hot Lakes'*, courtesy Babette Tregent

FIG. 26: Whakatāne sketches including the centenarian Apanui and the Dobie sisters in a waka. *'Trip to the Hot Lakes'*, courtesy Babette Tregent

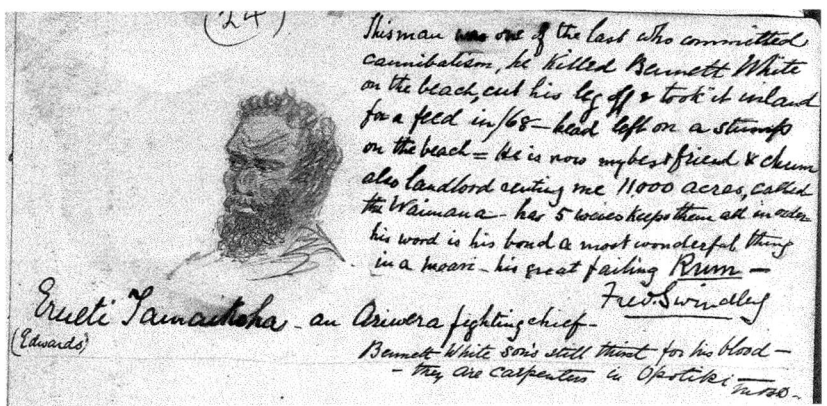

FIG. 27: Mary's sketch of the last cannibal with Captain Swindley's condescending caption. *'Trip to the Hot Lakes'*, courtesy Babette Tregent

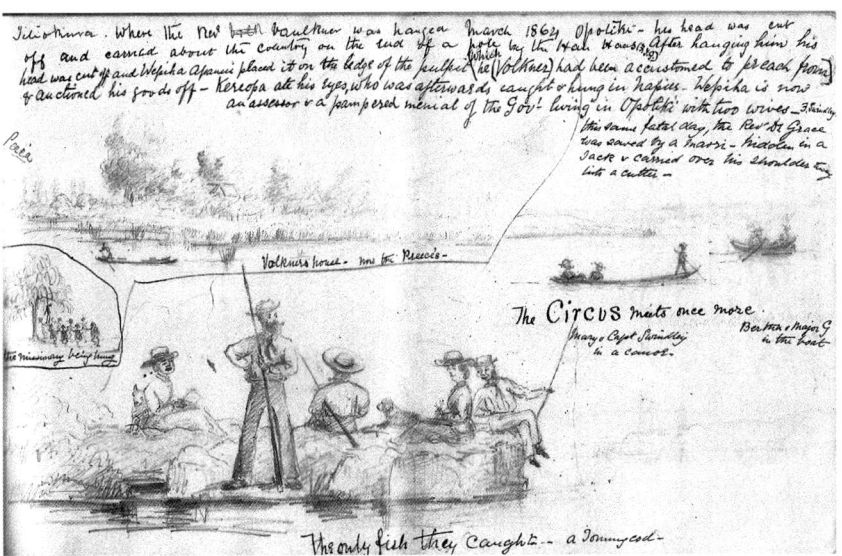

FIG. 28: A day's fishing and the horror story about the murder of Carl Völkner. *'Trip to the Hot Lakes'*, courtesy Babette Tregent

FIG. 29: At Rotomahana where Bertha and Forster went for a moonlit stroll on the White Terraces. *'Trip to the Hot Lakes'*, courtesy Babette Tregent

FIG. 30: Forster follows the departing steamer carrying the Dobies downstream as though he could not bear to let a certain someone out of his sight. *'Trip to the Hot Lakes'*, courtesy Babette Tregent

FIG. 31: The Dobie sisters trekking through the bush during their five-month stay in Fiji. *Mary Dobie,* New Zealand Graphic

FIG. 32: Cave diving in the Yasawa Islands. *Mary Dobie,* New Zealand Graphic

FIG. 33: An evening in Fiji where it seemed that Mary and Bertha co-opted the British administration and a good proportion of the traditional hierarchy to do their bidding. *Mary Dobie,* New Zealand Graphic

QUAGUARIOOLO.—CAVE IN YASAWA-I-LAU

LIFE IN FIJI — EVENING

FIGS 34 & 35: Bertha and Forster were married on a chilly and crisp winter's day in 1880. *Family album*

FIG. 36: When the Parihaka ploughmen asserted their mana whenua in the winter of 1879, many settlers feared it was a prelude to bloodshed. *Illustrated London News*

FIG. 37: Major Charles Stapp signed up 849 volunteers in June 1879 to reinforce the state's presence in Taranaki. *PHO2002-66 PA*

FIG. 38: Forster was officer in charge at the Egmont lighthouse when Mary and her mother came for their farewell visit in 1880. *David Hastings*

them. The blood seemed fresh.[40] About 12 metres from the road and near the bloody trail another member of the search party found the headstall of an old bridle tied together with string.[41]

In the mind of Sergeant McKeon, who was still leading the investigation on Friday morning in the absence of the civilian police, the new evidence, especially the bridle, cemented Stannard's guilt. Not only had the accused been smeared with blood but he had been seen leading a bridle-less horse near Te Namu soon after the murder. There was great excitement when the search party returned in triumph to the redoubt, bearing what they thought was the key to the mystery. But John Shearman, one of the guards, was not convinced and thought that in their understandable eagerness to solve the case his comrades were rushing to condemn an innocent man. The evidence that aroused his suspicion was the moleskins rather than the bridle. He knew a man who wore trousers like those and it was not Stannard. He asked McKeon if he could view the exhibits. When shown the trousers he instantly recognised them as belonging to Tuhi from Pūnehu, the other horse-catcher who was in Ōpunake on the day that Mary died.[42]

With the air of a man whose mind was firmly made up and tightly insulated against alternative interpretations, McKeon brushed off the constable. Many men who had been in town on the day of the murder had seen the trousers and none recognised them, he said. Shearman refused to back down despite his superior's closed mind and insisted that McKeon go to Goring with the trousers and declare Tuhi, and not Stannard, the murderer. His was not the most tactful method of persuasion. McKeon thought he was going to solve the case before the civilian police had even reached town, and, as so often happens when a cherished theory or opinion is undermined by evidence, he refused even to contemplate the possibility that he had made a mistake. And he had plenty of support from his men. 'I was ridiculed by the Sergt and the other men,' said Shearman. 'Both the Sergt and others said they knew [Tuhi] was innocent.' McKeon called Shearman a fool though Shearman was anything but a fool and he did not lack courage either. He delivered a bold ultimatum: he would tell Goring about the trousers if McKeon would not. At this the sergeant had no choice but to concede defeat.[43]

Goring showed none of McKeon's defensive scepticism; he immediately saw the point and ordered that Tuhi should also be arrested. Emphasising the delicacy of the task he reminded the chastened McKeon that any clumsy mistake might cause trouble at Pūnehu and give the man they were hunting an opportunity to escape. Shearman volunteered to be part of the arresting party but McKeon, perhaps still smarting at being shown up by the constable, excluded him from the group of six sent to bring in Tuhi.

They found Tuhi on Friday morning hoeing his potato patch.[44] Thomas Knowles, the leader of the party, said at the inquest he had no orders to arrest him but to get him to Ōpunake the best way he could.[45] By Knowles' account it all went smoothly. 'I asked him to come along and look for horses lost on the previous day – I did not speak in Māori. He understood me. He stood talking some time – he showed no unwillingness to go with me.' Other accounts suggest the detention of Tuhi was more fraught than Knowles made out. A report by Goring said that instead of declaring the real reason they wanted to talk to him, they claimed a dispute had arisen over a horse he had sold to a constable and they wanted him to come and sort it out. Tuhi was not about to fall for the trick.

He replied that the horse had belonged to his father and so his father should be the one to go. 'No, I want you,' said one of the constables firmly, and, again, Tuhi refused. The constable, who was on horseback, then began to dismount as though to seize Tuhi and, for the third time, insisted that he should come. This time Tuhi agreed.

Another version, from the *Wanganui Herald*, said the pretext was to question him about sheep-stealing.[46] By this account he scented danger in a few moments and began to sidle towards the bush as though to make his escape. But Knowles placed himself between Tuhi and the bush and the others surrounded him. Under supervision of the constables, Tuhi saddled his horse, his father put the bridle on and they rode off. On the way to Ōpunake, Knowles stayed close, keeping his knee level with the tail of Tuhi's horse in case the wanted man tried to bolt. They stopped briefly two or three times on the way, the last time about 200 metres from the redoubt to give Tuhi the chance to light his pipe. Goring was convinced that had they not acted so promptly Tuhi would have fled to Parihaka, seeking sanctuary like Hiroki had done. Indeed, he claimed that Tuhi later said as much himself.[47]

Some of this information – Carey's declaration that there was no rape, the discovery of the bloody trousers and the arrest of a Māori man – made it into the Saturday editions of the evening papers and started to shake the assumptions about what had happened. But the details were not widely known until the evidence was presented at the inquest which began at midday on Saturday.

The usual frivolity of the billiard room of the Middletons' hotel gave way to the solemnity of a legal inquiry to decide which of the two men should be sent for trial on a charge of murder, with a certain death penalty if the verdict proved to be guilty. But the case was about much more than just deciding who had most likely done it. People wanted to know why. Was the motive rape, robbery or political? Or was it a combination of some or all of these factors? Or did the answer lie with some other motivation that no one had mentioned or was too difficult to put into words?

7.

THE MANY DEATHS

Mary's funeral was on Saturday afternoon. For a moment attention was redirected from the murder investigation as soldiers and townsfolk turned out to pay their respects. The funeral procession was held in silence but the mourners found out later that simultaneously a constabulary band at Camp Egmont, where Mary had first stayed in Taranaki, played Handel's 'Funeral March in Saul' as a regal tribute to their former commander's sister-in-law.[1] Her body was lowered into the ground in the little cemetery between the redoubt, the tennis court and the vegetable garden.[2] In the absence of a minister, Colonel Roberts intoned the words that drew a line under Mary's short life: 'Earth to earth, ashes to ashes, dust to dust, in sure and certain hope of the resurrection to eternal life through our Lord Jesus Christ...'

Bertha laid a floral cross on the grave.[3] The flowers were the only public expression of grief by the family at the time. But the following Saturday a poem titled 'In Memoriam' appeared in the Auckland *Observer*, putting their feelings into words:

> Cover her gaping wounds dark night!
> Compose the fair and shapely limbs
> With weeping, and with solemn hymns
> Bury our dead from out our sight![4]

Although it was anonymous, someone in the family was probably the author, either Bertha or Herbert. The family had cooperated with the paper giving it access to Mary's last letter to her brother and to a photograph which was the basis of a drawing that appeared on the same page as the poem (Figs 47, 48). Of the two, Bertha is more likely to have been the author than the pragmatic Herbert. Although they were both writers she was the one who had a great love of poetry; in her memoir she quoted liberally from all the greats. She was especially fond of Tennyson, her distant relation by marriage, but the verse on Mary's death owed little other than its metre and its title to his 'In Memoriam', one of the most famous and complex literary works of the Victorian era.

There could be many reasons why the family did not make some public declaration at the funeral. It could be, as one paper put it, that they were crushed.[5] Or that they kept a British reserve which inhibited public displays of emotion. Or maybe it was because they had told Ellen that Mary had been gored to death by a bull. Newall said that at the funeral, 48 hours after Mary's murder, Ellen still did not know the truth.[6] If he was right she must have been deeply alone when surrounded by the mourners, all of whom knew what had happened to her daughter and had been talking about it obsessively for more than a day.

Ellen was not to know that she was by herself in a parallel world constructed from a white lie. But she could not have been insulated for long from the storm of anger, fear and speculation that was raging around Ōpunake and across the country. If the gossip did not reach her ears first, sooner rather than later she would have read about it in a newspaper. The only certainty was that Mary had not been gored by a bull. Within two days of the murder seven potential suspects had been identified or mentioned. As well as Tuhi and Stannard they included groups of two or three men and the allegation that a dishonourably discharged constabulary man had killed Mary for revenge.[7] Thomas Hughson reported that guards had been put on the beach between Egmont and Ōpunake to arrest anyone on suspicion. He heard that two men had been detained but then released.[8]

Lined up with the suspects were six potential motives. Rape was at the head of the list but robbery was also considered seriously as well as a political motive that had Te Whiti accused of being responsible, if only indirectly. Then there was the revenge motive linked to the constabulary man and, as so often happens in such crimes, the victim was perversely blamed for having put herself in harm's way. For some the motive was too hard to discern accurately so it was put down to 'savagery' or maybe just 'bloodthirstyness'.[9]

These theories and suspicions in various combinations were formed and reformed by prejudice and fear as much as by developments in the evidence. By the time of the funeral the universal belief that rape was the motive and Stannard the man had been shaken by news of Tuhi's arrest and his appearance at the inquest. The change in opinion came about partly because of the testimonials in Stannard's favour but also because the evidence was magnified and distorted through the lens of racial prejudice.[10] The Christchurch *Star*, for instance, argued that the killer must have been Māori because a European would have been too cunning to commit such an atrocious deed in daylight unless he happened to be a Pākehā-Māori, one of the lowest of the low of the human species.[11] And as for the motive, the *Star* doubted rape because, it said, Māori lived 'a life of social freedom, absence of restraint and what may be termed promiscuous intercourse' and so presumably would not feel the need to satisfy lust with an unwilling stranger on a lonely road. A more likely motive was robbery or perhaps revenge for some unknown slight.

Other papers published variations on the theme that one or more Māori were to blame. The *Taranaki Herald* carried a report saying three Māori men had been arrested on suspicion.[12] One of the Taranaki men who visited the Auckland *Star* to vouch for Stannard was convinced that Mary had died because of her sketching around Parihaka, which he believed Māori thought of as spying.[13] He was not to know that Mary's sketches were done with Te Whiti's blessing but in the back of his mind may have been the fate of the missionary Carl Völkner whose horrific killing was in part motivated by the belief he was a spy.

Even as the case against Stannard was crumbling there were still many who argued the murder was not the sort of crime a Māori man would commit. Nervous settlers could take some comfort from the opinion of the old chief Matakātea who had just been released after serving time for his part in the ploughing protest. He was asked whether the killer was Māori, and after viewing the body he shook his head; Māori did not kill in that way he said.[14]

All of these versions of Mary's death were revised over the weekend as the police investigation uncovered more evidence. The soldiers had done a good job on the first day, finding important clues and detaining two suspects. But their work was rough and ready by comparison with the efforts of the civilian police who had been converging on Ōpunake since Friday afternoon. Superintendent William James, the most senior officer in the area, rode through the night from Whanganui and arrived early on Saturday morning to take charge. He was not satisfied with some aspects of the constabulary's work and immediately ordered a new and more thorough search of the crime scene.[15] He greatly increased the size of the search area and had the flax cut down to see what might be revealed. James in the meantime measured everything. The distance between Te Namu and the telegraph office at Ōpunake (1 mile 191 yards or 1.8 kilometres), between the telegraph office and the hotel (one and a half chains or about 30 metres) and between the road and the place where the body was found (90 feet or 27 metres).[16]

Partly by the more rigorous detective work and partly by good luck the searchers came up with three more pieces of crucial evidence. The first was a bridle with its reins tied to a flax bush about 90 metres from where the body had been concealed.[17] The second was a pocket knife with bloodstains on it, found purely by chance by 11-year-old Francis Hickey when he was playing near the redoubt.[18] It was in the exact spot where the party escorting Tuhi the day before had paused so he could light his pipe. As a result of this discovery James sent the soldiers back to Pūnehu to search Tuhi's whare. It was there on Sunday morning that they found the final piece of evidence – the coat that Tuhi had worn on the fatal day was hanging on a peg and its sleeve was stained with blood.[19] When Constable Knowles returned to the redoubt with the coat rolled up under his arm Tuhi saw it and exclaimed 'that is my coat'.[20]

William Skinner followed these developments closely and by Sunday was in no doubt about who had done it. He listed in his diary the accumulated evidence of the knife and the bloodstained trousers in the flax bush and noted how strong it was against the Māori.[21] The more the evidence pointed to Tuhi the more the levels of anxiety in the settler community rose. Fear gave wings to rumour again, just as it had done when the ploughmen first appeared on settler land eighteen months ago.

One story spreading like an epidemic through the AC camps said that Te Whiti had prophesied there would soon be a startling awakening and that someone – possibly a surveyor – would die like a pig, in other words with his throat cut. Stuart Newall recorded it in his diary highlighting the similarity between the prophecy and Mary's death – her throat was cut in the way a pig would be slaughtered. He said that one of his fellow officers, perhaps all too aware of the pressure the road-makers were putting on Māori, had been making solemn predictions of coming evil and these were 'thickening daily'.[22] The same or a similar story was doing the rounds of the settlers and appeared in the Auckland *Star*. 'Many old military settlers believe that the murder has been committed by natives and it possesses political significance,' reported the *Star* on Saturday afternoon, implying Te Whiti's people were preparing for war by selling up their livestock and buying food for Parihaka.[23]

The weight of the new evidence pointing to a Māori man as the killer and the portentous rumours at the weekend proved irresistible to the *New Zealand Herald* which, on Monday morning, reversed its original judgement. Neither rape nor robbery were motives, the paper now argued, and the killer was a Māori who had acted for political purposes.[24] 'It seems extraordinary that a lady should be murdered to mark the anger of the Maoris at their land being taken, but consideration makes the event quite possible,' the paper said, yet again inadvertently conceding that the land belonged to Māori.

Perhaps influenced by the settlers quoted in the *Star* on Saturday, the *Herald* now believed Mary's sketching around the district had something to do with her death. It cited its own Taranaki source as saying Māori feeling in the district was alarming and that they would not yield the land without acting in revenge. 'They know that they have no chance in attempting to go to war, that they would be beaten easily by the constabulary now on the plains. But they will commit murders wherever they can, and commit them in such a manner that it will be exceedingly difficult to find out the perpetrator.' Terrorism is the word that would be used today. And the paper linked the prophet of Parihaka to the murder even as it admitted there was no evidence and no possibility of finding any. 'Te Whiti does not command such murders, but he works the natives up to the necessary frame of mind. It will be impossible to connect him with these crimes.'[25]

The implications of this line of reasoning were potentially catastrophic for Te Whiti and his people. If it could be proved the motive for Mary's murder was Māori vengeance over the land then a forceful response would be justified and what some editorial writers and politicians had in mind was nothing less than an attack on the settlement at Parihaka. The *Herald* argued that if the case were proved against the Māori then the government should be prepared to demand Hiroki and break up the settlement. This was exactly what the Native Minister John Bryce was vigorously advocating in cabinet at the time.

The *Herald* qualified its opinion by saying *if* the case were proved. It was an important 'if'. No one had been committed for trial yet, much less found guilty of the charge. The first opportunity to test the evidence formally came at the inquest. It sat late into the night on Saturday and then Monday, hearing from 39 witnesses in a room crowded with people exercising the same public interest and curiosity that had driven many to the scene of the crime on Friday morning.

At first it did not look good for Stannard. Two crucial pieces of police evidence pointed directly to him. Constable McGrath, who rode north with him on the fatal day, swore that he had no blood on him at the time.[26] And yet Stannard's clothes and boots were stained with blood when he was arrested that night. Then there was the bridle found on Saturday morning. Find a man leading a horse without a bridle, the logic ran, and you will have found the killer. As it happened Stannard had been seen bringing a horse without a bridle back to Ōpunake soon after Mary disappeared.[27] But Stannard had perfectly reasonable explanations. Most of the blood had come from a cut on his horse's nose which was the result of a fall while chasing a stray colt. And when he brought the horse back to Ōpunake, of course it had no bridle, it was a stray.[28]

After the first few witnesses the case against Stannard looked weak and the tide turned swiftly against Tuhi. The trousers were crucial. Despite what McKeon had said in his argument with Shearman, a number of witnesses swore they had seen Tuhi on the morning of the fatal day wearing a pair of torn moleskins over a pair of tweeds which were visible through a tear. Their evidence was corroborated by others who said that by the early evening, when Mary was surely dead, they saw Tuhi back in Ōpunake but wearing only the tweeds. The moleskins were gone and they matched the trousers found streaked with blood near the scene of the crime.

Other evidence filled out the picture.[29] Tuhi had also been seen riding a horse without a bridle and on the night of the murder had gone to the saddlery at the hotel to see if he could borrow one. A constable identified the bridle found tied to a flax bush; he had seen it on a bay horse that Tuhi had offered to sell him six weeks previously. Caroline Paki, who travelled with Hone Pīhama from Parihaka on the fatal day, said she had seen a black horse in the flax near the scene of the crime and other members of the party said they had seen it too. Then William Eyes told the inquest that he had noticed Tuhi riding fast up the road on a black horse about half an hour after Mary, inviting the conclusion that he had followed her.[30] Three more exhibits added important links to the chain of circumstantial evidence: the knife found near the spot where Tuhi lit his pipe, the coat recovered from Tuhi's whare and a threepenny piece – every item stained with blood.

However, the story of the coin was not clear-cut. It appeared to be the same one given to Mary as change when she bought her pencil from Coffey on the afternoon of her death, then tendered by Tuhi when he bought a box of matches from Coffey that evening and, on the Monday morning after the murder, passed on in another transaction to Dr Carey who immediately realised its significance.[31] The coin evidence was full of contradictions and was to be repudiated and quietly dropped from the prosecution case. One important question was how could the storekeeper be sure, among all the coins he handled, that this was the one that he had given to Mary? There was no satisfactory answer but that did not prevent the story of the threepenny piece encouraging those who thought Tuhi was the killer and robbery the motive.

In the coming days and weeks, public comments from the courts and in the press laid great stress on the importance of the Māori witnesses.[32] In private correspondence, though, Superintendent James expressed his frustration with them, saying they were apathetic and reluctant.[33] The most reluctant of them fled to Parihaka rather than give evidence.[34] But the others corroborated the story of the black horse near the scene of the crime and fleshed out details about Tuhi's suspicious behaviour on the evening of the fatal day, after he had broken the news of the murder to Stannard.[35] Rona Matiu, who had spent the day drinking on the beach and in the pub, said Tuhi rode up to him as he was heading towards the whare of a friend, about a kilometre from the hotel. He was intending to join Tamati Kawino and his wife Miha for dinner, and at his suggestion Tuhi tagged along. Although Miha thought there was nothing unusual about Tuhi's behaviour, both Rona and Tamati described it as odd. 'He looked unnatural,' Rona told the jury. 'I observed him frequently looking at the door.' Tamati noticed this too. Their evidence must have created an impression in the jurors' minds of a hunted man worrying about his pursuers.

What these Māori witnesses said was similar to an account given by the settler William Eyes, a neighbour and friend of Tuhi at Pūnehu. Eyes happened also to be the foreman of the jury but he did not hesitate to accept the appointment despite the conflict of interest. Tuhi often visited his whare and he had appeared that night about 9 p.m. He knocked and was invited to enter but drew back when he saw an armed constable inside. Instead of coming in he said good night and left quickly. He appeared 'rather scared', said Eyes.[36] However, Eyes was uncertain about the time, which must have been much later given that Tuhi had informed Stannard and Stevenson about the discovery of the body after 9.30 p.m.

All day and into the night on Monday the evidence was mounting against Tuhi and one observer noticed that his confidence was breaking down as 'all the horrid details of his crime were passed before his view'.[37] Never was this clearer than when Carey stood up to give a demonstration of his evidence from the autopsy. A special reporter for the *Wanganui Herald* wrote that Tuhi displayed 'marked attention' when the doctor produced Mary's dress and showed how the knife allegedly used in the murder fitted the cut on the bloodstained collar. Then Carey used a beardless constable to demonstrate where the five cuts had been made on Mary's neck. 'Tuhi's gaze at this juncture was intense and strained,' said the reporter, 'and he gave an audible sigh at the conclusion of the description.'[38]

It was late on Monday night when the last witness was heard and the coroner began to read over the evidence, but the jury stopped him saying it was unnecessary.[39] They were unanimous that there was no evidence against Stannard who should be released immediately. The coroner accepted their verdict and, turning to Stannard, said, 'I congratulate you . . . you leave this room without a stain on your character'.

What happened next caught everyone in the room by surprise. At the suggestion of the coroner, the interpreter Charles Hursthouse asked Tuhi if he had anything to say.[40] Hursthouse later swore that he warned Tuhi to be cautious because anything he said might be used in evidence against him.[41] The warning is not recorded in the published transcripts but if it was made, Tuhi paid no heed. He stated bluntly, 'I did it.' Despite the weight of the evidence, no one expected to hear a confession and one reporter said the thrill of horror that passed through the courtroom at that moment was indescribable.[42] Everyone was deeply affected, including the coroner and Hursthouse, who, in an agitated but loud and clear voice, repeated the question as though he could not believe what he was hearing.[43]

'It was done by me,' said Tuhi.

'Do you know what you have really said?' asked Hursthouse. 'Do you know your position?'

'I know I killed the woman. It was a great sin and crime. I know it,' replied Tuhi.

He appeared to be the calmest person in the room after the confession, reported the *Taranaki Herald* correspondent. And he was again asked if he had anything further to say. 'I desire to be questioned,' was his response but the coroner ruled this was inadmissible. Tuhi then said, 'I have nothing more to say except that I committed the murder.' The excitement reached a crescendo when he approached the table to sign his confession and have it attested by the interpreter.

The coroner was so moved by the dramatic moment that he became muddled over procedure and told the jury there was nothing further for them to do, even though they had not yet delivered their verdict on Tuhi. It must have seemed unnecessary in the light of the confession which was such hot news that Superintendent James rushed a telegram to the commissioner of the constabulary, Colonel Henry Reader, within half an hour.[44] A further half-hour passed before the coroner gathered his wits and remembered to ask the jury for a formal verdict.

After only a few seconds of whispering among the jurors, Eyes stood up to declare: 'That the deceased Miss Mary Dobie was wilfully murdered by the prisoner Tuhi (or Te Karea) on the afternoon of November 25, between the hours of 2 and 5 p.m.' With that, the coroner committed the prisoner to stand trial in the Supreme Court. But Tuhi did not want to wait. 'I do not wish for any more trials; I want to meet my death here now,' he said.[45] But that was not going to happen. The wheels of justice were speeding along but they were not that fast.

Tuhi was handcuffed and led away. Preserving the same calmness he had shown for most of the day, he looked in the eye all the curious people who had come to see justice done. His confession would cause a sensation across the land almost as profound as the news of the murder itself. It settled the first of the burning questions that had been on everyone's mind for four days. If any suspicions about Stannard had survived the weekend's revelations they were now swept away and there were no doubts about the killer's identity.

For one newspaper the confession was enough. In its Saturday edition the Christchurch *Star*, using pure prejudice as its only analytical tool, had predicted against the known evidence that the killer would turn out to be Māori. Now it felt vindicated and boasted to its readers of its insight. 'Tuhi has confessed to the perpetration of the crime and thus all difficulty in reference to this fearful tragedy is at an end.'[46] But all difficulties were not at an end. Tuhi had made only a bald confession, he had not explained exactly what happened and, as William Skinner noted in his diary, there was still no answer to the final burning question: why did he do it?[47] This was a much more difficult question to answer, and not just because the coroner had stopped Tuhi before he could go beyond a basic declaration of guilt. At the same time as the inquest delivered an unambiguous answer to the 'who' question it reopened the 'why' question with a detail that suggested the motive might have been robbery after all.

The detail was the bloodstained threepenny piece mentioned by Coffey and Carey at the inquest. Added to proof of Tuhi being hard up, begging for clothes and alcohol on credit, it suggested that he had robbed Mary and then killed her. Although the evidence of the coin was not credible, the *Hawke's Bay Herald* was quick to join the dots: 'His motive seems to have been robbery, but he obtained only a threepenny piece and two coppers.'[48] Robbery may have been the most favoured explanation in the days after the inquest but it was by no means universally held, nor advocated with great conviction, as more possibilities were added to the many deaths of Mary Dobie. Of all the papers that supported robbery as the motive the *Taranaki Herald* was the most certain. 'Murder pure and simple for the sake of gain,' was how their editorial put it.[49] More typically the *New Zealand Times* on Tuesday declared robbery as the prime motive but on the following day argued that as the killer had made no attempt to take her jewellery 'lust and unbridled passion must have been at the bottom of this hideous deed' after all.[50]

The *New Zealand Herald* found itself having to make even greater adjustments. By the time of Tuhi's confession it had already switched from rape to politics as the motive. Like the *Times*, it discounted robbery on the grounds that Mary was still wearing her jewellery when found.[51] It was possible that Mary had given the money to Tuhi not because he demanded it but because she was frightened of him. The *Herald* also ruled out the political motive that it had advocated so forcefully on the

Monday morning. There was no evidence for such a motive, the paper now argued, and if the crime had been political Tuhi would have sought refuge at Parihaka and no Māori would have given evidence against him. The best it could come up with was an 'uncontrollable impulse of slaughter'.

Despite their disagreements over whether the motive was rape or robbery, most papers had declared explicitly, by the middle of the week after the murder, that whatever else it might be, it was not politics. And yet the insinuation that Te Whiti was in some way to blame, even if not directly, persisted. The Auckland *Star* – which said the motive was 'one of those sudden outbreaks of bloodthirstiness which shew that some human beings are but little removed from wild beasts' – could not let go of the idea that Te Whiti was somehow behind it. It echoed the *Herald*'s now abandoned view from Monday morning when it said his responsibility was a question that naturally arose. 'Though the degree . . . is difficult to estimate, it cannot be denied that he is in some sort culpable.'[52]

The idea that Te Whiti and Parihaka were linked to the murder persisted with the pathological power of a rumour that retained its currency not because it was supported by any evidence but because it neatly fitted the fears, prejudices and political objectives of those who spread it and believed it. More than one paper argued that, even though the murder was not political, it was time something was done about Parihaka and Hiroki.[53] The *Taranaki Herald*, in trying to calm anxieties, said that although there was no political significance it was only natural that uneasiness and distrust should be provoked by a murder so close to an AC camp.[54]

It was a forlorn hope to expect that such a strong and malevolent idea could easily be extinguished. Three weeks after the murder, the *Observer* in Auckland published a letter from a woman who set out to blame the victim and, in the process, connected her death to Parihaka and its people. The I-told-you-so letter came from one of the gossips who had been so critical of Mary's adventures on her grand tour. 'I am not surprised that if a victim was needed to appease the Maoris of the Plains, Miss Dobie was selected,' she declared self-righteously. 'I cannot imagine that unless some idea had been first suggested to Tuhi, a young fellow such as he, would wantonly have committed so terrible a crime.'[55]

Probably influenced by what she read in the *New Zealand Herald* and the Auckland *Star*, she was convinced that the crime had its genesis in Mary's sketching trip to Parihaka. 'Not many days before the fatal event, Miss Dobie was sketching in Te Whiti's kainga. Possibly Tuhi might have seen her and marked her down.'[56] In her eyes the crime was political – Tuhi must have been put up to it – and Mary had offered herself as a victim in her 'utter innocence and ignorance'. The *New Zealand Times* and the *Otago Daily Times* did not explicitly blame Mary but they made similar points when commenting that her death should make women in the out-settlements cautious about putting themselves in a vulnerable position.[57] What the papers and the letter-writer meant was that women should stay in their places, safe behind the invisible social boundaries that Mary and her sister had always boldly negotiated on their travels across the world and around the Pacific.

Some of the papers seemed to sense that they were setting themselves an impossible task in attempting to answer the 'why' question with one-word answers such as rape, robbery and politics. After the confession the *Taranaki Herald* correspondent covering the inquest said it might be all of the above:

'As yet nothing has transpired as to the motive for the crime; it may have been lust, plunder, or an innate hatred of the pakeha, and a savage delight to kill combined.'[58] And after all of its contradictory attempts to explain why, the *New Zealand Herald* acknowledged there was an 'entire absence of any known motive'.[59]

The *Otago Daily Times* suggested that a full understanding may well be beyond reach: 'possibly plunder, possibly of a kind that we cannot more particularly indicate'.[60] Faced with such a difficult task the papers' first instinct was to fall back on racial explanations, which they could do easily once the killer was identified as Māori and not Pākehā. Savage and savagery were words that recurred.[61] But still the papers persisted in uncovering a motive. The uncertainty was a great mystery, said the *Evening Post*, and from the endeavours of the newspapers it was clear they thought their readers deserved nothing less than an answer to the question of why.[62] One place they looked for that answer was in the character of the man who was about to go on trial for his life.

8.

SON OF A DIVIDED WORLD

Tuhi's conduct made a deep impression on everyone who gathered for the inquest. Observations made during the hearing contrasted with descriptions of the ragged man who had spent the morning of 25 November hanging around the pub pathetically trying to persuade someone to sell him a new pair of trousers on credit. The *Hawera Star* correspondent in the billiard room noted that throughout the hearing he had been calm; the few questions he asked were well put. Even when he approached the table to sign his confession, he held himself together admirably and his hand did not shake as might have been expected. At that moment, said the reporter, he appeared to be the coolest man in the room.[1] His physical presence impressed onlookers as much as his demeanour. He was a fine, handsome young man somewhere between 20 and 24 years old who was estimated at between 5 foot 10 inches and 6 feet tall (1.79 and 1.83 metres). He was of muscular build, weighing about 12 stone (76 kilograms), and stood straight.[2]

The contrast between how Tuhi was described on the fatal day and his appearance and demeanour at the inquest is highlighted by the only known photograph of him (Fig. 62). Tuhi stands wrapped in a kahu huruhuru – a feather cloak – holding the eye of the camera with a steady, confident gaze. Rather than a shiftless, bedraggled man down on his luck the picture shows someone high-born and it suggests that despite Tuhi's liking for drink and his tendency to rack up debts, the family enterprise was not doing so badly; apparently they had enough money to pay for a studio portrait.[3]

And yet all may not be as it seems. It is possible, even probable, that the carte-de-visite style picture was not taken in a studio but in The Terrace gaol in Wellington where Tuhi was held during his trial. It was not unknown for jail authorities to allow photographers to take pictures of notorious prisoners in the nineteenth century. For instance, a photo of Kereopa Te Rau was taken at Napier prison in 1871 where he was held on a charge of murdering the missionary Carl Völkner, and in 1866 four men accused of the Maungatapu murders were photographed in Nelson jail.[4] Unfortunately the provenance of Tuhi's picture was not preserved by the archive where it was found but it was probably the same one that was for sale to a morbidly curious public at Deveril's photo shop in Cuba Street, Wellington, after his trial.[5] It may also be the same one displayed by the Grand Sightascope, a travelling curiosity show which highlighted historic events and famous or notorious people through picture displays, wax works and dioramas. In the summer of 1880–81 the show was in Thames, featuring a wax work of Ned Kelly in armour and a monster sea lion as well as photographs of Mary and Tuhi.[6]

The most likely explanation for how Deveril's obtained the photograph of Tuhi is that they took it themselves in the prison and possibly provided the feather cloak as well. No description of Tuhi published in the press ever mentioned him wearing a garment like the one in the picture. In *Journey to a Hanging*, Peter Wells argues convincingly that the Māori garb worn by Kereopa when he was captured on camera in Napier prison was not his own but a photographer's prop and the same may have applied to Tuhi.[7] The idea created by the picture of a prosperous, high-born man may well be false, the cloak concealing the ragged fellow beneath. With this in mind a second look at the image suggests passivity rather than confidence and defensiveness in the way he has wrapped the kahu huruhuru around him.

Despite the ambiguity of what the photograph reveals about Tuhi's social status and frame of mind, it confirms the reporter's description of his physical bearing. He stood straight and even the cloak could not change the impression that he was tall. His good looks and grand physique were said to be inherited from his mother Te Huripoto whom the *New Zealand Herald* described as one of the 'handsomest Māori women on the coast'.[8] It was an observation made repeatedly in the Pākehā press and, like much of the speculation about who had killed Mary, it carried a racist sting: they admired her beauty because they thought she looked more European than Māori. 'She has few of the distinctive features of the race, her lips being thin, and her nose of Grecian type, whilst her whole expression is amiable and pleasing,' said the *Taranaki Herald*.[9]

Tuhi's tribal affiliations were reported as Ngāti Ruanui and Tītahi, those of Hone Pīhama who declared Tuhi to be one of his people.[10] Both groups could trace their line of descent back to the waka *Aotea* which, about 30 generations ago, sailed across the wide Pacific Ocean from Mahaena in the northeast of Tahiti to Aotearoa.[11] So, like Mary, Tuhi had seafaring in his ancestry. And his forbears, like hers, also had plenty of experience at warfare. Inter-tribal conflict was endemic and became bloodier with the introduction of muskets in the early nineteenth century, resulting in raids such as the Waikato attack on Te Namu Pā when Matakātea made his name in 1833.[12]

And then there were the wars with the Pākehā in the 1860s. Tuhi's father, Te Wharengaro, said to be a man of vile temper and bad disposition, was suspected of being one of the war party that killed three sawyers near Ketemarae in 1868, triggering Tītokowaru's war of resistance.[13] If that was true, it meant the families of Tuhi and Mary had a history which began long before the murder at Te Namu. They would have been ranged against each other with Tuhi's father on the side of Tītokowaru and Mary's brother-in-law in the AC force that was defeated at the battles of Te Ngutu-o-te-manu and Moturoa.

For a time, when he was about 20 years old, Tuhi worked as a servant for a solicitor in Whanganui.[14] He evidently spoke some English – for instance he was quoted as claiming his bloodstained coat in English and he understood Knowles when he spoke in English – but not so well that he could do without a translator when facing court on a capital charge. Various pieces of testimony have him spending some time at Parihaka with his family.[15] An Ōpunake correspondent wrote to the *Taranaki Herald* to say that Tuhi, accompanied by his wife, parents and about a dozen others, had returned to Pūnehu from Parihaka shortly before the murder so, as many suspected, he was probably there at the same time as Mary and Bertha.[16]

Everyone in Ōpunake knew Tuhi. He was known at the pub and in the shops. Major Goring knew him as did most of the constables. From what they said, their relations were usually friendly. Despite this and the obvious admiration for his conduct at the inquest, character sketches published after his arrest and confession stressed his unsavoury reputation. As had happened to Stannard, when the finger of suspicion was first pointed, no one could find a good word to say. The *Wanganui Herald*, for example, reported that he did not have a good character and four years earlier had been convicted of robbing a guest at a hotel.[17] He was reputed to be a drunk and the *Taranaki Herald* said 'he is of notoriously bad character, even amongst his own people, and subject to fits of uncontrollable passion'.[18]

The only example given of this uncontrollable passion was a fight he had with his father in the week before the murder. According to the story, which was widely published, father and son were working with a bullock team when the dray ran over Tuhi's right foot. Tuhi cried out in pain and Te Wharengaro dismounted from the dray and bent over to examine the injury. But Tuhi was not looking for sympathy. He blamed his father and attacked the old man, throwing him to the ground, attempting to throttle him. He would probably have succeeded if not for the intervention of their friends.[19] The injury to his foot and ankle failed to heal and became a bloody, suppurating sore which stained the bottom of his moleskins' right leg and was an important piece of circumstantial evidence linking him to the trousers and through them to the murder. Dr Carey, who examined both Tuhi and the trousers, said the stain had soaked through the fabric, unlike the streaks of blood at the front and on the outside and back of both legs.[20]

Many who knew him did not agree with this portrait of a thoroughly bad man who had no redeeming features, although no one said anything in support of him at first. They doubted he was violent and, if he did drink, it was not much. Pīhama and a Māori constable, both of whom had known Tuhi all his life, were among those who gave a different account to the stories appearing in the papers. The constable said he was a quiet man, he was not quarrelsome and did not drink.[21] And Pīhama had never seen him quarrel with anyone.[22] But endorsements of Tuhi were not unequivocal like those given for Stannard. When questioned at his trial other friends and acquaintances would not confirm that he was a peaceful and sober man. They would say only that they did not *know* whether he was quarrelsome and had never *seen* him drunk.[23] Such faint support from people who claimed to know him well left the door ajar for the suspicion that he was, indeed, inclined to violence and to drink too much.

Rona Matiu, his companion on the evening of Mary's murder, said he did not drink heavily.[24] This may sound like a solid statement of support except that Matiu was the man who had spent the morning on the beach drinking beer and the afternoon in the pub; his definition of heavy drinking is likely to be less rigorous than, say, that of a teetotaller. Harry Middleton the publican had known Tuhi for only four months but, unlike some who had known him all his life, had seen him drunk enough times to form an opinion on what he was like when he had imbibed too much. Tuhi, he said, was stupid and silly when drunk rather than 'excitable', by which he meant agitated or hot-tempered.[25] Taken together, the testimony suggests that Tuhi was indeed a drinker but whether he was given to fits of violent rage was less clear-cut.

Unlike Mary, Tuhi came from a fractured, divided and disrupted world. To a great extent her confidence and certainty came from being a daughter of a great empire. Wherever she went in her travels, even when far away from the beaten track, she was enveloped by the laws and power of that empire and protected by its officers. Tuhi, on the other hand, occupied a smaller world with closer horizons, full of uncertainty because of the dramatic changes brought about as Mary's empire spread its foreign customs over his land and went to war with the tangata whenua. The span of his short life stretched from the first and second Taranaki Wars in 1860 and 1863 to General Duncan Cameron's campaign to take the land between Pātea and Whanganui in 1865 to General Trevor Chute's ruthless scorched-earth campaign the following year which brought havoc to Ngā Rauru, Taranaki and Ngāti Ruanui between the Waitotara River and the mountain.[26] Still it was not over. In late 1866, when Tuhi was about ten years old and the imperial troops had been withdrawn, colonial forces picked up where the army had left off, raiding the villages and cultivations of Māori who were opposed to the survey of the Waimate Plains.[27] And after that came Tītokowaru's war of resistance in which Tuhi's father reputedly fought.

The original inhabitants had difficult decisions to make as their world was shaken by these upheavals. Pīhama had thrown in his lot with the Pākehā state but others chose to fight and Tītokowaru was the most famous of them. Then there was Te Whiti who devised a strategy of peaceful resistance to protect the land and his people's way of life. One thing they all had in common was that there was no certainty to how their various strategies would work. Another was fear. With such great upheaval, disruption and dispossession, fear weighed on the Māori as heavily as it did on the Pākehā. In 1866 Pīhama said the real cause of war was the fear of the Pākehā spreading 'as the tide overspreads the sandbank'.[28] Just as settlers had reason to be afraid because of atrocities committed within living memory, so the Māori would have recalled shocking acts by colonial troops and the British Army. Māori would have been able to match every horror story the Dobie sisters heard on their travels.

General Chute, for instance, had marched from the Waitotara River to the mountain attacking pā, burning villages, forcing people from their homes and, in Tony Sole's words, driving a bayonet deep into the economic heart of Ngāti Ruanui.[29] The pitiless nature of his tactics was captured in a note written after a battle at Ōtapawa. 'The native loss is not known,' wrote Lieutenant Colonel Gorton, commander of the Wanganui District, 'but it must have been very great as the General spares none – and the Natives are overwhelmed with fear.'[30] The general mounted a vigorous pursuit of Māori fleeing their homes. The indiscriminate terror he spread was so great that even Pīhama was forced to seek refuge with Gorton at Ōpunake. Sole estimates that in five weeks Chute took seven fortified pā and 21 open kāinga and created 'heightened levels of insecurity and mistrust among the iwi in the area'.[31] During Tītokowaru's war a few years later there were two incidents in which colonial troops and their Māori allies killed children who were trapped at the edge of the fighting.[32] In 1869 three Māori men were shot and two women captured for the offence of attempting to return to land north of the Waingongoro River that had been deserted after the uprising.[33]

A long period of superficial calm followed the wars of the 1860s but at the end of the 1870s the fears of Māori as well as Pākehā were rekindled. The latter by the challenge of the ploughmen and the former by the attitude of the government and the relentless work of the AC in pushing ahead with road building, surveying and installing the telegraph, all preludes to occupying the land. In the year to March 1880 they built 30 kilometres of road between the Stony and Waingongoro rivers and the pace was accelerating; the following year it was nearly 50 kilometres.[34] Work parties were armed and escorted by teams of 20 to 50 constables, among them Thomas Hughson, who were led by men like Forster and who had all been thoroughly drilled at target practice. As they inched closer to Parihaka they built a series of temporary camps which were then abandoned as they advanced. Every one of them justified the term 'stronghold' which Mary had incongruously applied to the pacifist prophets' unfortified settlement. Official reports boasted of how the constabulary was busy building and extending breastworks, blockhouses and palisading.[35] It was a form of strangulation by road building.

By the middle of 1880 the work parties were forcing their way through cultivations of potatoes and maize on the seaward side of Parihaka. Their forward base at Pungarehu was just 3 kilometres away and by knocking down Parihaka's fences they made the crops vulnerable to stray livestock.[36] Far from worrying about this they were only too happy about the trouble they were causing. Newall summed it up one day when he realised the plantation he had just driven through belonged to Te Whiti himself. 'He will have an opportunity tonight to chew the cud of bitter reflection for we have turned neither to the right hand nor the left with our line but gone straight through his clearings,' he wrote in his diary.[37]

The work was easily observed from Parihaka and the people there were acutely aware of the road builders' relentless progress and what was going on in the background. Redoubts were being strengthened and all were connected by the telegraph. The numbers of AC men were up and they were being intensively drilled at shooting ranges dotted around the district.[38] In his diary Newall mentioned the officers coming out to the roadworks for a spot of shooting for sport.[39] But their targets were game birds; the men practising on the shooting ranges with 100 rounds each were being trained to kill a different kind of quarry.

Even deeper in the background political developments were making it appear more and more likely that – as articulated by Pīhama – the tide was overspreading the sandbank, and coming ever closer. Te Whiti was to use a similar metaphor when he spoke of the land being inundated.[40] Despite the protests and the stand-off between the government and Parihaka, the selling of land was already under way in December 1880.[41] And if this was not enough, Native Minister John Bryce was pressing to deal with the government's Parihaka problem head-on by marching to the village and arresting Hiroki and possibly Te Whiti as well.[42] The idea was being seriously discussed in cabinet and they decided against it only because a sufficient number of ministers worried about the bad press New Zealand would get in England. Yet the initiative was supported in some colonial newspapers. On the day before Mary was murdered the *New Zealand Herald* complained about a new push to disrupt the survey with protesters pulling up settlers' pegs and flags. The time had come to act, it argued, the crisis had arrived and the constabulary should march on Parihaka.[43]

Such was the extent of the coverage given to the case against Tuhi and the insinuations about Te Whiti and Parihaka that it is easy to assume there was no counter-argument in public, that Māori people were mute in the face of the onslaught. And yet their voices were there, though less prominent, often indirect and filtered through the medium of the Pākehā press. The papers closest to Parihaka and the scene of the crime – the *Taranaki Herald* and the *Hawera Star* – picked up on how Māori were reacting to news of the killing and the storm of controversy that raged around it. The week after Tuhi was committed for trial the *Taranaki Herald* published Te Whiti's comments – obtained third-hand through a 'reliable source' – explicitly dissociating himself from the accused and the murder. 'I am in no way responsible. He must bear his own punishment since he followed his own way,' he said, presumably referring to Tuhi's refusal to join the ploughmen. 'I have always preached against bloodshed. My song is the song of peace. The Maori has bitten like a cur; let him die like a dog.'[44] Another report had Te Whiti stressing that Tuhi was the author of his own tragic misfortune. Had he gone ploughing he would have been imprisoned at the time of Mary's last walk and not in a position to commit the crime for which he seemed likely to forfeit his life.[45]

Parihaka people generally were eager to distance themselves from Tuhi. They said that he had very little to do with them, having been no more than two or three times to the monthly meetings.[46] From what the *Taranaki Herald* reported they were horrified by the murder of a woman. 'They talk over it far more than if it was a man who had been the victim,' reported the paper. 'They say it is the work of a pononga kino (a bad or vile slave).' They believed Tuhi must have been drinking before he did it.[47] They feared not only the possibility of an irrational

FIG. 39: Mary was a prolific sketcher of people and places wherever she went. These undated pictures were probably done soon after she arrived in New Zealand. *Courtesy Drake Brockman family*

FIG. 40: Loaves for the Parihaka meeting in January 1880. Spiritual, political and cultural guidance were on offer at these monthly meetings as well as generous hospitality. *William Francis Gordon, PHO2008-1811 PA*

FIG. 41: Mary's sketch of Parihaka with Mount Taranaki in the background. She described it as a stronghold, but she drew a peaceful village. *Mary Dobie,* The Graphic, *Schoolhistory NZ*

FIGS 42 & 43: Mary's sketches of Te Whiti show where she stood on the contradictory spectrum of Pākehā opinion about him. The Graphic, *pk100014, pk 100015, Schoolhistory NZ*

FIGS 44 & 45: Wiremu Kingi Matakātea in old age. The hero of Te Namu joined the Parihaka ploughmen and was arrested. Hone Pīhama chose a different way of survival for his people. *Matakātea PAColl-5800-31, ATL; Pīhama PHO2012-0495, PA*

FIG. 46: The great Ōpunake redoubt with the surf boats used for unloading cargo and passengers from ships anchored in the bay. One of a series of watercolours depicting scenes linked to the Dobie murder which decorate the margins of artist Henry Hobson's photograph album. *E-814-017, ATL*

FIGS 47 & 48: Ready for a walk. Mary and dog in a photo taken before the fatal day and how the Auckland *Observer* reproduced the image after her death. *Family album,* Observer, *4 Dec 1880*

FIG. 49: The road that Mary walked on the fatal day. *Henry Hobson album, E-184-018 ATL*

FIG. 50 (LEFT): Major Goring joined the search for Mary as soon as he returned from a day trip to Ōeo, and was called to view her bloody corpse in the flax bushes. *PA3-0176, ATL*

FIG. 51 (RIGHT): Lieutenant Colonel Roberts rode from Pungarehu to Ōpunake in the early hours of Friday, 26 November 1880, after he was woken with the news of Mary's murder. *William Francis Gordon, PHO2011-2303, ATL*

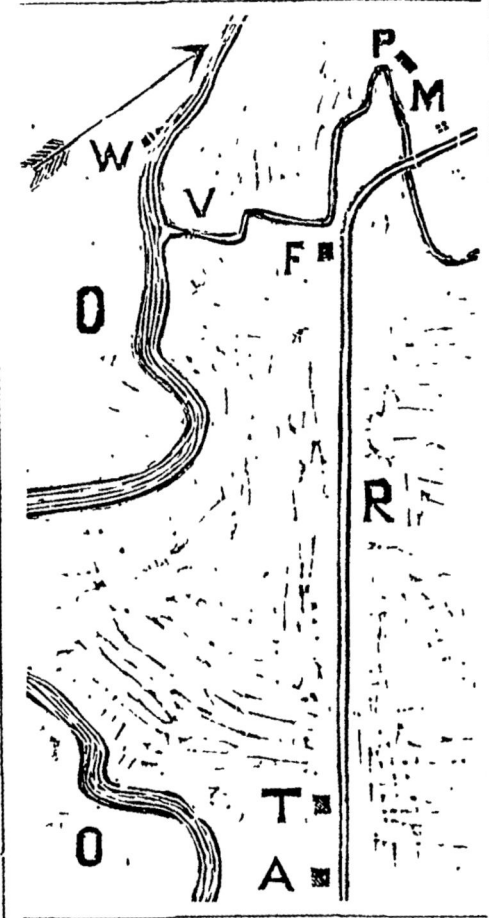

FIG. 52: Map from the *Taranaki Herald*, 30 November 1880, showing Middleton brothers' hotel and the spot where Mary was murdered.

DIABOLICAL MURDER AT OPUNAKE.

MISS DOBIE FOUND DEAD IN THE FLAX.

(BY TELEGRAPH, OWN CORRESPONDENT.)

NEW PLYMOUTH, this day.

INFORMATION has just been received from Opunake that Miss Dobie, the sister-in-law to Captain Goring, has been found murdered about two miles south of the Opunake camp.

The unfortunate lady went out for a walk during the afternoon, and not returning as expected a search party was sent to look for her, when her body was found in the flax with her head severed nearly from her body.

It is supposed that the unfortunate girl had been ravished, and then murdered.

Mr Bullen and the coroner have proceeded to Opunake to hold an inquest.

MISS DOBIE WAYLAID WHILE SKETCHING.

Miss Dobie, with her mother, were about to proceed to England, and had been on a visit to her sister, Mrs Goring, at the Camp at Cape Egmont, where Captain Goring is stationed. She had been sketching all parts of the country, and even at Parihaka, where she had been most kindly treated by Te Whiti and the natives.

Mrs Dobie and her daughter had gone to Opunake, and it is supposed that Miss Dobie had gone to sketch Te Ngamu Bay, where the Lord Worsley was wrecked, about a mile and a half from the township, when she must have been waylaid by a ruffian who had ill-treated and then murdered the poor girl.

There is great excitement here over the affair, as the young lady had been on a visit and was well known to many. Great sympathy is generally expressed for the mother and sister.

FINDING OF THE BODY.

The body of the murdered Miss Dobie was found at 9.30 last night. The clothes were nearly torn off.

DREADFUL MURDER AT OPUNAKE.

A YOUNG LADY KILLED.

HER HEAD NEARLY SEVERED FROM HER BODY.

MAN ARRESTED ON SUSPICION OF THE MURDER.

It is many years since we have had to record a murder in this district, but never has intelligence reached us of a more cowardly and brutal affair than that which took the town by surprise this morning. It is very satisfactory, however, to think that the atrocious deed has not been committed by the Maoris, nor any one connected with the settlement, as the suspicion points to a man whose character has never been of the best, and who, from information to hand, we find has blood upon his clothes.

The particulars as far as we can gather them are that Miss Dobie, a sister-in-law of Major Goring, of the A.C. Force, went for a walk yesterday afternoon, and as she did not return by dusk, a search party was sent out to look for her, when her body was found near Umuroa, a little off the main road, amongst the flax, with her clothes in great disorder, and with her throat cut—her head being nearly severed from her body.

On the discovery of the body, it was difficult at first to connect the dastardly murder with any one, but after the body of the unfortunate young lady had been brought into the camp, suspicion somehow pointed to a man named Walter Stoddard, who, on it being discovered that he had blood upon his clothes and boots, was at once arrested on suspicion of being connected with the atrocious crime.

On the information reaching town this morning, Mr. Bullen, accompanied by Dr. Gibbes, the Coroner, at once proceeded to the camp, where the latter will hold an inquest on the body, when full particulars of the dreadful occurrence will be gathered, and the whole affair thoroughly investigated.

From further information we have gathered we learn that Mrs. Dobie and her daughter (the young lady who has been so cruelly murdered) were about to proceed to England, but before taking their departure they went on a visit to a daughter of Mrs. Dobie. The ladies had made a long stay at the camp, and the young lady who has been murdered had made several sketching tours, even going to Parihaka, where she was most kindly received by Te Whiti and the natives.

The visit to Cape Egmont camp had come to a close, and Major Goring escorted the ladies to Opunake previous to their leaving the district. Miss Dobie, we surmise must have gone to take a last view of Te Namu Bay, the scene of the wreck of the Lord Worsley, one of the most beautiful spots in the district, and of an evening, and when the sun is setting, the scene is a most magnificent one. For an artist, this spot would have more than usual charms, and no doubt wishing to see the place again for the last time she was attracted thither, not fearing that she would in any way be molested, but where it appears she has met with such an unnatural and untimely death. Much sympathy is generally expressed for the friends of the unfortunate young lady in their bereavement.

TELEGRAMS.

(PER PRESS ASSOCIATION.)

WELLINGTON.

This day.

Brutal Murder.

Miss Dobie, of Auckland, was brutally murdered at Opunake last night, the head has been severed from the body.

LATER.

The body of the murdered Miss Dobie was found at 9.30 last night, all her clothing was nearly torn off. A man named Walter Stoddard, from Hawera, has been arrested on suspicion. Blood was found on his hat, clothes and boots, which he accounted for by his horse having cut his nose. This morning a pair of fustian hose were found within six feet of where the body was found lying and also a piece of a bridle.

Further Particulars.

Miss Mary Dobie, sister-in-law to Major Goring, went out for a walk towards Te Namu, and not returning, a search party was organised and bonfires lighted along the coast line. Miss Dobie was found forty yards off the main road to Te Namu pah. Her throat was cut from ear to ear, and life was extinct, her body presenting a dreadful appearance. Stannard, who has been arrested, said he passed the scene of the murder at or about the time. Honi Pihima's daughter saw a horse with saddle tied, at the scene of the murder. Col. Roberts, Mr Hursthouse, and Hone Pahama have just returned from the scene, and they found an old saddle and a bunch of wild flowers evidently gathered by the deceased. Blood was found from ten feet to forty yards off the road, and the ground shows traces of a desperate struggle. The scene is within 100 yards of the uninhabited pah of Te Ngauui, great consternation and sympathy prevails for the relatives, Mr Hursthouse is very energetic in pursuing the enquiry, also Col. Roberts and Honi Pahama. It is understood here that the wife of a storekeeper at Hawerau iped some blood off Stannard's clothes before he started for Opunake. The people here do not think him the culprit. Major Paris has left Hawera for Opunake this morning. Stannard was married by the Registrar early in the week to a Miss Prosser.

FIGS 53, 54 & 55: Diabolical, dreadful and brutal: the headlines on Friday, 26 November 1880, from left the Auckland *Star*, the *Taranaki Herald* and the *Thames Star*.

FIG. 56: Watercolours by Armed Constabulary man Eugene Charles Buckley showing Tuhi and the scene of the crime. In the second search of the area, on the Saturday after the murder, police cut the flax which explains why it does not appear to be as thick as described in evidence at the inquest. The portrait of Tuhi was painted in the Ōpunake redoubt library on the day after he had made a damning confession to Constable George Taylor. *Eugene Charles Buckley, PHO2011-2281, PA*

FIG. 57: Ellen Dobie was a strong woman and yet, according to Armed Constabulary captain Stuart Newall, her family could not tell her the truth about Mary's death. *Family album*

IN MEMORIAM.

Beside the lonely Pah she fell,
Beneath the dying light of Heaven,
Her young, defenceless beauty riven,
Her blood ensanguining the dell

And 'mid the bugle's warning note,
And past the blazing beacon fire,
With choking grief and burning ire,
And sobs that died within the throat.

Of strong men, crushing down their pain,
They bore her back where once she stood
In young and joyful womanhood,
To those she ne'er will greet again.

She had gone out, bright, fresh, so late
Gone out, their joy, and hope, and pride,
For whom they gladly would have died
To keep one shadow from her fate.

Cover her gaping wounds, dark night!
Compose the fair and shapely limbs
With weeping, and with solemn hymns
Bury our dead from out our sight!

Oh lay her in her mother earth!
With reverent hands, and requiem sweet,
And from the clay above her feet
May wild flowers take their fragrant birth.

She loved them, as she loved to look
On nature's loved and mystic grace
Her artist pencil loved to trace
The lines of that unwritten book.

So for her dark and tragic doom
Soft tears, and tender memories blent,
And echoes of one wide lament,
Shall deck the turf around her tomb.

FIG. 58: From the Auckland *Observer*, 4 December 1880. The poem owed its title and metre to Tennyson's great work but little else.

FIG. 59: Mouth of the Pūnehu River where Tuhi lived. Police found a bloodstained coat in his whare. *David Hastings*

FIG. 60: The Middleton brothers' hotel about 20 years after the murder. Tuhi spent six or seven hours in the pub on the fatal day. Two days later the coroner convened the inquest on Mary Dobie's death in the billiard room. *Feaver Photo, PHO2010-0216*

FIG. 61: The diary of surveyor William Skinner shows how quickly news spread, even to those working in the bush. *Hartley Webster PHO2008-1852*

and violent backlash from the Pākehā but also the damage the murder might do to their cause. They told the *Hawera Star*'s correspondent that, far from being an act directed by Te Whiti or inspired by his teaching, it was diametrically opposed to everything the prophet stood for.[48]

The *Hawera Star*'s correspondent in Ōpunake noticed a growing wariness among Māori living in the area and travelling to Parihaka. Where there had been a degree of intermingling – whether drinking in the pub, working, shopping or trading in horses – Māori were now giving the town a wide berth. Fear gave wings to rumour in Māori circles just as it did among the Pākehā, and one story doing the rounds was that the town had been closed against them. The correspondent said it had been noticeable that few Māori were visiting until a party of Te Whiti's supporters passed through on their way to Ōeo to buy tools to prepare a new cultivation. Like others before them, they stressed that the murder had no political significance; it was a 'murder without a cause'. Nevertheless, just to be on the safe side and guard against the distinct possibility that Pākehā would not see it that way, Te Whiti had advised them all to remain in his care at Parihaka, 'which injunction they appear to adhere to, as all are anxious to return quickly'.[49] Tuhi's own family and about a dozen other people from Pūnehu had been scared away and had gone to Parihaka before he confessed.[50]

Far and wide Māori people were deeply affected by Mary's murder and freely expressed their shock and condolences, especially in places where Forster had been known and liked. 'Great indignation is expressed by the Maoris here at the horrible murder of Miss Dobie,' reported the *Bay of Plenty Times*. 'The greatest sympathy is felt for the unfortunate young lady. And the murderer's crime is universally regarded with feelings of abhorrence and loathing.'[51] From the King Country, the *New Zealand Herald* correspondent wrote that the people of the Kīngitanga movement were not at all sorry for Tuhi's capture. 'I have heard a great many express their satisfaction that he did not make his escape to Hikurangi, and as they express it, "take his trouble there",' he wrote. 'Major Goring, when in charge of this district, was greatly liked and respected, and general sympathy is felt for him and other relatives of the deceased.'[52]

Closer to home, newspaper reports suggested some of the feelings of local Māori were cool and qualified by selfishness or cynicism. The *Taranaki Herald* paraphrased what they were saying: 'if Tuhi had killed a white man, especially a surveyor or an A.C., we should have sympathised with him, but as he has slain a woman we are indifferent'.[53] And the Auckland *Star* reported that Rona Matiu and others who gave evidence against Tuhi were angry that the crime had been committed on their ground and suggested they would not have minded if he had done it closer to where he lived.[54]

After the inquest and his confession, Tuhi was held at the redoubt under a heavy guard of six men. It must have been the loneliest time of his life. He cannot have been unaware of the clamour for his death or of the attitudes of his own people who had disowned him. The calm, confident demeanour – which had been shaken during the inquest only briefly when Dr Carey demonstrated Mary's shocking wounds – now showed signs of breaking down. One of his guards, Constable Dennis Connor, saw Tuhi crying and complaining of his loneliness. He asked after his father and even made a request to see Stannard, though it is not known what he wanted to say to him or if a meeting between them ever took place.[55]

The prisoner sent a message to his father to come and collect his horse but urged him to come alone; Tuhi did not want his wife or his mother to see him like this. From the redoubt he sent a farewell message to his family which was transcribed, translated and published by Charles Hursthouse. The message overflows with remorse: 'Salutations to you all who remain over there! Great is my love for you all at this time. You will not see me again. I have given myself for food for the birds of Heaven. This is all the adieu. A long love cannot return me to the house. Where is the fear? We were in the first sunny days overtaken by sin. This is all.'[56] To his father he made an explicit confession and urged that he should be forgotten: 'Let not your minds be troubled about me. I have sinned – murdered. On no account let the thought return to me. Cry not at all. With the great priest is the thought for me. This is all.'

Not even the most insensitive reader could miss the poetry in Tuhi's language. The *Manawatu Times* though could not help but sneer. 'Shakespeare tells us that there are villains who can "smile and murder while they smile",' it said, 'but the Ōpunake tragedy has developed a new species of scoundrel – a poetical cut-throat.'[57] Despite the sneers, there is no mistaking the depth of Tuhi's remorse, most eloquently expressed in the phrase 'food for the birds of heaven' which occurs a number of times in the Old Testament, twice in the book of despairing Jeremiah. This is the ultimate punishment for those who have sinned or departed from the word of God, who are cursed to die and their bodies cast out with no care or ceremony to be left as carrion.⁵⁸ Tuhi, who may well have picked up the phrase at Parihaka where Te Whiti often quoted from the Old Testament, had accepted he would be facing the harshest possible sentence even before it had been passed down. It was not just a matter of surrendering his life but being cast out and forgotten.

In his remorse and his loneliness, Tuhi was prepared to unburden himself by confessing to anyone who would listen. Including his statement at the inquest, he confessed at least seven times to various people and he had no doubts about where it was leading. He told one of his guards at the redoubt, Constable George Taylor, who was part-Māori, about a portentous dream he had during the inquest. 'I saw a person felling a tree upon my house,' he said. 'The house fell down with the exception of two posts at each end and the ridge-pole. I know now it was a dream concerning death either for me or my younger brother. I know now the dream concerns myself.'⁵⁹

9.

THE LAST BURNING QUESTION

On the morning after his sensational confession Tuhi received a visit from the coroner and the interpreter Charles Hursthouse. Worried about contaminating Tuhi's right to a fair trial, the coroner had ruled out any public questioning at the inquest once he had admitted his guilt. Naturally people still wanted to know the full story, exactly what had happened, whether he had any accomplices and the answer to the last burning question: Why? Now, in private, the coroner and Hursthouse aimed to fill in the gaps and they sat Tuhi down to place on record his own narrative of what happened on the afternoon of the fatal day.

It was the second of seven confessions he would make. When the coroner's questioning was over Tuhi would send the letter to his father that contained the third. The following day he would confess again, this time to one of the guards. He told the story for a fifth time to another guard on the steamer taking him to Wellington for his trial and twice more while he was held in prison there. The stories he told and the explanations he gave were not consistent. There were moments when it seemed that even he could not give a crisp answer to the question 'Why did you do it?' He told the Bishop of Wellington, Octavius Hadfield, who visited him in his prison cell, that he had 'no motive whatever for what he did, that he had drunk too much, got suddenly excited, and immediately afterwards realised what he had done'.[1] And if he could not explain it what chance did anyone else have? Maybe the motive was beyond reach, as some newspapers said or, in the words of some of Te Whiti's supporters, it was a murder without a cause.

Hadfield thought Tuhi was perfectly candid during their meetings but his substantial confessions show him skipping details of what happened and glossing over the motive, skirting around any admission that he had robbed Mary before killing her and no mention of rape. As the letters to his family made plain, he was deeply remorseful; his confessions read like a man trying to find some detail, however slight, that might give him a chance of redemption no matter how slim, and avoiding anything that might reduce that chance. Those who heard his confessions and passed them on also had their biases not to mention difficulties with the language. The many confessions each add another layer to the many deaths of Mary Dobie. And yet, when weighed against each other and the physical evidence, they can be reconciled and lead, step by step, to an explanation of what exactly happened on that fatal afternoon and to an answer to the last burning question.

A summary of Tuhi's confession to the coroner was sent to the justice minister in Wellington in an urgent telegram just after midday on Tuesday.[2] Two versions of it appeared in the morning papers on the following day, apparently leaked by Hursthouse.[3] The three versions – one official and two unofficial – were not identical but, apart from variations in phrasing, they told essentially the same story. Tuhi said he left Ōpunake to look for a horse and had no intention of committing a crime. This was to counter evidence from William Eyes and Dennis Connor that suggested Tuhi may have followed Mary from Ōpunake, thus implying some degree of premeditation.[4]

North of Te Namu he met Mary. He got off his horse, tied it to a flax bush and followed her. She was frightened when he overtook her on foot and gave him 6s 4d. Having taken the money, he killed her. The telegram quotes him as saying: 'I then took out my pocket knife & stuck it in her throat holding her by her dress in front. She fell down but was not dead'. He dragged her to a flax bush where, as she struggled for her life, he cut her throat again before dragging her further away to the spot where she died and he concealed her body. He took off the moleskins and threw them away, washed his hands in the Ōtahi Stream and went to catch his horse which had slipped its bridle. He hid when Hone Pīhama and his party came down the road. After they passed he retrieved his horse and swiftly rode back to Ōpunake, catching up with them near the telegraph office on the outskirts of town.

At the end of the narrative part of the confession, Tuhi made a series of important admissions. He admitted the knife found by Francis Hickey near the redoubt at the weekend was the one he used to kill Mary. The bloodstains on his moleskins and coat came from Mary, he said, but the stains on his other trousers were from pigs. He gave an account of the money he spent that day. He had five shillings in the morning and when he came back in the afternoon he spent three shillings and sixpence in the pub. He gave three shillings and sixpence to a man from Parihaka and spent threepence on a box of matches at Coffey's and bought a pipe for half a penny. Including the sum he took from Mary, that leaves four shillings unaccounted for. Towards the end of his confession he repeated his desire to give up his life. 'I want now at once to be killed I do not want any more trials,' he said. 'May not her relations kill me or may I kill myself?' He added that she had called out once before he stabbed her and she made no attempt to run away when he got off his horse.

The narrative accords loosely with the physical evidence. The pool of blood and the drag marks in the flax and his admissions about the knife and the bloodstains on his clothes matched his description of how he had driven her from the road and stabbed her to death. And although he mentioned stabbing or cutting Mary only twice, when she had six wounds, his account of the attack was fairly close to the way Carey had described it which could explain why Tuhi was so discomfited when the doctor gave his demonstration at the inquest.

One important difference between the *Taranaki Herald* version of this confession and the other two is that it provides the first attempt at an explanation by Tuhi himself. A sentence at the end, which does not appear in the official telegram, says 'I had no desire but to kill her. It was a momentary impulse and I acted on it.' His inability to explain clearly – reflected in what he said to Hadfield later – left the burning question of 'why' unanswered. The confession, which gave a narrative far more comprehensive than any so far, raised other important questions which were also left hanging. How and why did Mary come to give him the money? What was said? And does this version adequately account for the great distance – about 90 metres according to Superintendent James' measurement – between where the horse was tethered and where the murder took place?

Added to these questions were doubts about the abilities of the interpreter Hursthouse and suspicions about his motives. Hursthouse, a civil engineer and surveyor by trade, was with Newall when they cut through Te Whiti's cultivations on the outskirts of Parihaka a few months before the murder.[5] From time to time he acted as an official interpreter and Captain Louis Knollys, aide-de-camp to the new governor, for one admired his linguistic ability, reporting that he was 'a gentleman who speaks thoroughly the Maori language, has resided with the Natives all his life, and is acquainted with their customs'.[6] But others had grave misgivings about him. The *Thames Star*'s Auckland correspondent was sceptical of Hursthouse's reasons for making public the Tuesday confession – a 'private and alleged' conversation he called it.[7] He quoted a letter he had received from a Taranaki contact who scorned Hursthouse's capability as an interpreter – an appointment not looked upon with favour in either Ōpunake or Hawera he said – and questioned his role as the supplier of sensational details to the newspapers. The source was particularly concerned about Tuhi's motive. 'I am not without hope that when the Supreme Court is engaged calmly getting at all the facts, it will be found that there were motives which are not already published but will be got out at the trial to account in part for the awful deed,' he wrote.[8]

Another problem with the inquest confession was not immediately apparent but would become an important issue at the trial: had it been obtained legally? At issue was whether Tuhi had been cautioned properly and whether the confession had been extracted by questioning or by threats and inducements. In court Hursthouse insisted that Tuhi had been properly cautioned. 'I told him that he must be cautious because anything he said might be used against him in evidence.'[9] Hursthouse said the caution was repeated after the confession at the coroner's insistence.[10] But defence counsel Charles Forwood objected, arguing that the warning was insufficient because it should also have explicitly stated that Tuhi had nothing to fear from any threat and nothing to gain from any inducement. The cross-examination shows Forwood was trying to build a case to suggest that Tuhi's guards had pressured him to confess with threats on the one hand and promises that nothing would happen to him on the other.[11]

Chief Justice James Prendergast was inclined to accept the caution despite the defence's objection but when Hursthouse explained how the confession was made he raised an objection of his own. This issue was whether Tuhi had made a statement voluntarily or whether it had been extracted by a process of questioning. Prendergast noted that after Tuhi said he had done it, Hursthouse asked him a follow-up question – 'Was it you?' – and this made all the difference in deciding whether the answer was admissible. Hursthouse explained that he had asked the question simply to be sure of Tuhi's meaning but the judge was deeply worried by how it was done. 'What I have to consider is whether it is a voluntary statement on the part of the prisoner, but this involved questions and answers,' he said to the court.[12] He ruled that the brief confession made at the end of the inquest was inadmissible and it followed that the same applied to the confession made to Hursthouse and the coroner on the following day.[13]

Problems with Tuhi's interviews were far deeper than the discussion of admissibility at the trial suggested. Questioning of him began long before the inquest. Hursthouse was the translator on Saturday morning when Tuhi was interviewed in the redoubt by a police sergeant.[14] He was questioned about his clothing, the bridle and his movements on the day and given no reason and no formal caution although he must have known why.[15] The Tuesday morning confession showed signs that it, too, had been obtained by questioning which would certainly have made it inadmissible if it had been put to the court. In parts of the statement, especially towards the end when additional information is given out of narrative sequence, it is clear that questions had been cut out as was common practice at the time in official transcripts and press coverage of court cases and public meetings.

But even more significant, the Tuesday morning confession did not read like the translated words of a Māori man speaking spontaneously. It was too neatly tailored to fit the legal case against him with its economical narrative setting out what had happened and then the list of important admissions at the end to complete the stitching. The language is functional and precise, unlike the language in the letters that Tuhi wrote to his family. There is no poetry, no flowery turns of phrase which were usual in translations of Māori documents and speeches in the nineteenth century, nor does it end with a characteristic verbal punctuation mark such as 'this is all' or 'that is all'.

Another reason to doubt the Hursthouse confession was that it included the dubious story of the threepenny piece linking Tuhi to Mary. The story had originated with Dr Carey who went shopping at Coffey's store on the Monday morning after the murder while the inquest was still in session. In his change was a threepenny piece stained with what he thought was blood and signs that someone had tried to scrape it off.[16] It was all too easy to jump to the conclusion that this was the coin that Coffey had given to Mary when she bought her pencil.

But neither Carey nor Coffey had been a persuasive witness on this point. At the inquest Carey could not say for sure that the stain was blood. Coffey was uncertain and then changed his story.[17] 'I believe I recollect having served him with a tin box of matches for threepence. I also believe he paid me for it with a threepenny piece.' What needs emphasising is that he merely believed he recollected and believed he was paid with a threepenny piece. One other point underscored the weakness of the evidence. It was highly unlikely, he said, that a threepenny coin would remain in his till for four days. Coffey then contradicted the whole story saying that after some haggling he had sold Tuhi a penny box of matches for a halfpenny. Unsurprisingly the coin, which had been the focus of so much attention on the second day of the inquest, was dropped from the prosecution case. At the trial Coffey repeated that he had sold the matches for a halfpenny 'subject to my impression that I sold him a threepenny box before'.[18]

From the way this story emerged and quietly disappeared it is possible to infer that the police had suggested it to Coffey in an attempt to frame Tuhi before he admitted anything. On the other hand, Coffey's confusion and contradictions may have been the result of the police rushing evidence into the hearing before they had thought it through, much as Sergeant McKeon had done with Stannard's stained clothing. The investigation and the inquest were conducted in haste and so this may have been more of a muddle than a conspiracy, the result of over-excitement when Carey produced what he wrongly thought was a piece of conclusive evidence. However, a less charitable view is necessary of the coin's appearance in the confession to Hursthouse. Tuhi had no incentive to get this fact wrong and every reason to tell the truth. Therefore the mention of the threepence reinforces the conclusion that the statement was tailored to strengthen the case against him. Like the newspaper that seized on the story as evidence of motive, the person who did the stitching failed to see that it was not credible.

Loss of the dubious Tuesday confession did not destroy the prosecution's case. The coin evidence would not be led and, more importantly, they had another, more comprehensive and more convincing confession to offer, which was admitted. It was made on the Wednesday morning in the library at the redoubt, the place where Mary's body had been subjected to a post-mortem examination a few days before and where, on the next day, AC man Eugene Charles Buckley painted Tuhi in watercolours, smoking a pipe with his arms folded and a faraway look in his eyes (Fig. 56). Six men were on guard, among them Constable George Taylor. Tuhi opened the conversation by asking Taylor if he had seen his father going to Parihaka that day. Taylor said no and agreed to write a letter to the old man. Tuhi then told him about his portentous dream before volunteering a confession which was much fuller and more revealing than anything he had said before.[19]

Tuhi made his confession in te reo Māori and that was how Taylor gave it in court before translating it into English.[20] The court record preserves only the translation. Like the Hursthouse version, it begins with a denial of premeditation only it is much more explicit. 'I had no intention of killing the woman when I left,' he said, and from this point the differences are profound. According to the Taylor confession, Tuhi spoke to Mary when they met on the road saying 'Where do you come from?' She did not understand him at first but as he kept asking the question, she kept responding in English which he did not understand. 'That woman was frightened and gave me money,' said Tuhi. He was still on his horse at the time and after handing over the 6s 4d she threatened to report him. 'She said she would tell the soldiers of me or about me. I was then afraid of my crime of taking the money from that woman.' This was the catalyst for the murder. 'I got off my horse and tied it to the flax. The woman ran away when she saw me tying up the horse.' Tuhi then went on to describe the last terrifying moments of Mary's life. He ran after her, caught her and, in contrast to the Hursthouse version, he did not stab her but threw her on the ground and strangled her, just as he had done in the fight with his father the week before.

He thought she was dead and left her, but he was wrong. Mary was still alive and pulled herself to her feet in a desperate attempt to resume her flight. But it was futile, Tuhi sprang on her like a great cat. 'I then ran to her and cut her (or stabbed her) with a knife,' said Tuhi and he spared nothing in his description of the ferocity of the assault. 'I took her by the back of the neck and drove her along that she might be a distance from the road. When she had arrived a distance from the road she fell and died.'

The rest of the narrative followed Hursthouse's Tuesday version. He concealed the body and hid when the Pīhama party appeared. 'When they had passed I caught my horse and went,' said Tuhi. He ended the confession with the customary verbal punctuation so conspicuously lacking in the Hursthouse version: 'That is all.'

Unlike the Hursthouse confession, this one was kept secret until the trial where the court accepted Taylor's evidence that it was volunteered by Tuhi and made without any questions to prompt him. The style of the language and the verbal punctuation at the end give it a note of authenticity which is lacking from the other one and in substance it is more credible. The Taylor confession corrects the original narrative and answers some of the outstanding questions. For instance, it now became clear that the money changed hands while Tuhi was still on his horse and, far from being unconcerned when he dismounted, Mary started to run immediately. Another important point of difference was that the first attack was not a stabbing but an attempt at strangulation. The similarity with the attack on his father the week before adds to its credibility. Mary's end was neither quick nor merciful. Her fight for life covered much ground – 90 metres down the road and 30 metres into the flax – as it went through several phases of escalating horror from the moment of the first meeting to Tuhi running her down and trying to strangle her, then her renewed flight and finally the bloody climax as she was killed in the bushes.

But the most important difference between the Hursthouse and Taylor versions was that in the former the drama played out as though it was a silent movie except for Mary's one cry before death. Otherwise they met on the road without speaking, she gave him money apparently without exchanging a word and then, with not a syllable passing between them, he stabbed her. But, as became apparent in the Taylor confession, much was said in the few dangerous moments before the struggle for Mary's life began in earnest.

Mary and Tuhi were separated by a deep chasm of mutual misunderstanding. Tuhi spoke some English. Constables Connor and Knowles as well as the archdeacon who visited him in prison testified to that.[21] But it is equally clear he did not speak it well, which is why he had translators for his police interviews and when he appeared in court. Similarly, it is likely Mary knew a little Māori. All the records of her travels with her sister show their interest in the people they encountered included learning something of their languages. Within days of landing in New Zealand they were playing with Māori words and phrases and surely she had picked up a few more in the intervening three years. But it is not likely that she spoke the language with the kind of fluency that was needed for an awkward meeting on a lonely road with a strange man apparently intent on robbery. The words they spoke in those few terrifying moments were, as Napoleon would have said, all confusion and discord to each other's ears.

The language difficulty adds an extra barrier to understanding what happened but the money is the best evidence to support the robbery explanation. She did hand over a few coins and he did admit the crime of taking them. But there are still other possible interpretations. It was not unknown for Māori to demand payments from Pākehā travelling along the road from Ōpunake to Pungarehu. A few weeks before the murder, the *Hawera Star* reported that a Pākehā businessman had been bailed up on the road and told to pay 20 shillings or be hauled before a tribunal. He paid the money and doubtless regarded it as robbery while the Māori thought of it as a legitimate charge.[22] Tuhi may have had something similar in mind when he accosted Mary.

On the other hand, Tuhi may have been telling the truth when he said he had simply asked her where she was from. She, misunderstanding him and influenced by her knowledge of the fees charged at the Pink and White Terraces, may have assumed he was demanding cash. At the Hot Lakes, it appears she would not pay, but this time maybe she did because she was alone and frightened. Although the confession may look like an admission of robbery – and thus negate this idea – considered more carefully it admits only that Tuhi took the money, not that he demanded it.

A host of reasons prevents any certainty on this point. To begin with the only evidence for what was said came from the accused man. Most people in his position would tell the story in a way calculated to give them at least a chance of some sort of moral redemption even if there was no realistic hope of a not-guilty verdict. Compounding that were the profound language and cultural barriers. It was not just that Mary and Tuhi did not fully comprehend the words each other spoke but they may have had different cultural understandings and expectations which could not be resolved in time to prevent the tension and uncertainty leading to a fatal outcome. It is not even possible to completely write off the idea that rape was Tuhi's original intention. He did not mention it and although it was clear that no rape took place, and Dr Carey was adamant no attempt was made, who can say for sure what flickered across his mind that afternoon?

Despite all of these imponderables, the Wednesday confession provides a certain answer to the final burning question. It begins with the misunderstandings but goes on to show how the encounter was made fatal by two other factors reacting with each other to produce the terrifying last few minutes of Mary Dobie's life. Both are clear in the narrative that Tuhi told to Taylor. The first was fear and the second was the imbalance of power. Whatever the truth about the genesis of the confrontation, fear was decisive in the way it played out. Tuhi said he could see that Mary was frightened at his sudden appearance on horseback. It seems she panicked, handed over the money and then invoked the power of her empire, in the form of the AC, in the hope that it would protect her. 'She said she would tell the soldiers of me,' was how Tuhi put it to Taylor.

Mary could not have foreseen that the threat would spawn a sense of fear, perhaps even greater than her own, in the man who loomed before her on his black horse and that he, too, would panic. Whatever the limits to Tuhi's grasp of English, it seems he understood well enough the words and implications of what she said. For her part, she was not to know that he had a deep, perhaps irrational, fear of imprisonment and this, by more than one account, was the reason he had refused to join Te Whiti's ploughmen.[23] He made the point himself to a prison visitor in a seventh, informal confession after his trial, which was reported by a special correspondent of the *Otago Daily Times*.[24]

The correspondent did not identify his source saying only that it was a friend who had several 'earnest conversations' with Tuhi in prison. It is highly unlikely that any one of three churchmen who spent time with him in The Terrace gaol would have committed such an egregious breach of confidence. The most likely source was Ebenezer Baker, who would be the official interpreter at the trial. A prominent Anglican minister, Archdeacon Arthur Stock, had sought and been granted permission for Baker to go to the prison independently so Tuhi would have someone to talk to in his own tongue.[25] It is likely that the reporter used these conversations to construct his account of Tuhi's seventh confession.

Tuhi said he was not drunk but he had been drinking enough to make him reckless and violent if the occasion arose which it did after he had 'extorted' money from Mary and she threatened him with the soldiers. 'He was seized with a sudden and irresistible homicidal impulse,' wrote the correspondent, 'which urged him to kill her there and then, both in revenge for her sharp words and as a sure means of preventing the fulfilment of her threat which ... meant lengthened imprisonment.'

The correspondent admitted this was a 'free rendering' of the substance of Tuhi's words. But it is consistent with the Taylor confession which revealed for the first time the decisive role that fear played in the tragedy. To Taylor, Tuhi said that Mary was 'frightened' when he approached her and he, in turn, was 'afraid' when she threatened to tell the soldiers. The initial crime may well have been robbery – the prison visitor's version referred to 'extortion' – but robbery itself is not a sufficient motive for the killing. If robbery was his intention, then he succeeded the moment Mary handed over the money. Something else was required for him to commit murder and that something was the fear sparked by her threat of telling the constabulary.

Some newspapers and even Tuhi himself had difficulty explaining the motive because it could not simply be condensed into a single, convenient word whether that be robbery, rape, politics or just savagery. The *Otago Daily Times*' special correspondent fell into a similar trap when he went on to reduce Tuhi's motive to a calculated gamble staking his life against the chances of being caught. 'He resolved that he would *not* be imprisoned, and that if either captivity or death must befall him the latter should be his fate'. Although this rightly hints at the fear of imprisonment as a factor, it contradicts the correspondent's first, and more persuasive, statement that the crime was sudden and impulsive. The calculated gamble was more likely to be a reflection of Tuhi's state of mind since his arrest as he repeatedly expressed a death wish. Rather than being the result of such a macabre calculation, the crime was a rapidly unfolding series of events provoked by irrational emotions that in turn reacted against each other. It could be understood properly only when related as a story and not in a phrase or a simplistic formula, much less a word.

What may have started as a robbery, extortion or just a misunderstanding was transformed by fear and made fatal by the second crucial element, power. Or, more specifically, an unstable relationship of power. At first Tuhi, the tall, strong man, exercised power over a terrified woman and took her money. But she tilted the balance against him when she threatened to tell the soldiers. Then it was his turn to be afraid and he raised the stakes to tragic levels when he exercised his physical power by chasing her down the road and killing her in the flax bushes.

But the balance of power was to tilt once more and Tuhi's fate would be decided by the imported laws and customs of the settler government. He declared that he wanted to die immediately without trial. No one publicly commented at the time but it seems he wanted to expiate his sin through Māori law and custom rather than the trial by jury. In giving up his life he would satisfy the requirements of utu in its full sense, not simply revenge but a restoration of balance.[26] His death wish would be fulfilled, and swiftly, but not as quickly as he wanted and under the law of his victim's empire rather than the customs of his own people. The trial was set down for the Supreme Court sessions at Wellington starting on 9 December, fourteen days after the murder. It was not much time to organise the witnesses and the paperwork let alone the logistics of moving 20 or 30 people to the capital where they would have to be fed and watered for about four days.

The first person to be moved was the prisoner who was taken to Wellington on the government steamer *Hinemoa*, confined to the forecastle and guarded by three armed constables.²⁷ Hursthouse visited Tuhi on board and commented that his bold indifference had vanished and been replaced by a careworn, anxious look.²⁸ He was feeling more isolated and lonely than ever and was planning to face his trial defenceless. 'I . . . have no witnesses no wish for any of my friends to see me,' an official telegram quoted him as saying shortly before his departure.²⁹ The *Hinemoa* steamed through the night and during the voyage Tuhi made another confession, his fifth, to a guard. He repeated that he had killed Mary after she threatened to tell the soldiers.³⁰

In the morning he was greeted by a large crowd on the wharf in Wellington.³¹ It was only with some difficulty that the police held them in check while the constabulary commissioner Colonel Reader went on board to escort the object of their curiosity from the ship. When Tuhi was brought up on deck they saw a young man described by one reporter as carrying himself erect, with nothing remarkable about his features. He wore a striped shirt in brown cotton and a checked shawl wound Māori-fashion around his loins. He had no hat, his legs were bare – revealing the still festering injury to his ankle – and he was shoeless as he had been on the day he killed Mary.³² The reporter remarked that as he came on deck he gave a broad grin which made him appear sarcastic and defiant. This was not how he came across in his confessions and letters to his family or in the observation of Hursthouse. In the last days of his life Tuhi was described variously as despondent and despairing or arrogant and careless. These differences may reflect swings in his mood but they may also reflect the expectations of those who observed him.

As the police led him down the gangway and along the wharf to where a covered cab was waiting to take him to jail, the crowd, which had been so pushy, now hung back. Not a single expression of indignation escaped their lips, said the reporter. Yet despite his isolation in Ōpunake, Tuhi had his supporters in Wellington. The only sound came from an old woman who made 'terrific lamentations during which the word "pakeha" was frequently uttered, followed by shaking her clenched fists'. The reporter wrote that as Tuhi passed her she tried to console him in Māori by saying that he was 'going home to his father'.[33]

The police put Tuhi in the covered wagon and drove him through the streets of Wellington to The Terrace gaol. On the way he seemed to have been mightily impressed with what he saw of the town. 'He gazed hard at some of the principal shops,' wrote the *Taranaki Herald*'s reporter, 'and frequently remarked, "Kapai Poneke!" (Wellington is a fine place!)'.[34] This positive reaction even extended to the jail which he also declared 'kapai', surprisingly, given his phobia about being imprisoned and old photographs which show it as a typically grim Victorian penal establishment (Fig. 68).[35] The walls were topped with 'murderous looking spikes' and armed guards occupied a 10-metre tower which enabled them to keep all of the prison's yards and outside walls under surveillance at all times.[36] Inside there were cells, half-underground, for solitary confinement and, even worse, two 'dark cells' with double doors where especially wicked prisoners could be cut off from all light for up to 48 hours at a time.

Yet it was not all bad according to *Evening Post* reporter James Oakley Browne who toured the prison a few months after Tuhi's stay.[37] For a start it was 'exquisitely clean' and the diet of boiled beef, potatoes, soup and tea was good enough even though it was monotonous. Space was tight with three and sometimes four prisoners locked up at night in cells measuring 12 feet by 12 feet (3.6 metres by 3.6 metres), although Tuhi had one of the single cells which measured 7 feet 9 inches by 6 feet (2.35 metres by 1.82 metres). He would have slept on a mattress on the floor with a blanket to keep him warm but no pillow for his head. Browne reported a combination of good food, cleanliness and plenty of outdoor exercise in the form of hard labour meant the prisoners were generally in good health. When he visited, not one of the six beds in the prison infirmary was occupied. At night prisoners used the ventilation system to communicate between cells. It seems there was no attempt to stop them although, in contrast to their pristine surroundings, the talk was not particularly refined or clean, as Browne delicately put it. 'The god of the average criminal is Beelzebub, the deity of filth,' he wrote, 'and the conversation of the criminal is, therefore, often filthy.'

In a photograph of the prison taken from the rear, the land looks rough as though newly cleared (Fig. 68). But in front there were seven acres of prettily laid-out grounds with walks between fir and pine trees. The exotic trees were reminders that Tuhi was about to face judgment in a strange new world. Even so, his anxiety, which Hursthouse had observed on the steamer, seemed to vanish once he arrived. And yet there was much to be anxious about. The jailers were detailed to watch over him day and night lest he try to pre-empt the law's prerogative over life and death.[38]

10.

MAY GOD HAVE MERCY ON YOUR SOUL

The accused killer found unexpected support in the strange city where he had come to meet his fate. It first appeared among the many Māori people who were on the waterfront to greet him, all in silence except for the old woman who shouted words of defiance and encouragement as Tuhi passed by. It continued during his trial when they turned out in numbers every day. And it came in a pragmatic form too when the Māori people who lived at Te Aro organised a lawyer to defend him.[1] Without their intervention it is doubtful that he would have done it himself given his state of mind since the dramatic late-night confession at the inquest.

The man they briefed had an impressive record, on paper at least. Charles Forwood had been in the legal profession for 30 years and his CV included a brief stint as acting chief justice of

Fiji as well as showing he was once considered a front-runner for the job of second magistrate in Wellington.[2] But this was not as impressive as it might seem. Forwood did not get the job as magistrate and he acted only briefly as chief justice in a small colony so the title was not nearly as exalted as it sounded. His record as a lawyer in Wellington for the two years before Tuhi's trial did not suggest any special ability to defend a man on a capital charge. Most of his work was dealing with bankruptcy or petty crime and licensing cases in the Magistrate's Court. He came perilously close to bankruptcy himself when, just four months before the murder trial, he was forced to declare that he could not pay his debts and his creditors appointed trustees to navigate him through his difficult patch.[3]

Before Forwood could devote his attention to Tuhi's case he had another job to finish. While the *Hinemoa* was on its way north to collect his next client, Forwood was appearing in the Magistrate's Court to apply for a liquor licence for a notorious sly-grog shop which was evidently trying to go straight after too many inconvenient brushes with the law. The result of that case did not bode well; had Tuhi or the people of Te Aro cared to notice, the application was rejected. Ill-equipped as he was, Forwood faced a task which would have been of daunting difficulty even for a defence lawyer experienced in the dark arts of defending a murder charge. His problems could be neatly categorised as lack of time, lack of resources and a client who was far too talkative for his own good.

The problem of time was simply stated. Forwood took up his brief on Monday 6 December and the Supreme Court session at which Tuhi was to be tried began on the following Thursday. Forwood's first move was to persuade the reluctant court to delay the start of the trial until after the weekend.[4] It was a small victory, gaining him at most three days, but it counted as something special in a case where wins for the defence were few. Usually Forwood failed on points small and large, as he did when he tried to persuade the state to help with money and resources. When he took the brief from the Te Aro people he assumed his expenses would be covered but on the day the trial started he found they had no money and he would have to make do with the £10 10s allowed to him by the government. He wrote to the Crown Solicitor Harry Bell arguing it was not nearly enough to cover costs for such things as cabs to and from the jail, the interpreter and clerical assistance let alone his own fee. He stressed that this was no ordinary trial because it was a matter of life and death, and also related to the status of the Māori around Ōpunake.[5] Therefore the government should deal with it 'in a larger & more liberal spirit than may be justified in ordinary cases'. The request was rejected after being referred to Native Minister John Bryce; £10 10s was all he would get and that would be paid only on the understanding that it would not be supplemented from private sources.[6]

The result was the same when Forwood sought help from the state to track down witnesses and bring them to Wellington. Tuhi had told him he was drunk at the time of the murder and Forwood therefore wanted people who had been with him at the hotel on the fatal day. The trouble was that Tuhi had supplied no names so Forwood was left to beg the state to help with his legwork. In explaining the problem to Justice Minister William Rolleston he said Tuhi had been drinking at the hotel with Europeans and Māori people for some hours before the murder. 'As I think it highly desirable to show his condition at the time I have to urge upon the Government to give orders that this be rigidly enquired into and that any persons able to speak to this, should be sent down as well as the proprietor of the hotel,' he wrote in a telegram on the Tuesday afternoon before the trial was scheduled to begin.[7] However, he was still unable to provide any names and was feeling frustrated at official reluctance to help in what, to him, did not seem too difficult a task. 'I am told the hotel is close to the Camp of Constabulary & surely the fact of the prisoner having been drinking there must be known to the Police of the district.' He was certainly right about that; the crew who had unloaded the steamer that morning had been in the pub for some hours with Tuhi.

As this exchange was taking place, the government witnesses were already being rounded up and embarked on the *Hinemoa* at Ōpunake. Bell went to see Forwood late in the afternoon and gave him a deadline: he had to come up with the names of the witnesses by 8 p.m. or the *Hinemoa* would sail without them.[8] Forwood lamely managed just four names, all of whom had already been called for the prosecution and none of whom had been in the bar at the critical times. Forwood's final word to Bell was a telegram half an hour before the deadline expired saying he had no more names but making one final plaintive appeal: 'I cannot give you the names of any other witness. If a telegram be sent to send down anyone drinking in the Hotel with him... I think no more can be expected'.[9] But not even that could be expected. 'I have already explained to Mr Forwood,' wrote an exasperated Bell to Colonel Reader, 'that while the Government will afford him every facility for bringing his witnesses here we cannot bring the whole population of the coast on the chance of someone being able to give evidence.'[10]

These behind-the-scenes manoeuvrings before the trial give some hints to what Forwood was planning for the defence. In his plea for more funding, he said the case, as well as being a matter of life and death, also related to the status of Māori near Ōpunake. The reference is enigmatic but suggests he may have seen the possibility of a defence built out of some unspecified social or political argument. If so, it would not have been something the state would care to hear and in any case it was dropped in favour of two simpler and more conventional defences. The first was to try to knock the damning confessions out of the trial and the second, a fall-back position, to plead that alcohol was to blame.

A new Supreme Court building was under construction so the trial was staged in the old Provincial Council building on the site of what is now the Parliamentary Library at the corner of Aitken and Molesworth streets. It was a two-storey, neo-classical structure with two wings and large, gothic windows at the front which would have been familiar to those brought up in a European tradition but as foreign and exotic to the man in the dock as the pine trees outside his prison.

On the first day of his trial – as with every occasion that Tuhi had appeared in public since his arrest – a crowd gathered to see him. Among them were the witnesses who had arrived that morning on the *Hinemoa* and the *Evening Post* reported a number of Māori women, dressed in gay mats and brilliant dresses, squatted in the passages outside the courtroom.[11] The only people who did not want to be there were the potential jurors; a succession of 22 men were called and excused for one reason or another. Once the jurors took their seats the focus switched back to the man in the dock. The *Post* reported that he looked around the court and smiled when brought in. To the reporter's eye he seemed to have become much thinner in the week since he had landed in Wellington. When asked to plead he again smiled and seemed unconcerned when he said not guilty in Māori: 'kahore'. During the morning he kept his arms folded and his head averted from the jury. He was probably the only person in court who showed no interest in proceedings, commented the *Post*, and added that this was probably because he was only slightly acquainted with English although he had his own interpreter.[12]

Prosecutor Charles Izard laid out the case against Tuhi with a chain of circumstantial evidence, each witness who had come down on the *Hinemoa* constituting an unbreakable link which mocked the prisoner's denial of his own confessions. One by one they told their stories about what they had seen on the fatal day and afterwards. The torn and bloody trousers, the bridle, the knife and the bloodstained coat were all identified and linked to Tuhi. His actions after the event were recalled by Māori witnesses who portrayed him as behaving like a guilty man on the evening that Mary was murdered. And then there was the confession to George Taylor, spelled out in all its damning detail.

It was the confessions that Forwood attacked first, and both the Chief Justice James Prendergast and prosecutor Izard were irritated by the difficulties he raised. When Forwood argued the inquest confession was inadmissible, Izard – keen to get on with what he thought was an open-and-shut case – dismissively insisted that it was perfectly proper, having been made in front of the coroner, the jury and the public. Izard seemed to be winning the argument so Forwood pressed for an adjournment but the judge said he needed some definite grounds for that. No doubt feeling that a confession obtained in dubious circumstances was definite enough, Forwood began to speak: 'Your Honour seems to fancy . . .' But the learned judge cut him off: 'I don't fancy anything, Mr Forwood; I know the law and don't fancy it.'[13] The tone was set, although after a good deal of prevarication the judge eventually ruled the inquest confession inadmissible. But nothing could stop the jury hearing the Taylor version.

Forwood's fall-back position proved to be no more successful. Chief Justice Prendergast cut the ground from under the drunkenness defence when he said the question of whether the prisoner was insane, drunk or sober was not a matter for the jury.[14] But Forwood persisted, knowing that drunkenness could never possibly be the basis of a not-guilty verdict but presumably hoping to save a life, albeit the life of a man who apparently no longer wanted to live. He cross-examined every witness who had encountered Tuhi on the day of the murder about whether his client was drunk. Eleven of the twelve gave answers that were taken as confirming sobriety. The only one to state categorically that he had had too much to drink was Coffey the storekeeper, referring to their encounter in the evening at the time Tuhi bought the matches.

Despite what the witnesses said, the accumulated effect of the evidence suggests that Tuhi was drinking heavily that day, even in the morning. He spent six or seven hours in the pub, from 11 a.m. to 2 p.m. in his first session and from about 5 p.m. to 8 p.m. in his second. The second session may have been considerably longer because John Stevenson said it was Tuhi who broke the news of the murder to him and Stannard which means he was still in Ōpunake well after 9.30 p.m. when the body was found. It is impossible to imagine that a young man would spend that amount of time in a crowded pub without drinking. Even in the morning he had shown all the signs of losing his inhibitions as the alcohol coursed through his veins and did its work. He was thrown out of the pub's kitchen, then was spotted play-wrestling in the street and, finally, after some persuasion from his companions, performed a haka in the bar just before he broke away for his ride to Te Namu. His behaviour fitted publican Harry Middleton's description of his tendency to become silly or stupid when drunk. Alcohol may also have provided the confidence for his importunate begging for a pair of moleskins from Coffey, Pīhama and Middleton.

The big weakness in claims that Tuhi was sober is that most of the witnesses gave evidence about what they did not know as opposed to what they knew. Rather than saying for certain that Tuhi was sober, most said merely that they had not *seen* him drinking which is not quite the same thing.[15] This applied even to Harry Middleton who said he had not seen Tuhi drinking and yet insisted Tuhi was 'perfectly sober' at all times. Then he said Tuhi might have had a glass. In other words, Middleton was not sure. The publican in a busy hotel could hardly be expected to know exactly what every customer was doing. From all the scraps of information and hints inadvertently dropped by the witnesses, as well as the circumstantial evidence, it looks as though Tuhi drank some alcohol in the morning and then consumed a large amount in the evening when he returned to town.

For instance, Hone Pīhama bought a couple of rounds of beer for his party and Tuhi joined in. He later had drinks with three women, which one of the women shouted. That makes three pints and in his confession he admitted to spending 3s 6d in the hotel; at the standard price of 6d a pint that equated to seven more pints.[16] He may have spent more because he had taken money from Mary and four shillings remained unaccounted for, possibly slightly more given that he had spent only a halfpenny on matches rather than the threepence alleged at the inquest. Even allowing for the possibility that he spent some of the money on alcohol for others, it is more than likely he downed great volumes of beer that night. On top of it all he begged a bottle of brandy from Middleton which he promptly dropped in the stable, adding to the impression of a man who had had far too much to drink.

Middleton's evidence about Tuhi's drinking on that particular day followed the same pattern as his evidence about Tuhi's drinking habits generally. On the one hand he said he did not drink much, but on the other his evidence suggested Tuhi had a problem with alcohol. He spent far too much time in the pub and the money he owed to Middleton was mostly for drink. It is possible that Middleton was protecting his own reputation; he did not want to come across as an unscrupulous publican exploiting the weakness of a customer. However obvious the contradictions and inconsistencies in the evidence now seem, the net effect of Forwood's cross-examinations was the opposite of what he intended. Instead of building a picture of a man whose sense of right and wrong was eroded out of existence by too much alcohol, he was left with a series of witnesses implying, if not stating directly, that Tuhi was sober when he was alleged to have committed the crime.

Much of the evidence had already been published in newspaper reports and summaries of the inquest, but that did not diminish public interest in the case with the courtroom crowded daily. Among the spectators were the birds of heaven, six men haunting the trial in the hope of picking up the job of hangman. The six rivals tendered for the work early, confident that the result would mean the services of at least one of them would be required. It was not the first time they had competed against each other for the gruesome task, reported the *Taranaki Herald* and other papers. 'It would be a subject for

FIG. 62: The provenance of this photograph of Tuhi has not been preserved but it is likely to be the one sold by a Cuba Street photo shop after the trial, and was probably taken while he was in The Terrace gaol. *State Library of NSW P1/180*

FIG. 63: Tītokowaru drawn by William Gordon in 1885. The families of Tuhi and Mary were on opposite sides during his uprising in 1868. *O2005-074, PA*

FIG. 64: General Chute was pitiless in his campaign against Ngāti Ruanui in 1866 when Tuhi was a child. *002670-F, ATL*

FIG. 65: The Armed Constabulary's forward base at Pungarehu where the commanding officer Lieutenant Colonel Roberts had his headquarters in November 1880. *1077, ATL*

FIG. 66: At the time of Mary's death, Native Minister John Bryce was advocating a march on Parihaka to arrest murderer Hiroki and maybe Te Whiti as well. *William Gordon, PHO2011-2281, PA*

FIG. 67: Interpreter Charles Hursthouse recorded Tuhi's second confession on the morning after the inquest. *O5118F, ATL*

FIG. 68: Tuhi was incarcerated in The Terrace gaol, where the food was monotonous, the cells were clean and the prisoners foul-mouthed. *041383-F, ATL*

FIG. 69: A new Supreme Court building was under construction in 1880 so Tuhi's trial took place in the Provincial Council chambers. *003739-F, ATL*

FIG. 70: Prosecutor Charles Izard and the judge were irritated by Charles Forwood's defence tactics in what they regarded as an open-and-shut case. *00119-d-F, ATL*

FIG. 71: The Empire Hotel is the second building on the left, behind the *Evening Post* office. A *Post* reporter had a good vantage point for his observation that while Tuhi seemed to be wasting away, the jurors were stacking on weight thanks to the generous fare at the pub where they were staying. *PA7-04-23*

FIG. 72: One of Tuhi's last visitors, Bishop Octavius Hadfield. *05118-5, ATL*

FIG. 73: A bird of heaven, hangman David Marshall. Observer, *5 Feb 1881, p. 5*

FIG. 74: Archdeacon Stock read the funeral service over a living man. *081694-F*

FIG. 75: A picture page in the *Illustrated London News*, republished in a New York weekly, insinuates a connection between Parihaka and Mary's murder by including the sketch of her tomb among the images accompanying a report on the crisis of 1881. Some of the images match the watercolours in the Henry Hobson photo album (see Fig. 49). *LW 10058b, Schoolhistory NZ*

FIG. 76: Thomas Hughson, a soldier in the Armed Constabulary, wrote about the excitement when volunteers from Wellington and the South Island pitched camp at Rāhotu before the invasion of Parihaka. *Family album*

FIG. 77: The troops at Parihaka. A correspondent of the Christchurch *Star* said the men were determined to revenge the death of Mary Dobie if they had the opportunity. *1081, ATL*

FIG. 78: The officers who led the march on Parihaka: Gudgeon is first on the left in the back row; Stuart Newall is standing at the far back, nearest the fence; and Lieutenant Colonel Roberts is the third seated man from left. Forster is the beardless man at the front right, still looking every bit the boy in comparison to his grizzled comrades. *1070, ATL*

FIG. 79: Hiroki, captured after the invasion of Parihaka, was to suffer the same fate as Tuhi. *George Sherriff, The* Graphic, *pk1009 Schoolhistory NZ*

FIG. 80: Squat and incomplete. Mary's tomb without the cross in 2003. *Iolanthe Small*

FIG. 81: A fragment of the cross with its symbolic wreath of thorns has been rescued and now lies at the foot of the tomb. *David Hastings*

FIG. 82: Plantswoman Iolanthe Small left a tribute to Mary when she visited the grave in 2003 while helping with research into Herbert's pioneering botanical work.

FIG. 83: The stones near the spot where Mary's body was found. *David Hastings*

FIG. 84: Bertha and Forster during their hardscrabble years on an orange orchard in Whangārei. *'Orange Leaves'*

Hogarth to view the ghastly smile which played on each of their countenances when certain points of evidence were powerfully sheeted home to the culprit.'[17]

Tuhi himself appeared to be feeling the strain, even though he affected an unconcerned demeanour. The *Post* reporter observed that he was still losing weight and after three days in court his cheekbones stood out sharply.[18] The reluctant jury, on the other hand, were living off the 'fat of the land'. Although they were locked up for the duration of the trial, they had comparatively luxurious cells at the Empire Hotel in Willis Street, about 1 kilometre from the court. Every day they were marched to and from the trial under police guard. Some citizens mistook the maudlin parade for prisoners but the occasional embarrassment was more than compensated for by the catering provided by the Empire at the court's expense. The fare was so generous that, in a few short days, people began to notice that the privileged twelve were putting on weight. 'Already the jurymen and their guards have so materially expanded in bulk as to be scarcely recognisable by their friends,' wrote the reporter who was in a good position to observe because his office was next door to the hotel, 'and if the trial lasts much longer they certainly will have to go to the Wellington Hospital for a course of the Anti-Fat treatment for which that excellent institution is so famed.'[19]

Closing arguments from the lawyers were on Wednesday morning after the court had heard from 31 witnesses in two days. Forwood took only half an hour but in that short time he managed to tie himself up in an unresolvable contradiction when he denied the crime on behalf of his client at the same time as he offered an explanation for it.[20] Tuhi had no motive, he said, but if he was the one who killed Mary then he did it under the influence of liquor and because she had threatened to tell the soldiers on him. Having thus simultaneously denied and admitted the crime, he threw his client on the mercy of the jury. Tuhi was under their protection, he said, and they had to be satisfied not only that he had killed Mary but that he did it with malice aforethought. In conclusion, he begged the jury not to let the fact that Tuhi was Māori affect their decision, nor anything they had seen in the newspapers. They should give their verdict according to the evidence in court.[21]

In his summing-up Chief Justice Prendergast fell back on the murder-without-a-cause theory, telling the jury there appeared to be no motive in this case, specifically ruling out rape and robbery. He spent some time discussing the question of whether Tuhi was drunk. Although he clearly believed Tuhi was sober he said it did not matter one way or the other. Even if they accepted the defence submission that he was drunk, the charge could not be reduced from murder to manslaughter. He urged them to weigh the evidence carefully because a guilty verdict would bring the highest penalty possible. Although he did not review the evidence in detail he said it was simple, giving a definite steer to what he thought the verdict should be.[22]

The jury took 20 minutes to decide Tuhi's fate. When they returned the court was packed and although the verdict was guilty, as expected, it still caused a profound sensation.[23] Tuhi was asked if he had anything to say but this time the answer was no.[24] Justice Prendergast then put on his black cap and delivered the sentence of death. In his summing-up he had said there was no motive, but now he said the motive was the one that came out in the Taylor confession, that is, Tuhi killed Mary because of her threat to tell the soldiers. 'From your confession I believe that you have long since repented of taking the life of Miss Dobie,' he said. 'If you have not, no words of mine can affect you.' He then stressed that Tuhi had been convicted not just on European evidence but on the evidence of his own people. 'The sentence of the law is that you be taken from here... to the place of execution, and that you be there hanged by the neck until you be dead; and may God have mercy on your soul.'[25]

Prendergast was much affected when he passed sentence, said the *Post* reporter, in contrast to Tuhi who smiled in the coolest and most unconcerned manner when the last few words were spoken. The reporter thought he looked jaunty as he was led from the dock, and when Tuhi turned round to acknowledge some people in the court he laughed. He was taken through the Provincial Buildings to a yard at the back where a cab was waiting to take him to prison. The spectators from the court rushed round to get one last look at the prisoner before he was taken away forever. When Tuhi appeared at the back door – guarded by two policemen and Micaiah Reed the jailer – he seemed bewildered by all the attention. The large crowd followed him until he was put in the cab and driven away.

11.

FOOD FOR THE BIRDS OF HEAVEN

In the two weeks between sentencing and execution Tuhi was not left alone for a moment.[1] His main visitor was the Anglican archdeacon from St Peter's Church, Arthur Stock, who in the 1860s had famously run a seven-year campaign to save an innocent man from the gallows and ultimately to win his freedom.[2] Also visiting were Hitakara Warihi, a minister with the Wesleyan Church, and the Bishop of Wellington, Octavius Hadfield. Most of the published reports about Tuhi's meetings with the churchmen focused on Stock although the *Post* noted that he conversed most freely with Warihi.[3] Tuhi also had conversations with his jailers and the interpreter Ebenezer Baker at this time. He was turning the events of the day he killed Mary over and over in his mind and, as he had been doing since he was locked in the guardhouse at Ōpunake redoubt, explaining himself to anyone who would listen.[4]

The theme that came up again and again was that he was drunk at the time and had he been sober the crime would never have been committed. Even though he had resigned himself to his fate, he was still angry and bitter at the Māori who had given evidence against him, said the *Post*, and regarded them as traitors to their race. Equally he was bitter towards those Pākehā witnesses who had insisted he was sober, thus denying him the one sliver of evidence that might help to show he was not the unredeemable monster that his crime implied.[5] Sometimes his mind wandered, but usually he stuck to the theme that preoccupied him.[6]

And yet some of his visitors still commented on how relaxed he seemed. He ate and slept in a manner which suggested he either did not realise his position, or was utterly careless about his impending fate, commented the *Post*.[7] Some thought his demeanour expressed the same callous indifference to his own fate as he had shown to Mary. But a letter he wrote to the governor from the condemned cell gave a different impression: he wanted to atone in some way. 'Friend, greeting – I have heard that I am to be put to death on Wednesday,' he said, 'and I am willing to die on that day, but I have a word to say to you: Let my bad companions, your children, beer, rum, and other spirits die with me . . . they led us to commit wrong, and now let us die together one death on the day that I am to die.'[8]

Some responded with cynicism to the letter. The Nelson *Colonist*'s Wellington correspondent dismissed it as a crude attempt to shift the blame. Alternatively he argued it was really Tuhi's spiritual advisers who put him up to it. They knew the evils inflicted on Māori by drink and here was a golden opportunity to advance their campaign for prohibition.[9] But there were others who argued just as strongly that the letter was sincere. That is how the Wellington correspondent of the *Otago Daily Times* saw it. 'While he is willing and desirous to die in satisfaction for his crime, he shrinks from the idea that he should be remembered as a cold-blooded slayer of a woman, when he asserts, and I believe honestly, that the act was committed under alcoholic influence,' he wrote.[10]

But the letter was more than simply an attempt to save his reputation. It was an attempt at redemption; he wanted to leave a beneficial legacy despite his shocking crime. Out of evil, some good would come. In Tuhi's mind, the person who mattered most was Te Whiti. Even though he had refused to join the ploughmen and had been disowned after the murder, he now told Stock he was a follower of the prophet.[11] The letter to Gordon, therefore, was not so much a put-up job by the churchmen as an appeal to restore himself in the eyes of Parihaka's leader who had made a stand against the damage that drink did to his people.

On the eve of his execution, they moved Tuhi to the condemned cell. The prison governor's office was to the right of the main entrance of The Terrace gaol. Beyond that an iron-barred gate opened into a passage on the left of which was the cell where Tuhi spent his last night. From there the passage led to a courtyard where the jailers erected the scaffold on the evening before the execution. The cell was just a short walk to the 'drop'.

Tuhi had a flurry of visitors on the last day. Bishop Hadfield called in the afternoon and, as usual, Archdeacon Stock stayed late in the evening doing what he could to help the condemned man prepare to die. The time had been fixed for 8 a.m. and Tuhi must have heard the instrument of his death being constructed. By one account he restlessly paced up and down, prompting one of his jailers to urge him to get some rest. 'No matter,' he replied showing the coolness which some people admired and others loathed, 'I'll have plenty of that to-morrow.'[12]

Archdeacon Stock was back with him at daylight, and while Tuhi had breakfast, people began to gather outside the jail with the aim, wrote the *Post*'s James Oakley Browne, of being as near to the scene of the execution as possible.[13] For several days the sheriff had been flooded with applications from people wanting to bear witness to the deed. The applicants came from all quarters of society, said the *Colonist*, including a number of teenage boys who, needless to say, were given short shrift.[14] Yet one fifteen-year-old was so determined that he turned up with an admission order from the sheriff which had been issued in the name of someone who, at the last moment, found he did not have the courage or the stomach to watch a man being put to death.[15] The lad was turned away at the gate.

Only eight non-official observers were allowed in, four of whom were reporters: James Oakley Browne of the *Evening Post*, George Humphries of the Press Association, Henry Anderson of the Wellington *Chronicle* and John Chantry Harris of the *New Zealand Times*.[16] The official party consisted of the sheriff, Alexander Allan; the jail governor, Micaiah Reed; a doctor to certify death; the superintendent of police; Archdeacon Stock; Tuhi's defence counsel, Charles Forwood; the turnkey; and two police sergeants.

Browne commented that the reporters and the official party were not as eager as the crowd outside to witness the choreographed tragedy that was about to unfold within.[17] One of the spectators was overcome even before the ceremony of death had started and hurried away.[18] Browne and Harris wrote detailed descriptions of the scaffold. It had a flight of nine steps which led to a platform about 10 feet square (just under 1 square metre). In the middle of the platform was 'the drop', two hinged panels of flooring held in place by an iron bar attached to a lever concealed behind a black board. When the lever was pulled the flooring would fall away, like a gate suddenly blowing open in the wind. On each side of the panels was a narrow platform, one for the executioner and the other for the archdeacon and the official party.

The rope was attached to an iron bolt fixed to a heavy beam about 8 feet (2.4 metres) above the drop. When the reporters inspected the contraption the noose was already prepared.[19] On the far side of the platform was another set of steps which led to a door opening into an enclosed space underneath the gallows where the condemned man would fall when the hangman pulled the deadly lever.

The executioner had calculated a drop of 8 feet would exert the right amount of pressure to break Tuhi's neck and kill him instantly. According to Harris's calculations, this meant that Tuhi weighed less than 10 stone (63.5 kilograms), any heavier and the drop would have been consequently shorter.[20] The observers who had noticed Tuhi's thinning face in court had not been exaggerating; a man who was about six feet tall (1.83 metres) and weighed so little must have been just skin and bone. This was a measure of how much Tuhi had changed in the month since he was first arrested when he was described as being powerfully built and muscular. However arrogant, jaunty and careless he might have appeared to some observers, his physical condition suggests that beneath the veneer remorse and the knowledge of what was about to happen were eating away at him.

The reporters went on their tour half an hour before the appointed time. While they were acquainting themselves with the deadly space, Tuhi was closeted in his cell with Archdeacon Stock saying his final prayers. The passage outside was lined with jail warders and witnesses, waiting for the moment when the sheriff would produce his warrant and formally demand the body.[21] There could not be a greater contrast between the last few moments of Tuhi's life and the death of the woman he had killed. For Mary Dobie the end came suddenly and unexpectedly in a whirlpool of blood and violence after a desperate struggle to escape. For Tuhi the end was anticipated, scripted and ceremonial.

A few minutes before 8 a.m. Sheriff Allan accompanied by Governor Reed passed through the iron gate at the main entrance and walked down the passage to Tuhi's cell. At the door, Allan produced his warrant and demanded that Reed hand the prisoner over to the man who had been chosen from the six birds of heaven, executioner David Marshall. Reed then entered the cell and a few moments later emerged with Tuhi whose arms were pinioned in front of his body by a leather strap secured at his elbows. He was wearing an old blue jersey reaching to his knees and a pair of patched moleskin trousers, not unlike the ones he wore on the day he committed murder.[22]

The official party formed a line with the jail's governor in the lead. Behind him was the doctor who was followed by the chief warder leading the condemned man. Then came the hangman and, bringing up the rear, Archdeacon Stock. This melancholy procession moved down the passage to the sound of Stock reading the funeral service in Māori.

It was a sight not easily forgotten by those who saw it, wrote Browne, who felt strong sympathy for Tuhi despite his atrocious crime.[23] To him, Tuhi seemed calm though his face had a slight pallor and his expression was anxious and careworn; his cheeks appeared slightly drawn-in as was only to be expected in a man who had lost nearly 13 kilograms in a short time.[24] To Harris, Tuhi appeared stolid and unconcerned as he walked with a lounging gait towards his doom.[25]

As the official party ascended the nine steps of the scaffold – Tuhi with a stride as firm as the others, said Browne – the witnesses were ushered to their observation post, a toilet overlooking the courtyard. It had a grated window which allowed them to see everything that happened on the scaffold itself but when the executioner pulled the lever, the condemned man would drop from sight.[26]

From this vantage point Harris, Browne and the others watched as final preparations were made. Once at the top of the nine steps, Marshall took charge. He was thin, old and grey-bearded with a curious puckered face, said Harris. Browne described him in similar terms but could not conceal his distaste by adding that his wizened face was anything but pleasant. 'He made no attempt to disguise himself in any way, and seemed quite at home in the performance of his hideous task,' said Browne.[27]

If these descriptions were meant to depict Marshall as an angel of death, he went about his gruesome task like a skilled craftsman. He busied himself with unemotional efficiency, directing Tuhi to stand in the very centre of the drop, where the two gates would soon swing open and usher him out of this world.[28]

Marshall bent down and pinioned his ankles with a leather strap. Browne noticed Tuhi's expression of anxiety deepening at this point but he said nothing and did not tremble. He looked like a man who had strung every nerve so he could go through his last ordeal without flinching; his teeth and lips were tightly clenched.[29] Marshall fitted the noose around Tuhi's neck and adjusted a leather washer near his left ear to fix it in place. Then he pulled a white cap over the condemned man's head.

All the while, Archdeacon Stock was reciting the funeral service. The incongruity of it was not lost on one observer who wrote, 'It was a sad sight to see a finely built, and evidently intelligent young man – Maori though he was – standing on the hideous structure in the little prison yard, hearing the burial service read over him while he was so full of life and strength, and painful to reflect that in a few minutes he would be a corpse.'[30]

Marshall moved behind the black board towards the deadly lever but before he could pull it, Tuhi managed to free his pinioned arms enough to lift the white cap from his face. He wanted to speak but it was too late for that. Stock dissuaded him from saying anything more and Marshall readjusted the hood. He checked to make sure the leather ring holding the noose in place had not been disturbed and then retreated again behind the black board.

There was a hush as Tuhi stood alone on the drop for a moment. Stock resumed his recital of the funeral service and from his concealed position, Marshall pulled the lever. '[T]he flaps of the top fell with a loud crash; there was a kind of "boom" or "ping" of the straightened rope,' wrote Harris.[31] It was over in the twinkling of an eye, said Browne, death appeared to be instantaneous, no struggling and no convulsion.

In the aftermath there was much to do. The witnesses all had to sign certificates, an inquest had to be held and finally the burial. The reporters, too, had their tasks to perform. They wanted to interview Stock about Tuhi's state of mind in the last hours of his life and what he had said while the two were closeted in his cell waiting for the sheriff to come. But Stock was not talking. He was 'too much overcome by the awful spectacle' wrote Browne.[32]

At the inquest, held that morning, the doctor testified that Tuhi's neck had been broken and he had died instantly.[33] In the afternoon, two prisoners dug his grave in the front enclosure of the jail, next to those of three others who had been executed in the 1860s.[34] In the evening, Archdeacon Stock returned to read the funeral service again, this time over a man who was dead. It was a lonely burial; just Reed the prison governor with a few warders and prisoners looking on.[35] There was no gravestone, only a simple plaque on the wall to mark the spot inscribed with the year 1880. It did not even mention Tuhi's name.[36]

12.

POLITICS AND REVENGE

The December meeting at Parihaka took place two days after Tuhi was convicted and sentenced to death. Many in the Pākehā press expected that much would be said about him and his crime. On the eve of the meeting, one newspaper correspondent wrote, 'At present all that is authentic concerning Te Whiti's ideas is that he said, on hearing of the murder, that Tuhi's body alone should pay for his sin, and that he had been reserved for death when his parents refused to let him go ploughing.'[1] But those who thought there would be a further public statement were to be disappointed.[2] Te Whiti said nothing about Tuhi's sentence at the meeting; the only reference in the papers was to the effect that the people of Parihaka were sick and tired of attempts to connect all Māori criminals with Te Whiti.[3]

This moved the *Evening Post* to mockery. It was curious to note, said the *Post* in an editorial three days after the meeting, how month after month people expected something new and sensational out of Parihaka, only to be disappointed.[4] One example they gave was how, in March 1880, there had been widely published newspaper reports that Te Whiti had handed over leadership to Tohu in expectation that vigorous resistance – meaning violence – would be the new strategy. 'This seemed to promise something more acceptable to lovers of "sensation" than dry old sermons and pious exhortations,' said the *Post*, 'but Te Whiti ruthlessly dispelled all their rising hopes by pronouncing the whole story "a lie".' Something similar happened with the December meeting. A shocking murder had been committed. The victim was the sister-in-law of an officer commanding the constabulary that was building roads through sacred land. The murderer had been tried and sentenced to death, said the *Post*. 'Surely something would come of this? No; nothing. Friday's meeting passed in the customary dull and decorous manner. The murderer Tuhi was not even mentioned.'

The *Post* had a point, even though its sarcasm did nothing to explain why Te Whiti remained silent on the topic, especially as to Pākehā eyes the expectation that he speak must have seemed reasonable. Te Whiti had been quoted previously on the murder, albeit third-hand, and now that the legal process had run its course it might have been a good time to make a definitive statement. But Te Whiti had much greater problems to deal with than whether politicians, the press or the Pākehā public thought he was vicariously responsible for the murder.

About the time that Tuhi's trial reached its climax, the government began selling the land on the Waimate Plains. It was part of the process that began with the paper confiscation in the 1860s and continued with the surveying and road building in the 1870s and would end with a military invasion in 1881. It was the literal fulfilment of the fears expressed by Pīhama and Te Whiti of the rising tide flooding over the sandbank.

The sales began in the Hawera town hall on the day Tuhi was sentenced. Interest in the land was strong and over the coming days the papers were full of reports and details about how well it was selling and how much money was being raised to replenish the government's empty coffers.[5] The people of Parihaka would have been in no doubt that the land they had been cultivating was also earmarked for sale. When the governor's emissary Captain Louis Knollys reported on his visit to Parihaka he remarked that it would be a valuable asset to whoever eventually possessed it. The fields were well looked after, carefully fenced, and the crops of potatoes, maize and tobacco were looking very promising. So promising that a dozen influential New Plymouth gentlemen signed an open letter to the government suggesting that potential buyers should be taken to Parihaka where they could get a better idea of the extraordinarily fertile land of the region by inspecting the crops there.[6]

About the time of Mary's murder, Te Whiti's followers would also have been aware of support in the press for John Bryce's plan to raid Parihaka. Although he resigned in disgust as native minister when the raid did not go ahead, Bryce was not forgotten. When another crisis erupted in September 1881 he was recalled with the express task of dusting off his plan and putting it into action.

The murder of Mary Dobie was among the many factors shaping the way the crisis played out, even though it happened a year before and suspicions of political motives had been well and truly scotched at the inquest. Nevertheless, one of the most enduring themes in popular versions of the story was that Parihaka was somehow linked to the murder. It was an idea which would not die even when all the evidence was laid out to show it was false. The Auckland *Star*, for instance, had insisted immediately after the inquest that Te Whiti was in some way culpable despite the paper being unable to say how and admitting it could not provide a skerrick of evidence to support the claim.[7]

The connection was again insinuated in 1882 by the *Illustrated London News* which published an article with an accompanying picture page on the invasion entitled 'the last Maori trouble in New Zealand'.[8] Among the fourteen sketches – which include Māori heading off to Parihaka, an AC camp and soldiers at target practice – was a drawing of Mary's tomb (Fig. 75). The caption said simply: 'Memorial to Miss Dobie, murdered by a Maori', and the accompanying story said Mary's deplorable fate had 'excited the greatest horror and bitter indignation, both in New Zealand and in England'. Without saying so directly, the paper was strongly implying that Parihaka was connected to the murder. If there was a connection, it was the other way around; Parihaka was not to blame for the murder but the murder was linked to Parihaka in the public mind.

The clearest example of how the link was strengthened in retrospect came from Walter Gudgeon, an AC captain who led one of the companies at the invasion. In his book *Defenders of New Zealand* – written by Walter although published under the name of his father Thomas in 1887 – Gudgeon said that many of the men who rushed to sign up as volunteers for Bryce's invasion did so in response to the killing of Mary Dobie.[9] After Bryce resumed office he immediately sent the first contingent of 100 reinforcements to Taranaki. 'This was followed by a general volunteering throughout the North Island,' wrote Gudgeon, '*as in the meantime* the lamented Miss Dobie was foully murdered ... and the public mind was in a fever heat over the occurrence.' This is a serious time-shifting error. The murder had occurred nearly twelve months previously and the 'fever heat', which had been so intense in the few days after Mary's body was found, had long since died down, in public at least.

It is hard to escape the impression that Gudgeon's mistake was made because of his eagerness to find some sort of moral justification for what the men were about to do. His private letters, and those of William Rolleston, show they were at pains to persuade the public that the government was in the right and Te Whiti in the wrong.[10] And yet despite the mistake in the timing, Gudgeon was right about the attitude of the soldiers who not only remained angry about the murder but were bent on revenge if they could take it. Their intent was emphasised in a special correspondent's report published by the Christchurch *Star* in October 1881, as the invasion force was gathering. 'It is noticeable that the murder of poor Miss Dobie is as fresh in the minds of the men as though it had occurred yesterday,' the correspondent wrote. 'The effect appears to have been double, increasing their sense of treachery of the Maoris and their determination to take terrible revenge should the opportunity offer.'[11]

Less pointed, but no less significant, evidence of the way the murder played on the public mind can be found in private diaries and sketchbooks as well. Henry Hobson decorated the margins of his photograph album with watercolours of the same scenes associated with the Dobie murder that appeared in the *Illustrated London News* (Figs 46, 49). The *Timaru Herald* reported that artist Jas Ledger produced a page of Parihaka sketches which, like the British weekly, included Mary's tomb thus linking her death to the invasion.[12] An AC man, Eugene Buckley, preserved in his scrapbook the watercolour showing the crime scene and Tuhi, painted on the day after his confession to George Taylor (Fig. 56). And, as the troops were assembling for the invasion, William Skinner recorded in his diary how he had visited Mary's grave and retraced her steps to the place where she was murdered.[13]

The great political crisis was composed of the same unholy trinity that had played out on a personal level between Tuhi and Mary on the lonely road near Te Namu: misunderstanding, fear and an imbalance of power. Only this crisis came to a head with careful political calculation rather than an impulsive outburst of violence. Newspapers began reporting that at the September meeting at Parihaka, yet again, the prophets had supposedly reversed their strategy from peace to war. This time something really sensational had happened, which must have been music to the *Evening Post*'s ears. But alas, it was another misinterpretation just like the supposed reversal of the pacifist policy in March 1880. The central point was that Te Whiti had used the word 'pakanga' meaning 'fight' and thus shown his true colours. But, as Riseborough argues, the speeches at that meeting were more ambiguous than usual and were interpreted to fit existing preconceptions.[14] Te Whiti was angry about the reports and told an old friend that his words had been misrepresented in the press which quoted him as saying 'pakanga' when he did not mean it in the literal sense of 'fighting' but the common metaphorical sense of 'to dispute with the tongue'.[15]

The effect of the misunderstanding was immediate; fear gave wings to rumour yet again and encouraged men to reach for their guns just as they had done in the winter of 1879. Some expressed how the fear played on their minds in the privacy of their diaries. 'By this evening's paper Te Whiti's speech given on Saturday last, looks very bad, he says the time has passed for talking and they must act for themselves. Blow for blow and shot for shot,' wrote Skinner.[16] And he quoted a rumour picked up from a colleague that said the Māori could muster 1000 fighting men at a day's notice and were boasting they could take any AC camp without the slightest trouble.[17] In his diary Skinner comes across as a confident man who did not scare easily as he travelled through the bush doing his difficult and sometimes dangerous job as a surveyor. But now he was worried enough to stay at home the next day.[18] A few days later he was reporting that settlers and townspeople were in a great state of anxiety and some of those from the Parihaka block had fled to town.[19]

The rumour picked up by Skinner kept on spreading and growing. Two days later Anton Fromm, a German-speaking Swiss settler who joined the AC in 1881, recorded in his diary how the 1000-strong force of Māori, now supposedly under Tītokowaru's command, had broken camp and 'routed many farmers'.[20] The next day he went to New Plymouth and found the town in uproar, crowds of young men besieging the barracks to sign up with either the constabulary or the volunteer forces.[21] But not everyone was so certain about the threat. Major Stapp called a meeting in New Plymouth to revive the Volunteer Corps which had drooped so quickly when the scare of 1879 came to nothing. According to Skinner he was hoping to recruit 300 men but only nine stepped forward. 'Most of them said they had been humbugged so much by native scares that they would not join again,' he wrote.[22]

About this time the imbalance of power came in to play but unlike the killer on the lonely road, the state marshalled its superior forces and planned its action carefully. If some of the potential volunteers were filled with weary cynicism about yet another scare, the government of Sir John Hall – which had replaced the Grey government and included Atkinson as treasurer – knew the supposed threat was an illusion. They had plenty of first-hand reports to show that far from organising for war the people of Parihaka were going about the peaceful routines of agriculture.[23] And yet, once again, for their own political ends, they exploited the fear. An election was coming up and votes were to be won by a plan to settle the 'native difficulty' at Parihaka once and for all by using overwhelming force. Not only would this curry favour with anxious voters, but in the longer term it would be an opportunity to reduce the heavy costs associated with maintaining a small army in Taranaki, a point of extra concern to Atkinson in his new role. There was also a pressing tactical consideration: the governor Sir Arthur Gordon – Mary's host in Fiji – was out of the country on official business. Given his known sympathies with Parihaka, they needed to act quickly before he returned. In his absence Chief Justice James Prendergast – the man who had sentenced Tuhi to hang and who had declared the Treaty of Waitangi a 'nullity' – signed off on the plan to end the peaceful resistance movement.

The speed of the political manoeuvring was matched by large numbers of men hurrying to enlist. Despite his initial frustrations, by the middle of October, Major Stapp was swearing in a steady stream of recruits at places like Waitara, Egmont, Urenui, Stratford and Ōpunake to replace those who had resigned the year before.[24] Elsewhere the response to the government's call to arms was even more enthusiastic and reflected how far war fever had spread across the colony. Eager to take part in the decisive confrontation, men volunteered in droves. There was 'a perfect rush' to sign up in Christchurch, said one report, with more than 100 men sworn in on one day. The recruiting officer said he was mightily impressed by those who had been rejected and he could easily sign one hundred more if necessary.[25] It was this flood of volunteers that Gudgeon claimed was in reaction to the murder. The numbers were so great that Bryce had to say 'no more'.[26]

The symptoms of the war fever could be seen and heard on the streets of Ōpunake as the volunteers arrived. Settlers said the town was busy and bustling as the troops marched through.[27] One recalled as many as fifteen military bands playing. War fever radiated from the editorial columns of many newspapers as well. Some, like the Auckland *Star*, nervously supported the action but fretted about the possible consequences in damaging the colony's economic interests in Britain or provoking uprisings elsewhere. Only the *Lyttelton Times* was unequivocal in opposition. It pointed out that the people of Parihaka had never taken up arms and the confiscation of their land was illegitimate. The most likely outcome of the government's policy, which it described as ridiculous, cruel and evil, would be to prevent any chance of a peaceful settlement. The *Times* called on the country to protest in the strongest manner at 'the unnecessary spoliation of the remnant of a weak race that has many wrongs to be redressed'.[28]

By the standards of the great armies and great invasions of history this was a minute affair although there were profound moral and political issues at stake. The invading force consisted of only about 1500 men, just over half of whom were volunteers, under the command of Lieutenant Colonel Roberts (Fig. 77). Forster Goring was there, leading one of the companies, and so was Thomas Hughson who had written about Mary in his diary. Also there were Anton Fromm and Stuart Newall, the AC captain at Pungarehu who had recorded the hysterical rumours about Te Whiti's warmongering after Mary's death (Fig. 78). Hughson wrote about the excitement when volunteers from Wellington, Nelson and Blenheim arrived and pitched tents 200 metres from his camp at Rāhotu (Fig. 76). 'There being about 1200 all together things looked pretty lively in camp and drill every day,' he wrote.[29]

As well as the drill, the days before the invasion were taken up with shooting practice, war games and a reconnaissance in force. Newall and Goring joined a party of officers escorted by 30 men to check the lay of the land at Parihaka. Although Newall had been close to Parihaka before with the road-building and survey parties, he had not set eyes on the settlement until this day. The way he observed it was in marked contrast to Mary. She had looked through the curious, enquiring and friendly eyes of an artist. What she saw and described in words and pictures was a vibrant, prosperous and peaceful community. But Newall looked at it with a soldier's eye. 'As a fighting position I consider it quite untenable being surrounded by small hills from all of which a destructive fire could be poured into the place without any risk of one portion of the attacking party firing into another as the village occupies quite a hollow and appears to be quite devoid of any defensive work,' he wrote.[30] He concluded that if the people were going to fight it would be outside the settlement, but from his diary it seems they were paying very little attention to the soldiers manoeuvring around them.

At 6.30 a.m. on the morning of 5 November the little army marched off to Parihaka with the band playing.[31] Their weapons were loaded and they sent out an advance guard and skirmishers to protect their flanks. But no one impeded them and without opposition they were able to take up their positions overlooking the settlement. They pulled a great field gun to the top of one of the hills which later became known to the Pākehā as Mount Rolleston, after Bryce's predecessor as native minister, or Purepo to the Māori after the gun itself. It was from either this hill or a neighbouring burial hill that Te Whiti had allowed Mary to make her sketch of Parihaka.[32] Facing the cannon was not a band of armed warriors as might have been expected from the rumours and the rhetoric but the entire population densely packed on the ground in front of the marae and wearing their Sunday best with feathers in their hair.

After a tense stand-off lasting more than an hour, Newall's company formed a pathway through the throng down which they would lead Te Whiti, Tohu and Hiroki the murderer. The prophets were to go into three years of exile in the South Island and Hiroki was to suffer the same fate as Tuhi. Until this moment Newall had never had much time for Te Whiti but he was now deeply impressed. 'Not without dignity did he thus move through the lane of grey shirted and stalwart constabulary; for even in that hour of trial he was every inch a chief and his grizzled hair and beard and smiling handsome face created anything but an unpleasant impression.'[33]

On reaching the slope of the burial hill Te Whiti turned to his people and exhorted them to be stout-hearted, to live in peace and to hold on to their land. 'No outward expression of anger, sorrow or regret not even from Te Whiti's wife broke the silence of the Marae and the recumbent and enshrouded figures composing the dense assembly moved not,' wrote Newall. 'Nor did stolid composure in a single instance as far as could be observed give place to any symptom of emotion.'

The soldiers dismantled most of the houses and sent people from distant tribes back to their homelands, 1500 of them in about three weeks.[34] Two weeks after the invasion, a *New Zealand Herald* correspondent was able to evade the sentries for a moment and explore the dwellings being demolished. 'Pigs, dogs, and fowls roamed through them,' he wrote. 'They were all down, smashed, tottering to their fall. Some were well furnished and lined inside ... Most had the indescribable smell of smoke and closeness.'[35] But before he could go too far he was ushered away.

Bryce tried his best to keep the reporters out. They were banned from covering the invasion although a group of them managed to get inside Parihaka before the troops arrived and watched the whole drama unfold from close quarters. The aim of the ban was no doubt to protect the reputation of the colony by controlling and sanitising news reports going back to Britain. But like so many attempts to suppress or control the news, it also provided cover for the abuse of power. The soldiers engaged in the official task of demolishing the village also took the opportunity to do some looting on their own account and perhaps exact some of the revenge for Mary's death that the Christchurch *Star*'s special correspondent had predicted a few weeks ago. 'Orders had been given that no Māori property was to be touched, but I know there was a good deal of looting – in fact, robbery,' one of the officers told James Cowan years later. 'Many of our government men stole greenstones and other treasures from the native houses, among them were some fine *meres*.'[36] The *New Zealand Times* at first refused to believe reports of looting but then came to accept them with world-weary cynicism. The paper's special correspondent at Pungarehu commented that it was no doubt impossible to prevent petty depredations among a mixed collection of men in enemy country. 'It is rumoured that the removal of some Volunteers yesterday evening... was prompted by a knowledge of their freebooting propensities,' he wrote.[37]

An especially disturbing incident occurred one night when a group of AC men were sent to check on the number of people sleeping in each whare. The *New Zealand Herald*'s special correspondent reported that at one dwelling they discovered an unidentified gentleman taking part in 'semi-connubial relations' with a woman.[38] Given the circumstances it was an odd choice of euphemism. One of those used in the first reports of Mary's death would have been a better way of describing the man's behaviour: outraging, ravishing or, maybe, ill-treating.

It is worth observing that all the elements that combined to create the many different versions of Mary's death – politics, robbery and rape – were visited on the people of Parihaka in the spring of 1881. What happened there should have removed any doubts about Te Whiti's pacifism. The way he and his people conducted themselves during the invasion showed that settlers' fears – although real – were based on an illusory threat. Conversely, the dismantling of the settlement and the dispersal of its people showed that Māori fears, as defined by Te Whiti and Hone Pīhama, sprang from a genuine threat which was fulfilled in detail.

No serious history covering Parihaka mentions the influence of the Dobie murder on the events of November 1881. To some extent this is understandable because it does not appear to have been significant in the process of decision making that led to the invasion. However, Mary's murder did affect the attitudes of the troops and the civilian population. Although the extent of its influence is hard to assess with precision, the evidence of

Gudgeon and the newspaper correspondent who observed that the murder still played on the minds of the troops a year after it was committed, coupled with references in diaries and sketchbooks, suggest the effects lingered long after it had ceased to be a topic of public discussion. Indeed, even though the murder did not appear in the work of professional historians, the popular memory would not let go. In posterity, Mary was to have many more deaths and one of the most enduring was Gudgeon's time-shifting error that implied the crime happened on the eve of the invasion.

13.

IN MEMORIAM

Eight days after Tuhi was hanged, the *Hinemoa* returned to Ōpunake bringing home 30 of the Parihaka ploughmen who had just been released from prison in Dunedin. Also on board was a special cargo, the great tombstone that was to be the permanent tribute to Mary Dobie by the men of the AC.[1] A Wellington mason had fashioned it from white Italian marble.[2] At nearly 3 metres high, it must have been challenging to shift it from the steamer in the bay, across the surf and the shallows, and up the winding cliff path to the spot where it still stands, hemmed in by flax bushes.

While Forster was in Wellington giving evidence for the prosecution, Bertha and Ellen were back in Auckland spending a mournful Christmas with Herbert. They returned to Taranaki in February 1881, presumably for the dedication of the tombstone with no epitaph. Only then did Ellen resume her planned voyage back to England, without her two daughters who had done so much to enliven the outward passage on the *May Queen* three years before.

With the memorial in place the name of Dobie vanished from the headlines just as suddenly as it had appeared seven weeks previously. But the story was not forgotten; it was incorporated into local history alongside the stories of Matakātea's brave defence of Te Namu Pā, Betty Guard's rescue and the wreck of the *Lord Worsley*. The tomb became a must-see landmark for journalists and tourists.[3]

Among the first to visit was William Skinner who stayed in Ōpunake eleven months after the murder as John Bryce's little army was gathering in readiness for the invasion. He observed a brisk trade bringing timber up from the port and noted the Middletons' Telegraph Hotel was as rowdy as ever. Then he visited the white marble tombstone and retraced Mary's last steps along the road past the old flax mill and across the Ōtahi Stream to the place of her fatal encounter with Tuhi.[4] Skinner's observation was made in the privacy of his diary but in the coming years a visit to Mary's tomb became essential for all journalists who wrote about the coast.[5] The tombstone was so prominent they could hardly miss it and remained a permanent feature even as the landscape around it changed and other landmarks that connected the town to its history were dismantled.

A special reporter from Dunedin's *Evening Star*, who visited in 1883, thought it was one of the most interesting features in a town of about 400 people, including the AC men, which now had five stores and two banks as well as a school house, flax mill and brewery all watched over by the great redoubt.[6] A decade later Ōpunake presented a civilian face to its visitors. When a

Taranaki Herald reporter was in town to cover the local race meeting he found the Telegraph Hotel packed with convivial punters exchanging tips. There was no talk of uprisings or land disputes and not a soldier in sight. The redoubt was still there and although it had been unoccupied for years was remarkably well preserved, with its high sod walls, the officers' quarters and the former library where, he probably did not realise, Mary's lifeless body had been examined and Tuhi had made his damning confession to George Taylor.

But the redoubt's days were numbered; already one of its barrack buildings had been shifted away for a community hall at Rāhotu. Outside, grass had smothered the tennis court where Mary and Bertha had spent many happy hours in the spring of 1880 and the kitchen garden had long since been abandoned. The little graveyard, too, was deteriorating. The fence was rotten and had collapsed in places and the pathway had vanished beneath the undergrowth. The one structure that stood out as sharply as the day it was first erected was Mary's gleaming white headstone.[7]

In time, the redoubt was entirely dismantled, much to the disappointment of some who thought it should have been preserved as a tourist attraction and reminder of the district's turbulent past.[8] The only hint of it now is a subtle indentation in the lawn of a reserve near the cliff where the defensive trench was dug beneath the great walls. In the 1920s a lake was formed where the tennis court and the vegetable garden had been. Down on the beach, where the constabulary used to unload cargo from the government steamers, there is now a surf club and a camping ground. The little graveyard and its grand memorial to Mary Dobie is the most obvious physical reminder of the old days.

Although fixed in stone the grave marker was not immune to change. In the 1960s a visiting journalist said it was half-smothered at times by a mass of wild creeper.[9] Sometime after that the cross was broken off and the once elegant shape now looks squat and deformed. Some say it came off in a storm, but more likely it succumbed to vandalism just like so many of the gravestones in the Mission Cemetery at Tauranga.[10] But someone still cared. Part of the cross was rescued and now lies at the foot of the tombstone. And Iolanthe Small, a plantswoman who for many years worked in the fernery at New Plymouth's famous Pukekura Park, found a bunch of faded artificial flowers on the grave when she visited the cemetery in 2003. She was there to help with research into the pioneering botanical work of Mary's brother.[11] Before leaving she added some fern fronds as her own tribute to a woman who loved nature and whose artistic skills enhanced the first edition of Herbert Dobbie's classic work *New Zealand Ferns*.

As well as the physical reminders, the story of what happened on that November day in 1880 has changed over the years; in posterity Mary's many deaths continued to multiply. Bits and pieces of the evidence were reconstituted into different versions which had little in common with each other or with what had really happened. They included the account of an old chief who said Tuhi killed Mary with a red light dancing before his eyes after she had refused to give him tobacco.[12] Some of those directly connected with the investigation also scrambled their facts. One of the soldiers in the party who arrested Tuhi gave an interview on the forty-fifth anniversary of the murder in which his description of the crime contained traces of Tuhi's confession but, in the end, bore little resemblance to it.[13] Tuhi had pushed Mary after taking her money, he said, and she fainted. He thought she was dead but when she recovered, she screamed and so he killed her. The old soldier's credibility derived from him having been there but his fading memory let him down and he made many more mistakes including saying the trial was held in Ōpunake rather than Wellington, no doubt confusing it with the inquest.

Facts are also scrambled in a family version of the murder.[14] By this account Tuhi rode up and demanded money. 'She said that she had none, and in any case, if she had she wouldn't give it to him,' says a family history preserved in the Alexander Turnbull Library. 'He turned to ride off and Mary threatened to "tell the soldiers" about him. This enflamed him and he cut her throat.' In this version it was not detective work but the conscience of Tuhi's family that solved the crime; they supposedly turned him in after seeing blood on his clothes.

Many of the details are obviously wrong and although some are accurate the story is impossible to reconcile with the one that Tuhi told to George Taylor. There is no sense of the mutual incomprehension and fear that are so important to understanding what happened. Mary comes across as the confident woman of the *May Queen* diary and the trips to Fiji and the Pink and White Terraces, perhaps because that is the way the family wanted to remember her, courageous to a fault. But the isolated and terrified victim described in Tuhi's confession is a more credible and compelling image of Mary in the last moments of her life. Of course it is possible that he did demand money but the evidence shows that, rather than imperiously dismissing him, Mary handed over the 6 shillings and 4 pence she had in her pockets.

John Shearman, the constable who realised his colleagues had arrested the wrong man, always felt he had never received due recognition and he retold the story of his role in the investigation to support a long, but ultimately futile, campaign for promotion.[15] A magazine feature in the 1930s published yet another version of Mary's death, removing all the political and social context, and reducing it to a simple horror story like the ones the Dobie sisters heard at their mother's knee and later when they were visiting the Bay of Plenty.[16] In the twenty-first century the murder features briefly in studies of writers and women travellers in nineteenth-century New Zealand.[17] In *Country of Writing* Lydia Wevers contrasts Mary's fate with Constance Gordon Cumming who preceded her to Fiji and the Hot Lakes.[18] Cumming's work showed the lady traveller as artist and hero, writes Wevers, and is a story about entitlement, notably in the way she dismissed attempts by Māori to assert their property rights. Mary was the other, tragic, side of that heroic image and Cumming was shocked when she read about her fate in *The Times*.

Local lore has it that Tuhi accosted and killed Mary while she was sketching on the cluster of stones at the top of the gully where the Ōtahi Stream loops north and then south in a hairpin bend on its way to the sea.[19] The flax that was so dense in 1880 has long gone but it is the exact spot marked on the map published by the *Taranaki Herald* shortly after the murder (Fig. 52) and fits both the paper's description of the crime scene and Eugene Buckley's watercolour. The location is an ideal place to admire the grandeur of Mount Taranaki if the day is clear and the mountain deigns to show itself from behind the clouds, as it did on the day Mary died. And as the *Taranaki Herald* said at the time, it is one of the most beautiful spots in the district. To this day tourists travelling north along State Highway 45 are often so entranced by the view they stop to take photographs across the road thus unconsciously re-enacting a few moments of the last day of Mary Dobie's life.

The local story accords with first reports which said Mary was sketching at the time of her death.[20] But Tuhi's confessions made no mention of her sitting on a rock or sketching; he said only that he met her on the road.[21] And none of the witnesses who saw her on the afternoon of the fatal day mentioned a sketchbook nor did they find one despite a meticulous ground search. It is possible that it was overlooked or that Mary had just paused to admire the view when Tuhi came upon her. The newspaper map and the Buckley watercolour of the crime scene suggest this spot is where the body was found rather than where Tuhi and Mary first met. According to the measurements of Superintendent James, the fatal encounter began about 90 metres along the road where Tuhi tied his horse to a flax bush.

Whether Mary was sketching or just sitting on a rock or walking along the road will never be known for sure and is merely a tantalising detail. Of far more significance is the idea that somehow Mary's death was connected to Parihaka. It changed the story and had real consequences in forming the attitudes and determining the behaviour of the soldiers who raided and looted Parihaka in November 1881. The most influential example of this idea was Walter Gudgeon's time-shifting error which moved the murder to the period immediately before the invasion. It was later cemented into the story in an obituary of Te Whiti in 1907 and repeated in Dudley Dyne's 1969 book *Famous New Zealand Murders*.[22]

But this does not mean that Gudgeon is solely responsible for linking the murder to Parihaka or that the mistake was necessarily a deliberate attempt to mislead. His account was just a striking example of a widely held mindset which manifested itself in many different ways and resulted in distortions passed from individuals into the collective memory. Long before Gudgeon put pen to paper it was expressed in the Auckland *Star* editorial in the week after the inquest and was implicit in the *Illustrated London News* picture page on the Parihaka crisis published in 1882. The staying power of the idea could later be seen in a sign erected outside the old cemetery which said Mary had met her death at 'the hands of the enemy'. The sign was changed after a local doctor pointed out that the murder of Mary Dobie had no political significance.[23] An even clearer indication of the idea's stamina came from one who lived through those troubled times. W. K. Howitt grew up on a farm north of the Stony River in the 1870s and vividly recalled in the 1920s and 1930s the trying times the settlers faced. He was a great stickler for accuracy, rushing off letters to the editor whenever he thought someone had departed from the strict truth. But he, too, linked Parihaka to the Dobie murder by insisting that Tuhi had been given refuge there when nothing of the kind happened.[24] Once again the effect of the story was to imply some sort of moral justification for what happened in November 1881.

Two people who remained enigmatically silent about the murder – in their known writings at least – were Mary's brother Herbert and sister Bertha. Both wrote unpublished memoirs and yet neither mentioned Mary's fate. Herbert's eccentric memoir concentrated on his life from the late 1890s when he left New Zealand to work on building railways in Rhodesia, now Zimbabwe. After two years in Africa he went back to England to visit his mother shortly before she died in 1903 and to tour the countryside on a penny-farthing bicycle. He reasoned that nothing out of the ordinary had happened to him before the African trip. Although he introduced his memoir with a summary of his life before then he did not give the death of his sister, who had helped him with the first edition of his book on ferns, even a passing reference.[25]

Bertha's silence is, if anything, more puzzling than Herbert's. The diary-sketchbooks the sisters created together show how close they were throughout their great southern adventure. Bertha was the writer who went on to contribute short stories and journalism to New Zealand periodicals and yet, with the possible exception of the 'In Memoriam' poem in the Auckland *Observer*, she published nothing and made no public statement about her sister's horrifying death. Even her unpublished memoir, 'Orange Leaves and the Simple Life', makes no mention of Mary.

In some ways it is understandable that Bertha avoided such a grim topic in 'Orange Leaves', which aimed to be an upbeat account of how she and Forster came to terms with their new life as orchardists in Whangārei after he was forced to retire from his position as colonel because of failing eyesight. But amid the anecdotes of domestic bliss and the delights of rustic living, it is obvious that the Gorings had come down in the world and felt it keenly. Money worries were a constant theme, arising largely because Forster did not receive what they regarded as an adequate pension, so it was a relief when a family member – probably Ellen – gave them an allowance of £15 a year.[26] In 1899 when the local member of Parliament came door-knocking with Premier 'King Dick' Seddon in tow, Bertha, as forthright as ever, seized the opportunity to give him a piece of her mind about how badly the government had treated its loyal servants like Forster. But this time her persuasive powers had no effect. 'It did not trouble him much, you may be sure,' she wrote, 'but there is a satisfaction in having one's say'.[27]

Nostalgia played a big part in the memoir too. Much as her main aim was to give an account of her life and struggles on the orchard in the 1890s, she could not help but hark back to the old days in Taranaki and even before that. 'Each year we find it harder to make new friends and cling more and more, in thought, as we cannot in the flesh, to those olden days,' she wrote.[28] And yet there was never a mention of Mary or what happened to her.

Bertha's silence on her sister's fate is deeper than the muteness of the great tombstone in the little cemetery. Of all the people who might have come up with a suitable epitaph, Bertha was the one. Her knowledge of poetry could have led her to an apt quotation which eluded the soldiers more used to memorialising comrades who had fallen in battle than a woman brutally murdered. And she understood how important a memorial could be. Even if she was not as sensitive as her sister, she knew how deeply Mary had been touched by the epitaph on Private Manion's grave in Tauranga. And when she returned to England on a visit in 1893 she made a point of going to see Tennyson's grave in Westminster Abbey. He would have appreciated how someone had left a tiny bunch of violets on it, she wrote.[29]

Given her fondness for Tennyson, it is tempting to think that she would have looked to 'In Memoriam' for a poetic epitaph to mark the passing of an artistic life cut cruelly short. The imitation published in the *Observer* was a brief verse to express grief but the original, inspired by the poet's brilliant friend Arthur Hallam who died tragically young, encompassed great themes of remembrance, fear of forgetting, doubt and the changing nature of knowledge and wisdom as well as grief. Out of this immensely long poem – it runs to more than 130 sections in some editions – one line suggests itself as a possibility for Mary's epitaph: 'There must be wisdom with great Death'. In context it is a reference to the deceased living on after death and looking on the world with wise and forgiving eyes. As such it would have provided Mary's family and friends with some solace. It also had the potential of communicating something to future generations who would see Mary's many deaths in a different way. Not as an occasion of personal grief but as a story that captures the essence of the New Zealand tragedy in microcosm, a story of fear, misunderstanding and what happens when the balance of power becomes unstable.

But for all that she loved Tennyson, Bertha reacted to the tragedy in polar opposition to the way the poet grieved for Hallam. His poem was about remembrance, whereas her memoir avoids all mention of Mary. A recurring theme of 'In Memoriam' is how Tennyson is reminded of his friend on anniversaries and when he returns to places they visited together.[30] But similar triggers of memory appeared to have had no effect on Bertha, or at least on her writing. She did not mention her sister when she reminisced about her adventures in Fiji and the Bay of Plenty. And when she and Forster returned to Taranaki on holiday, she did not mention that this was where she had seen Mary for the last time.[31] Even when she wrote about witnessing the great comet of 1882 at Parihaka, where Forster was stationed after the invasion, it did not seem to remind her of Mary though this was the place of their last great adventure together.[32]

Another point of difference is the way Tennyson's poem faces up to doubt and the profound changes buffeting Victorian England as new scientific knowledge challenged the certainties of religious faith.[33] But Bertha was a stranger to doubt. She was, after all, a daughter of a great empire like her sister and she never questioned its customs and traditions or its role in her life. If the soldiers had asked Mary's literary sister to come up with a quotation she might have chosen something that had more in common with Manion's epitaph than 'In Memoriam'. Something that expressed the remote loneliness of her sister's death and the impossibility of making sense of it but also reaffirming the value of Mary's life. Rather than turning to the great works of Tennyson, she would have found it in a verse from *Poems*, published in 1868 by Uncle Frederick:

> Her quiet resting-place is far away,
> None dwelling there can tell you her sad story
> The stones are mute. The stones could only say,
> 'A humble spirit passed away to glory'.[34]

NOTES

CHAPTER 1: **TOMB WITH NO EPITAPH**

1. Headnotes, *The Graphic*, in 'British Newspapers 1600–1950', http://0-find.galegroup.com.www.elgar.govt.nz/bncn/start.do?prodId=BNWS&userGroupName=auclib.
2. 'Dreadful murder at Opunake', *Taranaki Herald*, 26 Nov 1880, p. 2.
3. Tony Sole, *Ngāti Ruanui: A history*, Wellington, 2005, pp. 139–40.
4. Ibid., pp. 154–65.
5. Walter Hugh Ross, 'Matakātea, Wiremu Kingi or Moki', in *An Encyclopaedia of New Zealand*, A. H. McLintock (ed.), Wellington, 1966. Also available at http://www.teara.govt.nz/en/1966/matakatea-wiremu-kingi-or-moki; Danny Keenan, 'Te Whiti-o-Rongomai III, Erueti', *Dictionary of New Zealand Biography*, Te Ara – the Encyclopedia of New Zealand, http://www.teara.govt.nz/en/biographies/2t34/te-whiti-o-rongomai-iii-erueti, updated 30 October 2012.
6. Dennis Connor, 'Notes of evidence and other documents re conviction of Tuhi for wilful murder', in inward letters, C490 149, J1 Box 283, 1881/5-50, ANZ, Wellington, p. 14; William Eyes, 'Notes of evidence and other documents', p. 10; Walter Stannard, 'Notes of evidence and other documents', p. 19.
7. 'The late Miss M. B. Dobie', *The Graphic*, 5 Feb 1881, p. 126.
8. Forster Goring, 'Notes of evidence and other documents', pp. 2–3.
9. 'Tragedy at Opunake', *Evening Post*, 26 Nov 1880, p. 2.
10. 'Miss Dobie found dead in the flax' and 'Lieut Col Roberts' report on the occurrence', *Auckland Star*, 26 Nov 1880, p. 3.
11. I am grateful to Len Stimpson for pointing this out.
12. John Bilcliffe, *Well Done the 68th: The Durhams in the Crimea and New Zealand 1854–1866*, Chippenham, 1995, p. 203.
13. *Collins Quotation Finder*, Glasgow, 2001, p. 217.

CHAPTER 2: **DAUGHTERS OF EMPIRE**

1. David Hastings, *Over the Mountains of the Sea*, Auckland, 2006, pp. 107–8.
2. Bertha Dobie and Mary Dobie, *Voyage of the May Queen*, Margaret Drake Brockman (ed.), Braunton, 1992, 11 Oct 1877.

3   'The late Miss M. B. Dobie', *The Graphic*, 5 Feb 1881, p. 126.
4   About Town, *Observer*, 4 Dec 1880, p. 97.
5   Walter E. Houghton, *The Victorian Frame of Mind*, Yale, 1985, pp. 364–72; Barbara Ehrenreich and Dierdre English, *For Her Own Good*, New York, 2nd edition, 2005, p. xiv; Hastings, *Over the Mountains of the Sea*, p. 184.
6   Bertha V. Goring, 'Orange Leaves and the Simple Life', unpublished manuscript, 1905, p. 109.
7   J. D. McCraw, 'Life of H. B. Dobbie', MSX 2730, ATL, Wellington, p. 2.
8   Richard J. Hall, 'Further papers re H. B. Dobbie and family', MS-Papers-6602, ATL, Wellington, p. 5.
9   Frederick Locker-Lampson, *My Confidences, An autobiographical sketch addressed to my descendants*, London, 1896. Also available at Open Library, https://archive.org/stream/myconfidencesan00lamgoog#page/n10/mode/2upp, pp. viii, 15, 18–22.
10 Roger Quarm, 'Locker, Edward Hawke (1777–1849)', *Oxford Dictionary of National Biography*, Oxford University Press, 2004. Also available at http://0-www.oxforddnb.com.www.elgar.govt.nz/view/article/16893, accessed 5 Oct 2014.
11 Locker-Lampson, *My Confidences*, pp. 23–28.
12 Richard Garnett, 'Locker, Arthur (1828–1893)', rev. Joseph Coohill, *Oxford Dictionary of National Biography*, Oxford University Press, 2004. Also available at http://0-www.oxforddnb.com.www.elgar.govt.nz/view/article/16892, accessed 5 Oct 2014.
13 Austin Dobson, rev. Katharine Chubbuck, 'Lampson, Frederick Locker (1821–1895)', *Oxford Dictionary of National Biography*, Oxford University Press, 2004. Also available at http://0-www.oxforddnb.com.www.elgar.govt.nz/view/article/16896, accessed 5 Oct 2014.
14 Goring, 'Orange Leaves', pp. 178–79.
15 'The Colonel's Lady', *Free Lance*, 24 June 1936, p. 12.
16 Goring, 'Orange Leaves', pp. 76–77.
17 Ibid., p. 60.
18 Death notice, *The Times*, 31 July 1854, p. 1.
19 Hall, 'Further papers', p. 3; McCraw, 'Life of H. B. Dobbie', pp. 2–3.
20 Goring, 'Orange Leaves', pp. 182–83.
21 Hugh Drake Brockman, 'Descendants of Robert Dobbie'.
22 Ibid.
23 'Female School of Art and Design, Gower St', *The Times*, 15 June 1860, p. 10; 'Employment of Educated Women', *The Times*, 14 June 1861, p. 12; 'Female School of Art and Design', *The Times*, 18 June 1862, p. 10; Female School of Art, UCL Bloomsbury Project.
24 Hugh Drake Brockman, 'Descendants of Robert Dobbie'.
25 J. D. McCraw, 'H. B. Dobbie – Fern Enthusiast', *New Zealand Journal of Botany*, 1988, vol. 26: 171–78; J. D. McCraw, 'Dobbie, Herbert Boucher', *Dictionary of New Zealand Biography*, Te Ara – the Encyclopedia of New Zealand, http://www.TeAra.govt.nz/en/biographies/3d9/dobbie-herbert-boucher, updated 30 October 2012; J. D. McCraw, 'Life of H. B. Dobbie', pp. 1–2; Hall, 'Further papers', pp. 4–7.

26 Hugh Drake Brockman, 'Descendants of Robert Dobbie'.
27 Hall, 'Further papers', p. 3.
28 *Voyage of the May Queen*, dancing 12 Oct 1877; reading parties 5, 9, 26, 29 Oct 1877; parlour games 19, 21 Nov 1877.
29 Ibid., 17 Nov 1877.
30 Ibid., 6 Oct 1877.
31 Ibid., 7 Oct, 18, 30 Nov 1877.
32 Ibid., 17 Nov 1877.
33 Ibid., 23 Nov 1877.
34 Ibid., 2 Oct 1877.
35 Ibid., 7 Oct 1877.
36 Ibid., 31 Oct 1877.
37 Ibid., 15 Dec 1877.
38 Ibid., 18 Oct 1877.
39 Ibid., 4 Oct 1877.
40 Ibid., 10 Oct 1877.
41 Ibid., 17 Nov 1877.
42 Ibid., 4, 5 Oct, 8, 9 Nov 1877; 2 Jan 1878.
43 Ibid., 8 Nov 1877.
44 Ibid., 31 Oct 1877.
45 Ibid., 3 Dec 1877; Hastings, *Over the Mountains of the Sea*, pp. 46, 59.
46 *Voyage of the May Queen*, 6 Dec 1877.
47 Ibid., 7 Nov 1877.
48 Ibid., 17 Nov 1877.
49 Hastings, *Over the Mountains of the Sea*, pp. 175–84.
50 *Voyage of the May Queen*, 17 Nov 1877.
51 Ibid.
52 Hall, 'Further papers', p. 3.
53 Goring, 'Orange Leaves', p. 2.
54 Ibid., p. 138.
55 'Personal notes from London', Auckland *Star*, 11 April 1900, p. 2.

CHAPTER 3: THE GRAND TOUR

1 Bertha Dobie and Mary Dobie, *Voyage of the May Queen*, Margaret Drake Brockman (ed.), Braunton, 1992, 6 Jan 1878.
2 Ibid.
3 Ibid., 7 Jan 1878.
4 Ibid.
5 Ibid., 30 Jan 1878.
6 Bertha V. Goring, 'Orange Leaves and the Simple Life,' unpublished manuscript, 1905, p. 32.
7 *Voyage of the May Queen*, 30 Jan 1878.
8 'The murdered lady', *NZH*, 27 Nov 1880, p. 5.
9 Jill Williamson, 'Outhwaite of Eden Hill, the Life and Times of an Auckland

      settler 1841–1879', BA (Hons) thesis, University of Auckland, 1999, NZMS1243, pp. 10–11.
10   Auckland *Star*, 25 June 1880, p. 2.
11   *NZH*, 25 June 1880, p. 5.
12   J. H. Kerry-Nicholls, *The King Country or Explorations in New Zealand*, London, 1884, pp. 95–96 in Lydia Wevers, *Country of Writing, Travel Writing and New Zealand 1809–1900*, Auckland, 2002, p. 188.
13   Wevers, *Country of Writing*, p. 201.
14   Ibid., p. 202.
15   Constance Gordon Cumming, *At Home in Fiji*, New York, 1883. Also available at Open Library, https://archive.org/stream/athomeinfiji00cummgoog#page/n10/mode/1up, p. 304.
16   Bertha Dobie and Mary Dobie, 'Diary of a Trip to the Hot Lakes', Sunday, 2 March 1879.
17   Ibid., p. 2. A combination of vandalism and the weather has ensured that none of the original inscriptions survive in the graveyard but they are preserved in John Bilcliffe, *Well Done the 68th*, p. 203.
18   'Trip to the Hot Lakes', 4 Mar 1879.
19   Margaret Drake Brockman, preface, in *The Voyage of the May Queen*, Margaret Drake Brockman (ed.), Braunton, 1992, p. 7.
20   Goring, 'Orange Leaves', p. 24.
21   T. W. Gudgeon, *Defenders of New Zealand*, Auckland, 1887, pp. 359–60. Also available at Early New Zealand Books, University of Auckland, http://www.enzb.auckland.ac.nz/document?wid=2188&action=null.
22   'Trip to the Hot Lakes', 5–7 Mar 1879.
23   Ibid., 11 Mar 1879.
24   Ibid., 9 Mar 1879.
25   Forster Goring, 'Notes of evidence and other documents re conviction of Tuhi for wilful murder', in inward letters, C490 149, J1 Box 283, 1881/5-50, ANZ, Wellington, pp. 3–4.
26   'Trip to the Hot Lakes', 8 Mar 1879.
27   Ibid., p. 23.
28   Ibid., p. 24.
29   Ibid., 8 Mar 1879.
30   Goring, 'Orange Leaves', pp. 182–83.
31   Judith Binney, *Redemption Songs: A life of Te Kooti Arikirangi Te Turuki*, Auckland, 1995, p. 121; James Belich, *The New Zealand Wars and the Victorian Interpretation of Racial Conflict*, Auckland, 1998, p. 217.
32   Evelyn Stokes, 'Völkner, Carl Sylvius', *Dictionary of New Zealand Biography*, Te Ara – the Encyclopedia of New Zealand, http://www.TeAra.govt.nz/en/biographies/1v5/volkner-carl-sylvius, updated 30 October 2012. Peter Wells argues that the spying allegation is an oversimplification and stresses that Völkner was made a scapegoat for the defeat in February 1864 of a Whakatōhea war party; see *Journey to a Hanging*, Auckland, 2014, pp. 93–94, 100, 104–5, 123.
33   'Trip to the Hot Lakes', p. 24.
34   Ibid., 4 Mar 1879.

35 Ibid., 17, 19, 20, 21, 22 Mar 1879.
36 Ibid., 11 Mar 1879.
37 Ibid.
38 'Our Opotiki Letter', *Bay of Plenty Times*, 18 April 1877, p. 3; *Bay of Plenty Times*, 15 Oct 1878, p. 3.
39 Goring, Bertha V. and Mary Dobie, 'A Trip to the South Seas', *New Zealand Graphic*, 6 Feb–9 April 1892.
40 Ibid., 13 Feb 1892, p. 148.
41 Ibid., 12 Mar 1892, p. 244.
42 Ibid., p. 245.
43 Ibid., 27 Feb 1892, p. 196.
44 Ibid., 20 Feb 1892, p 178.
45 Ibid., 6 Feb 1892, p. 125; 20 Feb 1892, p. 178.
46 Ibid., 27 Feb 1892, p. 196
47 Ibid., 6 Feb 1892, p 125.
48 Ibid., 20 Feb 1892, p. 178.
49 Ibid., 13 Feb 1892, p. 149.
50 Ibid., 2 April 1892, p. 325.
51 Ibid., 9 April 1892, p. 370.
52 'The late Miss M. B. Dobie', *The Graphic*, 5 Feb 1881, p. 126.
53 'A Trip to the South Seas', 27 Feb 1892, p. 196.
54 Cumming, *At Home in Fiji*, p. 268.
55 'The murdered lady', *NZH*, 27 Nov 1880, p. 5; 'A Trip to the South Seas', 6 Feb 1892, p. 124; 9 April 1892, p. 370.
56 An account of this trip by Isa Outhwaite, accompanied by sketches, appeared in *The Graphic* in March 1879. Isa said her travelling companion was 'a genuine English lady'. This comment seems to have led many contemporaries to assume the lady in question was Mary. Even though the style of the sketches and the adventures of the two women sound very much like Mary, records in the ATL suggest Outhwaite's companion was Gertrude Yarborough. The original article 'A New Zealand excursion by two ladies' appeared in *The Graphic*, 29 Mar 1879; it was reprinted in the *New Zealand Herald* as 'A New Zealand Excursion', *NZH*, 5 June 1879, p. 5. The assumption that Mary was Isa's companion on that trip appeared in 'The murdered lady', *NZH*, 27 Nov 1880, p. 5 and About Town, *Observer*, 11 Dec 1880, p. 109. The source suggesting it was Yarborough is a scrapbook held by the ATL. See Yarborough, Gertrude Flora Cooke, 'Scrapbook of watercolours, prints and photographs', E-881-f, ATL.
57 About Town, *Observer*, 11 Dec 1880, p. 109.
58 'A Trip to the South Seas', 9 April 1892, p. 370.
59 'Marriage', *NZH*, 28 June 1880, p. 4.
60 Goring, 'Orange Leaves', p. 9.
61 'Scientific conversazione', *NZH*, 11 Sept 1880, p. 4; Auckland Museum and Institute, *NZH*, 17 Sept 1880, p. 5; Auckland Museum and Institute, *NZH*, 11 Oct 1880, p. 6; 'The ferns of New Zealand, illustrated by H. B. Dobbie, Auckland, 1880', *NZH*, 1 Dec 1880, p. 6; Auckland *Star*, 6 Jan 1881, p. 2.
62 J. D. McCraw, 'Dobbie, Herbert Boucher', *Dictionary of New Zealand*

Biography, Te Ara – the Encyclopedia of New Zealand, http://www.TeAra.govt.nz/en/biographies/3d9/dobbie-herbert-boucher, updated 30 October 2012.

CHAPTER 4: ON MEASURED GROUND

1. 'Aggressive position of the natives', *The Budget*, 31 May 1879, p. 9.
2. 'Deputation to the Premier', *Taranaki Herald*, 2 June 1879, p. 2.
3. H. R. Richmond to C. W. Richmond, 4 June 1879, in Guy Scholefield (ed.), *The Richmond Atkinson Papers*, vol. 2, Wellington, 1960, pp. 466–67.
4. Charles Henry Taylor, 26 August 1879, diaries (transcribed by Margareta Gee), MSX-8142, MSX-8143, ATL, Wellington, p. 346.
5. 'The native difficulty', *Grey River Argus*, 4 June 1879, p. 2.
6. Editorial, *Taranaki News*, 31 May 1879, p. 8; *Taranaki News*, 5 June 1879 in Hazel Riseborough, *Days of Darkness, the Government and Parihaka 1878–1884*, revised edition, Auckland, 2002, p. 84; 'Defence of the Out-Districts', *The Budget*, 14 June 1879, p. 7.
7. Kate Mickelson, *The Clearing: A history of Opunake*, Christchurch, 1999, p. 119.
8. Thomas Pole Hughson, 'The History of the Hughson Family', part 1, ARC 2002-851, PA, New Plymouth, p. 7.
9. 'Arrival of the governor and ministers', *Taranaki News*, 7 June 1879, p. 11.
10. *Taranaki Herald*, 2, 3, 4, 5, 6 June 1879.
11. Ibid.
12. 'Aggressive position of the natives', *The Budget*, 31 May 1879, p. 9; 'The Taranaki affair', *NZH*, 31 May 1879, p. 5; Editorial, *NZH*, 3 June 1879, p. 4; 'An opposition opinion', *The Budget*, 14 June 1879, p. 7; 'Carlyle', *The Budget*, 14 June 1879, p. 7.
13. Judith Bassett, *Sir Harry Atkinson*, Auckland, 1975, pp. 56–57, 59–74.
14. 'Deputation to the Premier', *The Budget*, 7 June 1879, p. 5.
15. 'Deputation to the Premier', *Taranaki Herald*, 2 June 1879, p. 2.
16. 'Advance of the AC force', *The Budget*, 14 June 1879, p. 9.
17. 'Taranaki Rifle Volunteers, resignation of the corps', *The Budget*, 31 May 1879, p. 7; J. C. Davies to Editor, *The Budget*, 7 June 1879, p. 13.
18. 'Our volunteer force', *The Budget*, 14 June 1879, p. 9.
19. Riseborough, *Days of Darkness*, pp. 87–88.
20. William Skinner, 30 June, 5, 24, 25 July 1879, diaries 1880–82 (transcribed by Tania Pirini), ARC 2001-165, PA, New Plymouth.
21. Taranaki Provincial District, in 'Annual report on the New Zealand Constabulary', 31 May 1880, in *AJHR* 1880, H.-10, p. 23.
22. Ibid.
23. *Taranaki Herald*, 6 June 1879, p. 2.
24. 'Parihaka meeting', *Taranaki Herald*, 19 Mar 1880, p. 2.
25. 'Tohu's speech', *Taranaki Herald*, 19 Mar 1880, p. 2.
26. 'Annual report on the New Zealand Armed Constabulary', 31 May 1881, in *AJHR* 1881, H.-18, p. 2.

27 Bertha V. Goring, 'Orange Leaves and the Simple Life,' unpublished manuscript, 1905, p. 6.
28 'Descriptive account of the crime', *Wanganui Herald*, 1 Dec 1880, p. 2.
29 Ibid.; Forster Goring, 'Notes of evidence and other documents re conviction of Tuhi for wilful murder', in inward letters, C490 149, J1 Box 283, 1881/5-50, ANZ, Wellington, pp. 3-4.
30 Thomas Pole Hughson, diary, ARC 2002-851, R4/614, PA, New Plymouth, pp. 14-15.
31 Goring, 'Notes of evidence and other documents', pp. 3-4.
32 Riseborough, *Days of Darkness*, p. 23.
33 Ibid., p. 51.
34 Ibid., pp. 98, 128, 154, 162.
35 Parris to undersecretary Native Department, 18 April 1881, in *AJHR* 1881, G.-3, pp. 7-8.
36 'Parihaka meeting', *Taranaki Herald*, 19 Nov 1880, p. 2.
37 Captain Louis Knollys to the Governor, 31 Dec 1880, in *AJHR* 1881, A-1, pp. 23-24.
38 Ibid.
39 'The prophet Te Whiti and the Parihaka stronghold', *The Graphic*, 12 Nov 1881, p. 498.
40 'The colonel's lady', *Free Lance*, 24 June 1936, p. 12.
41 'The late Miss Dobie', *Taranaki Herald*, 15 Dec 1880, p. 2.
42 Ibid.
43 Herbert W. Williams, *A Dictionary of the Maori Language*, Wellington, 1975, p. 243; P. M. Ryan, *The Raupō Dictionary of Modern Māori*, Auckland, 2012, p. 203.
44 Captain Louis Knollys to the Governor, 31 Dec 1880, in *AJHR* 1881, A-1, pp. 23-24.
45 Belich, *New Zealand Wars*, pp. 294-98.
46 Parris to undersecretary Native Department, 18 April 1881, in *AJHR* 1881, G.-3, pp. 7-8.
47 Tony Sole, *Ngati Ruanui: A history*, Wellington, 2005, pp. 303-4.
48 Ian Church, 'Te Rei Hanataua, Hone Pihama', *Dictionary of New Zealand Biography*, Te Ara - the Encyclopedia of New Zealand, http://www.TeAra.govt.nz/en/biographies/2t28/te-rei-hanataua-hone-pihama, updated 30 October 2012.
49 Riseborough, *Days of Darkness*, p. 116; 'An important witness gone', Auckland *Star*, 29 Nov 1880, p. 2; 'Scintillations', Auckland *Star*, 30 Nov 1880, p. 2.
50 Riseborough, *Days of Darkness*, p. 139.
51 Ibid., pp. 47-48, 92-93.
52 Sole, pp. 373, 383.
53 'Parihaka meeting', *Taranaki Herald*, 19 Nov 1880, p. 2.
54 Sole, p. 370 and M. P. K. Sorrenson, *Ko Te Whenua Te Utu, the Price is the Land*, Auckland, 2014, p. 281.
55 Riseborough, *Days of Darkness*, pp. 73-74.
56 Ibid., pp. 29, 33; Sole, p. 367.

57 Riseborough, *Days of Darkness,* pp. 46–49.
58 Telegram from Mr Mackay and Mr Blake to Hon. Mr Sheehan on the subject of their visit to Te Whiti at Parihaka, Taranaki, 4 April 1879, in *AJHR* 1880, G-2, Appendix A, Part I, pp. 9–12.
59 'The native difficulty at Tapuae', *The Budget,* 31 May 1879, p. 8.
60 Riseborough, *Days of Darkness,* pp. 136–37.
61 'Parihaka meeting', *Taranaki Herald,* 19 Nov 1880, p. 2.
62 'Ominous speech by Te Whiti', Auckland *Star,* 19 Mar 1880, p. 2; Editorial, *Grey River Argus,* 20 Mar 1880, p. 2; 'The Taranaki difficulty', *Hawke's Bay Herald,* 20 Mar 1880, p. 2; Editorial, *NZH,* 19 Mar 1880, p. 4.
63 Riseborough, *Days of Darkness,* pp. 19–20, 25–26, 78–80.
64 Parris to undersecretary Native Department, 18 April 1881, in *AJHR* 1881, G.-3, pp. 7–8; Results of Census 1881 (approximate), in *AJHR* 1881, H.-21A, p. 1.
65 Sole, p. 370; Riseborough, *Days of Darkness,* p. 119.
66 W. H. J. Seffern, 'The history of a colonial newspaper', in *Taranaki Herald,* 27 Aug 1892, p. 8.
67 Riseborough, pp. 83, 88.
68 Editorial, Auckland *Star,* 14 Feb 1880, p. 2.
69 Sole, pp. 314–15.
70 Ibid., pp. 324–39.
71 *The Graphic,* 12 Nov 1881, p. 498.
72 Stapp to Under Secretary for Defence, 3, 25, 28 May, 3, 23 July, 2, 14, 16 Sept 1880, in Taranaki Militia and Volunteers Letter Book, Militia and Volunteers Office, New Plymouth, May 1880–Nov 1881.
73 Mickelson, p. 111.
74 Thomas Baker Blanchett, 'Colonial Experiences', diary, ARC 2001-465, PA, New Plymouth, p. 7.
75 Ibid.
76 Ibid.
77 Hughson, diary, pp. 5–6.
78 'Society', *Observer,* 11 Dec 1880, p. 112; 'The late Miss Dobie', *Taranaki Herald,* 15 Dec 1880, p. 2.

CHAPTER 5: THE FATAL DAY

1 Thomas Pole Hughson, 'Historical sketch re early settlement of West Coast with special reference to Rahotu', Hughson family papers, folder 1, ARC 2002-851, PA, New Plymouth.
2 'Annual report on the New Zealand Armed Constabulary', 31 May 1881, in *AJHR* 1881, H.-18, p. 2.
3 Kate Mickelson, *The Clearing: A history of Opunake,* Christchurch, 1999, p. 13.
4 Thomas Pole Hughson, diary, ARC 2002-851, R4/614, PA, New Plymouth, pp. 10–11.
5 Mickelson, p. 8.

6   William Skinner, 6 June 1880, diaries 1880–82 (transcribed by Tania Pirini), ARC 2001-165, PA, New Plymouth.
7   'The Parihaka meeting', Auckland *Star*, 16 Dec 1880, p. 2; 'Wellington', *ODT*, 31 Dec 1880, p. 5.
8   'Latest from Parihaka', *Wanganui Herald*, 16 Dec 1880, p. 2.
9   'The late Miss M. B. Dobie', *The Graphic*, 5 Feb 1881, p. 126; 'The ferns of New Zealand, illustrated by H.B. Dobbie, Auckland, 1880', *NZH*, 1 Dec 1880, p. 6; Auckland *Star*, 6 Dec 1880, p. 2.
10 Forster Goring, 'Notes of evidence and other documents re conviction of Tuhi for wilful murder', in inward letters, C490 149, J1 Box 283, 1881/5-50, ANZ, Wellington, p. 2.
11 Thomas Baker Blanchett, 'Colonial Experiences', diary, ARC 2001-465, PA, New Plymouth, p. 5.
12 Thomas Pole Hughson, diary, ARC 2002-851, R4/614, PA, New Plymouth, p. 4.
13 Thomas Pole Hughson, 'Historical sketch'.
14 Reports of the Royal Commission under the Confiscated Lands Inquiry and Maori Prisoners' Trials Act, 1879, 1880 in *AJHR* 1880, G-2, p. xxxiv.
15 Harry Middleton, 'Notes of evidence and other documents', p. 41.
16 William Eyes, 'Notes of evidence and other documents', pp. 10–14.
17 Middleton, 'Notes of evidence and other documents', p. 37.
18 Martin Coffey, 'Notes of evidence and other documents', p. 5.
19 Eyes, 'Notes of evidence and other documents', p. 10; Dennis Connor, 'Notes of evidence and other documents', p. 14.
20 Middleton, 'Notes of evidence and other documents', pp. 35–37; 'The Te Namu murder', *Taranaki Herald*, 27 Nov 1880, p. 2.
21 'Dreadful murder at Opunake', *Taranaki Herald*, 26 Nov 1880, p. 2.
22 Middleton, 'Notes of evidence and other documents', p. 35.
23 Eyes, 'Notes of evidence and other documents', p. 10; Connor, 'Notes of evidence and other documents', p. 14.
24 Walter Stannard, 'Notes of evidence and other documents', p. 18; 'The evidence at the inquest', *Auckland Star*, 29 Nov 1880, p. 2.
25 'Strong circumstantial evidence against Tuhi', *Evening Post*, 29 Nov 1880, p. 2.
26 'The evidence at the inquest', Auckland *Star*, 29 Nov 1880, p. 2.
27 Middleton, 'Notes of evidence and other documents', pp. 37–38.
28 Hone Pīhama, 'Notes of evidence and other documents', pp. 47–48.
29 'The late Miss M. B. Dobie', *The Graphic*, 5 Feb 1881, p. 126.
30 Forster Goring to Lieutenant-Colonel Roberts, 1 Dec 1880, in 'Murder of Mary Dobie by Tuhi', P1 (Box 281) 1892/222, ANZ, Wellington; 'Descriptive account of the crime', *Wanganui Herald*, 1 Dec 1880, p. 2.
31 'The evidence at the inquest', Auckland *Star*, 29 Nov 1880, p. 2.
32 Ibid.
33 'Descriptive account of the crime', *Wanganui Herald*, 1 Dec 1880, p. 2.
34 'Additional particulars', Auckland *Star*, 27 Nov 1880, p. 2.
35 Goring, 'Notes of evidence and other documents', p. 5.
36 'The Te Namu murder', *Taranaki Herald*, 29 Nov 1880, p. 2.

37 William Wilson, 'Notes of evidence and other documents', p. 20.
38 'The Te Namu murder', *Taranaki Herald*, 27, 29, 30 Nov 1880, p. 2.
39 *New Zealand Times*, 14 Dec 1880, p. 2; Wilson, 'Notes of evidence and other documents', p. 20; Joseph Tosland, 'Notes of evidence and other documents', p. 25.
40 Goring, 'Notes of evidence and other documents', pp. 2–3.
41 Wilson, 'Notes of evidence and other documents', p. 20; Tosland, 'Notes of evidence and other documents', p. 25; Dr Langer Carey, 'Notes of evidence and other documents', p. 30.
42 Wilson, 'Notes of evidence and other documents', p. 20; Tosland, 'Notes of evidence and other documents', p. 25.
43 William Ebbett, 'Notes of evidence and other documents', p. 28.
44 'The evidence at the inquest', Auckland *Star*, 30 Nov 1880, p. 2; 'Descriptive account of the crime', *Wanganui Herald*, 1 Dec 1880, p. 2.
45 Ibid.
46 Ibid.
47 Ibid.
48 'The coroner's inquest', *Evening Post*, 29 Nov 1880, p. 2.
49 'Report of Constable John Shearman re part taken [by] him in reference to the detection of Tuhi the murderer of Miss Dobie', in 'Murder of Mary Dobie by Tuhi'.
50 Stuart Newall, 26 Nov 1880, diary, MS-Copy-Micro-0740, ATL, Wellington.
51 Hughson, diary, p. 15.
52 Newall, 26 Nov 1880.
53 'Descriptive account of the crime', *Wanganui Herald*, 1 Dec 1880, p. 2.
54 Newall, 28 Nov 1880.

CHAPTER 6: BREAKING NEWS

1 William Wilson, 'Notes of evidence and other documents re conviction of Tuhi for wilful murder', in inward letters, C490 149, J1 Box 283, 1881/5-50, ANZ, Wellington, pp. 21–23.
2 'The Te Namu murder', *Taranaki Herald*, 29 Nov 1880, p. 2.
3 William Skinner, 26 Nov 1880, diaries 1880–82 (transcribed by Tania Pirini), ARC 2001-165, PA, New Plymouth.
4 'Diabolical murder at Opunake', Auckland *Star*, 26 Nov 1880, p. 3; 'Dreadful murder at Opunake', *Taranaki Herald*, 26 Nov 1880, p. 2; 'Murder of young lady at Opunake', *ODT*, 27 Nov 1880, p. 3; 'Brutal murder', *Thames Star*, 26 Nov 1880, p. 2.
5 Editorial, *NZH*, 27 Nov 1880, p. 4.
6 About Town, *Observer*, 4 Dec 1880, p. 97.
7 'The late murdered lady', *Thames Advertiser*, 29 Nov 1880, p. 3.
8 Reverend Vicesimus Lush, 4 Dec 1880, Lush family papers, folder 17 journal, MS 780, AWMML, Auckland.
9 Lionel Tennyson to Alfred, Emily and Hallam Tennyson, 26 and 29 Jan 1881, Tennyson Research Centre, Lincolnshire, UK.

10 Skinner, 26, 28, 30 Nov, 1 Dec 1880; Thomas Pole Hughson, diary, ARC 2002-851, R4/614, PA, New Plymouth, pp. 14, 15, 16.
11 'Later intelligence', Auckland *Star*, 26 Nov 1880, p. 3.
12 'Diabolical murder at Opunake', Auckland *Star*, 26 Nov 1880, p. 3; 'Tragedy at Opunake', *Evening Post*, 26 Nov 1880, p. 2.
13 'Opunake tragedy', *Manawatu Herald*, 30 Nov 1880, p. 2.
14 'Dreadful murder at Opunake', *Taranaki Herald*, 26 Nov 1880, p. 2; 'Brutal murder', *Thames Star*, 26 Nov 1880, p. 2.
15 Editorial, *New Zealand Times*, 27 Nov 1880, p. 2.
16 'The Opunake tragedy', *Evening Post*, 27 Nov 1880, p. 2.
17 'Dreadful murder at Opunake', *Taranaki Herald*, 26 Nov 1880, p. 2.
18 Editorial, *NZH*, 27 Nov 1880, p. 4.
19 'The Accused Stannard', *NZH*, 27 Nov 1880, p. 5.
20 Auckland *Star*, 27 Nov 1880, p. 2.
21 'Horrible murder', Christchurch *Star*, 27 Nov 1880, p. 3.
22 'The accused Stannard', *NZH*, 27 Nov 1880, p. 5.
23 'Horrible murder', Christchurch *Star*, 27 Nov 1880, p. 3.
24 'Scintillations', Auckland *Star*, 30 Nov 1880, p. 2.
25 'Favourable opinions of Stannard', Auckland *Star*, 27 Nov 1880, p. 2.
26 'Lieut. Col. Roberts' report on the occurrence', Auckland *Star*, 26 Nov 1880, p. 3;'The evidence at the inquest', Auckland *Star*, 30 Nov 1880, p. 2; 'Descriptive account of the crime', *Wanganui Herald*, 1 Dec 1880, p. 2.
27 'Favourable opinions of Stannard', Auckland *Star*, 27 Nov 1880, p. 2.
28 Mary Ann Ebbett, 'Notes of evidence and other documents', p. 29.
29 William Ebbett, 'Notes of evidence and other documents', p. 28.
30 Dr Langer Carey, 'Notes of evidence and other documents', pp. 30–34.
31 'The murder at Opunake', Auckland *Star*, 30 Nov 1880, p. 2.
32 'Trial of Tuhi', *Evening Post*, 14 Dec 1880, p. 2.
33 Carey, 'Notes of evidence and other documents', p. 34.
34 Wilson, 'Notes of evidence and other documents', pp. 20, 22.
35 Joseph Tosland, 'Notes of evidence and other documents', p. 25.
36 Forster Goring, 'Notes of evidence and other documents', p. 4.
37 'The body not violated', Auckland *Star*, 27 Nov 1880, p. 2.
38 Wilson, 'Notes of evidence and other documents', pp. 21–23.
39 Tosland, 'Notes of evidence and other documents', pp. 25–26; 'The evidence at the inquest', Auckland *Star*, 29 Nov 1880, p. 2.
40 Tosland, 'Notes of evidence and other documents', p. 26.
41 Ibid., p. 27.
42 'Report of Constable John Shearman re part taken [by] him in reference to the detection of Tuhi the murderer of Miss Dobie', in 'Murder of Mary Dobie by Tuhi', P1 (Box 281) 1892/222, ANZ, Wellington.
43 'Report of Constable John Shearman re part taken [by] him in reference to the detection of Tuhi the murderer of Miss Dobie', in 'Murder of Mary Dobie by Tuhi'.
44 Forster Y. Goring to Lieut-Col Roberts, 1 Dec 1880, in 'Murder of Mary Dobie by Tuhi'.
45 Thomas Knowles, 'Notes of evidence and other documents', pp. 71–74.

The official transcript mistakenly gives his name as Knollys.
46   'Descriptive account of the crime', *Wanganui Herald*, 1 Dec 1880, p. 2.
47   Forster Y. Goring to Lieut-Col Roberts, 1 Dec 1880, in 'Murder of Mary Dobie by Tuhi'.

CHAPTER 7: THE MANY DEATHS

1   'The Te Namu murder', *Taranaki Herald*, 29 Nov 1880, p. 2.
2   'Burial of the deceased Miss Dobie', *Hawera and Normanby* Star, 1 Dec 1880, p. 2.
3   'Descriptive account of the crime', *Wanganui Herald*, 1 Dec 1880, p. 2.
4   'In Memoriam', *Observer*, 4 Dec 1880, p. 100.
5   'Descriptive account of the crime', *Wanganui Herald*, 1 Dec 1880, p. 2.
6   Stuart Newall, 28 Nov 1880, diary, MS-Copy-Micro-0740, ATL, Wellington.
7   'Tragedy at Opunake', *Evening Post*, 26 Nov 1880, p. 2.
8   Thomas Pole Hughson, diary, ARC 2002-851, R4/614, PA, New Plymouth, p. 15.
9   Editorial, Auckland *Star*, 1 Dec 1880, p. 2.
10   For doubts about Stannard's guilt or rape as a motive: 'Stannard not supposed to be the man', *Taranaki Herald*, 27 Nov 1880, p. 2; 'The Opunake Tragedy', *Wanganui Herald*, 27 Nov 1880, p. 2; 'Favourable opinion of Stannard', Auckland *Star*, 27 Nov 1880, p. 2; 'The tragedy at Opunake', *Evening Post*, 27 Nov 1880, p. 2; Christchurch *Star*, 27 Nov 1880, p. 2.
11   Editorial, Christchurch *Star*, 27 Nov 1880, p. 2.
12   'The Te Namu murder', *Taranaki Herald*, 27 Nov 1880, p. 2.
13   Auckland *Star*, 27 Nov 1880, p. 2.
14   'The Te Namu murder', *Taranaki Herald*, 27 Nov 1880, p. 2.
15   Inspector James to Commissioner, Armed Constabulary, Wellington, 4 Dec 1880, in 'Murder of Mary Dobie by Tuhi', P1 (Box 281) 1892/222, ANZ, Wellington.
16   William James, 'Notes of evidence and other documents re conviction of Tuhi for wilful murder', in inward letters, C490 149, J1 Box 283, 1881/5-50, ANZ, Wellington, pp. 69–71.
17   Dennis Connor, 'Notes of evidence and other documents', pp. 15–16.
18   Francis Hickey, 'Notes of evidence and other documents', pp. 76–77.
19   Thomas Knowles, 'Notes of evidence and other documents', p. 72.
20   Ibid., p. 73.
21   William Skinner, 28 Nov 1880, diaries 1880–82 (transcribed by Tania Pirini), ARC 2001-165, PA, New Plymouth.
22   Newall, 29 Nov 1880.
23   'Possibility of Maoris being the murderers', Auckland *Star*, 27 Nov 1880, p. 2.
24   Editorial, *NZH*, 29 Nov 1880, p. 4.
25   Ibid.
26   'The evidence at the inquest', Auckland *Star*, 29 Nov 1880, p. 2.
27   Ibid.
28   'Descriptive account of the crime', *Wanganui Herald*, 1 Dec 1880, p. 2.

29 'The evidence at the inquest', Auckland *Star*, 29 Nov 1880, p. 2; 'The murder at Opunake', Auckland *Star*, 30 Nov 1880, p. 2.
30 'Strong circumstantial evidence against Tuhi', *Evening Post*, 29 Nov 1880, p. 2.
31 'The murder at Opunake', Auckland *Star*, 30 Nov 1880, p. 2.
32 'The verdict, sentence of death passed', *Evening Post*, 15 Dec 1880, p. 3.
33 Inspector James to Commissioner, Armed Constabulary, Wellington, 4 Dec 1880, in 'Murder of Mary Dobie by Tuhi'.
34 'An important witness gone', Auckland *Star*, 29 Nov 1880, p. 2; 'The murder at Opunake', Auckland *Star*, 30 Nov 1880, p. 2.
35 'The murder at Opunake', Auckland *Star*, 30 Nov 1880, p. 2.
36 William Eyes, 'Notes of evidence and other documents', p. 13.
37 'Maori confesses to the murder', *Taranaki Herald*, 30 Nov 1880, p. 2.
38 'Descriptive account of the crime', *Wanganui Herald*, 1 Dec 1880, p. 2.
39 'Inquest on the body', *Taranaki Herald*, 30 Nov 1880, p. 2.
40 'Confession by the Maori', Auckland *Star*, 30 Nov 1880, p. 2.
41 'This day', *Evening Post*, 15 Dec 1880, p. 2.
42 'The Te Namu murder', *Taranaki Herald*, 1 Dec 1880, p. 2.
43 'Inquest on the body', *Taranaki Herald*, 30 Nov 1880, p. 2.
44 William James to Henry Reader, 10.30 p.m., 29 Nov 1880, telegram, in 'Murder of Mary Dobie by Tuhi'.
45 'Inquest on the body', *Taranaki Herald*, 30 Nov 1880, p. 2.
46 Christchurch *Star*, 30 Nov 1880, p. 2.
47 Skinner, 30 Nov 1880.
48 *Hawke's Bay Herald*, 30 Nov 1880, p. 2.
49 Editorial, *Taranaki Herald*, 2 Dec 1880, p. 2.
50 Editorial, *New Zealand Times*, 30 Nov 1880, p. 3; Editorial, *New Zealand Times*, 1 Dec 1880, p. 2.
51 Editorial, *NZH*, 30 Nov 1880, p. 4; Editorial, *NZH*, 1 Dec 1880, p. 4.
52 Editorial, Auckland *Star*, 1 Dec 1880, p. 2.
53 Ibid.
54 Editorial, *Taranaki Herald*, 2 Dec 1880, p. 2.
55 *Observer*, 11 Dec 1880, p. 109.
56 Ibid.
57 Editorial, *New Zealand Times*, 1 Dec 1880, p. 2; Editorial, *ODT*, 30 Nov 1880, p. 2.
58 'The Te Namu murder', *Taranaki Herald*, 1 Dec 1880, p. 2.
59 Editorial, *NZH*, 1 Dec 1880, p. 4.
60 Editorial, *ODT*, 30 Nov 1880, p. 2.
61 'Arrest of a Maori', *Evening Post*, 29 Nov 1880, p. 2.
62 Ibid.

CHAPTER 8: SON OF A DIVIDED WORLD

1 'The Opunake murder', *Hawera and Normanby Star*, 1 Dec 1880, p. 2.
2 'Description of the murderer', *The Budget*, 11 Dec 1880, p. 9; 'The Te Namu murder', *Taranaki Herald*, 9 Dec 1880, p. 2; 'Description of the murderer',

Auckland *Star*, 6 Dec 1880, p. 2; 'The Opunake murder', *Hawera and Normanby Star*, 1 Dec 1880, p. 2.
3   Kelly Keane, 'Ngā manu – birds – Symbols of status', Te Ara – the Encyclopedia of New Zealand, http://www.TeAra.govt.nz/en/nga-manu-birds/page-1, updated 22 September 2012.
4   Peter Wells, *Journey to a Hanging*, Auckland, 2014, pp. 8, 195, 249; Group photographs of Messrs Sullivan, Burgess, Kelly and Levy, PA2-2593, ATL.
5   Photograph of Tuhi, Mitchell pictures, P1/1810, State Library of New South Wales, Sydney; 'Wanted known, Photographs of Tuhi the murderer, At Deveril's, the Photographer, Cuba-street', *Evening Post*, 31 Dec 1880, p. 3.
6   *Thames Star*, 4 Dec 1880, p. 2; 'Entertainment, The Grand Sightascope Exhibition', *Thames Advertiser*, 11 Dec 1880, p. 2.
7   Wells, pp. 195, 249.
8   'The murder of Miss Dobie', *NZH*, 1 Dec 1880, p. 5.
9   'Tuhiata's history', *Taranaki Herald*, 21 Dec 1880, p. 2.
10 Ibid.; 'The Opunake murder', *Hawera and Normanby Star*, 1 Dec 1880, p. 2; Hone Pīhama, 'Notes of evidence and other documents re conviction of Tuhi for wilful murder', in inward letters, C490 149, J1 Box 283, 1881/5-50, ANZ, Wellington, p. 47; Tony Sole, *Ngāti Ruanui: A history*, Wellington, 2005, pp. 111–12.
11 Sole, pp. 10–20, 111–12.
12 Ibid., pp. 110, 127, 139–40.
13 'Miss Dobie's murderer', Auckland *Star*, 6 Jan 1881, p. 2; 'The Te Namu murder', *Taranaki Herald*, 1 Dec 1880, p. 2; 'The Te Namu murder', *Taranaki Herald*, 6 Dec 1880, p. 2; 'The murder of Miss Dobie', *NZH*, 1 Dec 1880, p. 5.
14 *Wanganui Herald*, 30 Nov 1880, p. 2.
15 'Native opinion of the murder', *Taranaki Herald*, 8 Dec 1880, p. 2.
16 'Tuhiata's history', *Taranaki Herald*, 21 Dec 1880, p. 2.
17 *Wanganui Herald*, 30 Nov 1880, p. 2.
18 'Tuhiata's history', *Taranaki Herald*, 21 Dec 1880, p. 2.
19 'Miss Dobie's murderer', Auckland *Star*, 6 Jan 1881, p. 2; 'Native affairs', *New Zealand Times*, 3 Jan 1881, p. 3.
20 Dr Langer Carey, 'Notes of evidence and other documents', pp. 32–33.
21 Whatarau, 'Notes of evidence and other documents', p. 66.
22 Pīhama, 'Notes of evidence and other documents', p. 49.
23 Tuharangatai, 'Notes of evidence and other documents', p. 54 and Rahiri, 'Notes of evidence and other documents', p. 56.
24 Rona Matiu, 'Notes of evidence and other documents', p. 64.
25 Harry Middleton, 'Notes of evidence and other documents', p. 42.
26 Sole, pp. 262–80.
27 Ibid., pp. 280–94.
28 A. S. Atkinson, 6 Mar 1866, diary, in Sole, p. 272.
29 Sole, pp. 272–78.
30 Lieutenant Colonel Gorton, 18 Jan 1866, in Guy H. Scholefield, *The Richmond Atkinson Papers*, vol. 2, Wellington, 1960, p. 202.
31 Sole, p. 276.
32 Ibid., pp. 325–27, 337.

33 West Coast Commission, second report, II Aspect of affairs after the rebellion, in *AJHR* 1880, G-2, xiv.
34 Lieut-Colonel Reader to the Defence Minister, 31 May 1881, in *AJHR* 1880, H.-18, p. 2; J. M. Roberts to Commissioner of Armed Constabulary, 27 May 1880, in *AJHR* 1880, H-10, pp. 22–24.
35 Lieut-Colonel Reader to the Defence Minister, 31 May 1881, in *AJHR* 1880, H.-18, p. 2.
36 Captain Knollys to Gordon, 31 Dec 1880, in *AJHR* 1881, A-1, pp. 23–26.
37 Stuart Newall, 21 May 1880, diary, MS-Copy-Micro-0740, ATL, Wellington.
38 J. M. Roberts to Commissioner of Armed Constabulary, 27 May 1880, in *AJHR* 1880, H-10, pp. 22–24.
39 Newall, 15, 16 June 1880.
40 Riemenschneider's report, 1 Jan 1881, in William Rolleston, diary Sept–Oct 1881, qMS-1716, ATL, Wellington. Note although the report is entered under 1 Jan 1881 the content refers to the events of September 1881 and the internal evidence shows clearly that it must have been written in late September or early October.
41 Rolleston to Elliott, 22 Dec 1880, Rolleston correspondence, 77-248-03/2, 77-248-5/6, 77-248-09/3, ATL, Wellington.
42 Hall to Oliver, Dec 1880, in Sir John Hall, papers 1880–82, MS-Papers-106171-1, ATL, Wellington.
43 Editorial, *NZH*, 24 Nov 1880, p. 4.
44 'Te Whiti on the murder', *Taranaki Herald*, 9 Dec 1880, p. 2.
45 'Latest from Parihaka', *Wanganui Herald*, 16 Dec 1880, p. 2.
46 'Native opinion of the murder', *Taranaki Herald*, 8 Dec 1880, p. 2.
47 Ibid.
48 'Opunake', *Hawera and Normanby Star*, 8 Dec 1880, pp. 2–3.
49 Ibid.
50 'Tuhiata's history', *Taranaki Herald*, 21 Dec 1880, p. 2.
51 *Bay of Plenty Times*, 4 Dec 1880, p. 2.
52 'News from the King Country', *NZH*, 17 Dec 1880, p. 5.
53 'Maori feeling', *Taranaki Herald*, 9 Dec 1880, p. 2.
54 'Native feeling towards Tuhi', Auckland *Star*, 1 Dec 1880, p. 2.
55 Dennis Connor, 'Notes of evidence and other documents', pp. 17–18.
56 'Full confession by the murderer, letter to his friends', *NZH*, 1 Dec 1880, p. 5.
57 'A poetical murder', *Manawatu Times*, 4 Dec 1880, p. 2. The quotation is from *Henry VI*, part III, act III, scene 3. Gloucester (Richard III) says, 'Why, I can smile and murder while I smile'.
58 Deuteronomy 28.26; Jeremiah 7.33, 16.4; Psalms 79.2.
59 George Taylor, 'Notes of evidence and other documents', p. 85.

CHAPTER 9: THE LAST BURNING QUESTION

1 Hadfield to Rolleston, 17 Dec 1880, 'Notes of evidence and other documents re conviction of Tuhi for wilful murder', in inward letters, C490 149, J1 Box 283, 1881/5-50, ANZ, Wellington.

2   J. Murray Gibbes, coroner, to Minister of Justice, Wellington, 12.20 p.m. 30 Nov 1880, urgent telegram, 'Notes of evidence and other documents'.
3   'The murderer's confession', *Taranaki Herald*, 1 Dec 1880, p. 2; 'Confession of the murderer', *New Zealand Times*, 1 Dec 1880, p. 2.
4   William Eyes, 'Notes of evidence and other documents', p. 11; Dennis Connor, 'Notes of evidence and other documents', pp. 14–15.
5   Stuart Newall, 21 May, 15 June 1880, diary, MS-Copy-Micro-0740, ATL, Wellington.
6   Knollys to the Governor, 31 Dec 1880, in *AJHR* 1881, A-1, p. 23.
7   'Our Auckland letter', *Thames Star*, 13 Dec 1880, p. 2.
8   Ibid.
9   Charles Hursthouse, 'Notes of evidence and other documents', p. 80.
10 Ibid., p. 92.
11 Dennis Connor, 'Notes of evidence and other documents', pp. 61–62.
12 'Trial of Tuhi, this day', *Evening Post*, 15 Dec 1880, p. 2.
13 Ibid., p. 3.
14 Hursthouse, 'Notes of evidence and other documents', pp. 81–82.
15 Ibid.
16 'The murder at Opunake', *Auckland Star*, 30 Nov 1880, p. 2.
17 Ibid.
18 Martin Coffey, 'Notes of evidence and other documents', p. 9.
19 George Taylor, 'Notes of evidence and other documents', pp. 84–87.
20 'End of the trial', *Wairarapa Daily Times*, 17 Dec 1880, p. 2.
21 Connor, 'Notes of evidence and other documents', pp. 17–18; Thomas Knowles, 'Notes of evidence and other documents', p. 73; Stock to Rolleston, 6 Dec 1880, 'Notes of evidence and other documents'.
22 'News and notes', *Hawera and Normanby Star*, 6 Nov 1880, p. 2.
23 'The Parihaka meeting', Auckland *Star*, 16 Dec 1880, p. 2; 'Wellington', *ODT*, 31 Dec 1880, p. 5.
24 'Wellington', *ODT*, 31 Dec 1880, p. 5.
25 Stock to Rolleston, 6 Dec 1880, 'Notes of evidence and other documents'.
26 Ministry of Justice, 'Utu', Māori Perspectives on Justice, http://www.justice.govt.nz/publications/publications-archived/2001/he-hinatore-ki-te-ao-maori-a-glimpse-into-the-maori-world/part-1-traditional-maori-concepts/utu; Tai Ahu, Rachel Hoare and Māmari Stephens, 'Utu: finding a balance for the legal Māori dictionary,' in The New Zealand Association for Comparative Law, Te Roopu Whakaritenga O Nga Ture, yearbook 16, 2010, Victoria University, pp. 22–25.
27 'Tuhi landing at Wellington', *Taranaki Herald*, 9 Dec 1880, p. 2.
28 *Taranaki Herald*, 4 Dec 1880, p. 2.
29 James to Reader, 2 Dec 1880, in 'Murder of Mary Dobie by Tuhi', P1 (Box 281) 1892/222, ANZ, Wellington.
30 'Further confession', *Taranaki Herald*, 9 Dec 1880, p. 2.
31 'Tuhi landing at Wellington', *Taranaki Herald*, 9 Dec 1880, p. 2.
32 'Description of the murderer', *The Budget*, 11 Dec 1880, p. 9.
33 Ibid.
34 Ibid.

35 Ibid.
36 'The Wellingon Gaol', *Evening Post*, 14 April 1881, p. 2.
37 Ibid.
38 'Prisoner to be defended', *Taranaki Herald*, 8 Dec 1880, p. 2.

CHAPTER 10: MAY GOD HAVE MERCY ON YOUR SOUL

1 Forwood to Crown Solicitor, 13 Dec 1880, 'Notes of evidence and other documents re conviction of Tuhi for wilful murder', in inward letters, C490 149, J1 Box 283, 1881/5-50, ANZ, Wellington.
2 *Evening Post*, 22 April 1879, p. 2.
3 *Evening Post*, 12 July 1880, pp. 2, 3; 'Meeting of creditors', *Evening Post*, 20 July 1880, p. 2.
4 'The Trial of Tuhi', *New Zealand Times*, 10 Dec 1880, p. 3.
5 Forwood to Crown Solicitor, 13 Dec 1880, 'Notes of evidence and other documents'.
6 Bryce to Rolleston, 16 Dec 1880, 'Notes of evidence and other documents'.
7 Forwood to Minister of Justice, 7 Dec 1880, in 'Murder of Mary Dobie by Tuhi', P1 (Box 281) 1892/222, ANZ, Wellington.
8 Ibid., margin note.
9 Forwood to Bell, 7.30 p.m., 7 Dec 1880, in ibid.
10 Bell to Col Reader, 8 Dec 1880, in ibid.
11 *Evening Post*, 13 Dec 1880, p. 2.
12 Ibid.
13 'Trial of Tuhi', *Evening Post*, 13 Dec 1880, p. 2.
14 'Trial of Tuhiata', *Taranaki Herald*, 9 Dec 1880, p. 2.
15 Dennis Connor, 'Notes of evidence and other documents', p. 17.
16 'The beer tax', *NZH*, 11 June 1880, p. 5.
17 'Fuller particulars of the trial', *Taranaki Herald*, 15 Dec 1880, p. 2.
18 *Evening Post*, 15 Dec 1880, p. 2.
19 Ibid.
20 'Trial of Tuhi', *Evening Post*, 13 Dec 1880, p. 3.
21 Ibid.
22 'Verdict and sentence', *New Zealand Times*, 16 Dec 1880, p. 2.
23 'The end of the trial', *Taranaki Herald*, 20 Dec 1880, p. 2.
24 'The judge's sentence', *Taranaki Herald*, 16 Dec 1880, p. 2.
25 'The verdict, sentence of death passed', *Evening Post*, 15 Dec 1880, p. 3.

CHAPTER 11: FOOD FOR THE BIRDS OF HEAVEN

1 'Execution of Tuhi', *Evening Post*, 29 Dec 1880, p. 2.
2 David Hastings, '150 Years of Great New Zealanders', *NZH*, 23 Nov 2013, p. 10.
3 'Execution of Tuhi', *Evening Post*, 29 Dec 1880, p. 2.
4 'Wellington', *ODT*, 31 Dec 1880, p. 5.
5 *Evening Post*, 28 Dec 1880, p. 2.

6   'Execution of Tuhi', *Evening Post*, 29 Dec 1880, p. 2.
7   Ibid.
8   'Letter from Tuhi to the Governor', *Evening Post*, 29 Dec 1880, p. 3.
9   'Wellington', *Colonist*, 4 Jan 1881, p. 3.
10 'Wellington', *ODT*, 31 Dec 1880, p. 5.
11 Stock to Rolleston, 6 Dec 1880, 'Notes of evidence and other documents re conviction of Tuhi for wilful murder', in inward letters, C490 149, J1 Box 283, 1881/5-50, ANZ, Wellington.
12 *Nelson Evening Mail*, 4 Jan 1881, p. 2.
13 'Execution of Tuhi', *Evening Post*, 29 Dec 1880, p. 2.
14 'Wellington', *Colonist*, 4 Jan 1881, p. 3.
15 'Execution of Tuhi', *Evening Post*, 29 Dec 1880, p. 2.
16 'The execution of Tuhi', *Timaru Herald*, 12 Jan 1881, p. 2.
17 'Execution of Tuhi', *Evening Post*, 29 Dec 1880, p. 2.
18 "Wellington', *Colonist*, 4 Jan 1881, p. 3.
19 'Execution of Tuhi', *New Zealand Times*, 30 Nov 1880, in *Evening Post*, 29 Dec 1880, p. 2.
20 'The execution of Tuhi', *West Coast Times*, 7 Jan 1881, p. 2.
21 'Execution of Tuhi', *Evening Post*, 29 Dec 1880, p. 2.
22 Ibid.
23 Ibid.
24 Ibid.
25 'The execution of Tuhi', *New Zealand Times*, 30 Nov 1880, in *West Coast Times*, 7 Jan 1881, p. 2.
26 'Execution of Tuhi', *Evening Post*, 29 Dec 1880, p. 2.
27 Ibid.
28 'The execution of Tuhi', *New Zealand Times*, 30 Nov 1880, in *West Coast Times*, 7 Jan 1881, p. 2.
29 'Execution of Tuhi', *Evening Post*, 29 Dec 1880, p. 2; 'Wellington', *Colonist*, 4 Jan 1881, p. 3.
30 'Wellington', *Colonist*, 4 Jan 1881, p. 3.
31 'The execution of Tuhi', *New Zealand Times*, 30 Nov 1880, in *West Coast Times*, 7 Jan 1881, p. 2.
32 'Execution of Tuhi', *Evening Post*, 29 Dec 1880, p. 2.
33 Ibid.
34 'The execution of Tuhi', *New Zealand Times*, 30 Nov 1880, in *West Coast Times*, 7 Jan 1881, p. 2.
35 Ibid.
36 'The Terrace gaol, Wellington', *West Coast Times*, 20 Feb 1903, p. 3.

CHAPTER 12: POLITICS AND REVENGE

1   'The Parihaka meeting', Auckland *Star*, 16 Dec 1880, p. 2; see also *Wanganui Herald*, 16 Dec 1880, p. 2.
2   'Parihaka meeting', *Taranaki Herald*, 20 Dec 1880, p. 2; 'Te Whiti's speech', *Taranaki Herald*, 21 Dec 1880, p. 2.

3   'The Parihaka meeting', Auckland *Star*, 18 Dec 1880, p. 2; 'The Parihaka meeting', *Taranaki Herald*, 22 Dec 1880, p. 2; 'The close of the Parihaka meeting', *NZH*, 21 Dec 1880, p. 5.
4   'The Parihaka meeting', *Evening Post*, 20 Dec 1880, p. 2.
5   'The sale of the Waimate Plains', *NZH*, 16 Dec 1880, p. 5; 'Jobbery going on', *Taranaki Herald*, 15 Dec 1880, p. 2; 'The sale of the Waimate Plains', *NZH*, 21 Dec 1880, p. 5; 'Sale of Waimate Plains', *Taranaki Herald*, 17 Dec 1880, p. 2.
6   'Sale of the Parihaka land', *Taranaki Herald*, 21 Dec 1880, p. 2.
7   Editorial, Auckland *Star*, 1 Dec 1880, p. 2.
8   'The last Maori trouble in New Zealand', *Illustrated London News*, 28 Jan 1882, pp. 76–78.
9   Thomas Gudgeon, *Defenders of New Zealand*, Auckland, 1887, p. 313. Although the book is attributed to Thomas Gudgeon it was written by his son Walter, a captain in the Armed Constabulary at the time of the Parihaka invasion; see David Green, 'Gudgeon, Walter Edward', *Dictionary of New Zealand Biography*, Te Ara – the Encyclopedia of New Zealand, http://www.TeAra.govt.nz/en/biographies/2g23/gudgeon-walter-edward, updated 2 October 2013. The italics in the second quote in this paragraph are my emphasis.
10 Rolleston to B. J. Harman, 19 Oct 1881, William Rolleston letter book, 1880–1881, 77-248 Q0683, ATL, Wellington; Walter Gudgeon, autobiography, fms079, ATL, p. 62.
11 'The native difficulty', Christchurch *Star*, 5 Oct 1881, p. 3.
12 *Timaru Herald*, 2 Dec 1881, p. 2.
13 William Skinner, 21 Oct 1881, diaries 1880–82 (transcribed by Tania Pirini), ARC 2001-165, PA, New Plymouth.
14 Hazel Riseborough, *Days of Darkness, the Government and Parihaka 1878–1884*, revised edition, Auckland, 2002, p. 154.
15 Riemenschneider's report, 1 Jan 1881, in William Rolleston, diary Sept–Oct 1881, qMS-1716, ATL, Wellington.
16 Skinner, 19 Sept 1881.
17 Ibid.
18 Ibid., 20 Sept 1881.
19 Ibid., 21, 26 Sept 1881.
20 Anton Fromm, 21 Sept 1881, diary (M. Neuman, trans.), ARC 2002-721, PA, New Plymouth.
21 Ibid., 22 Sept 1881.
22 Skinner, 1 Oct 1881.
23 Riseborough, *Days of Darkness*, pp. 157–62.
24 Stapp, 8 Oct 1881 no. 138, 10 Oct no. 140, 12 Oct no. 141, 14 Oct no. 143, 14 Oct no. 144, 14 Oct no. 146, 15 Oct no. 147, 15 Oct no. 148, 19 Oct no. 156, 31 Oct no. 167/81, 1 Nov no. 168/81, in Taranaki Militia and Volunteers Letter Book, May 1880–Nov 1881, Militia and Volunteers Office, New Plymouth, May 1880–Nov 1881, ARC 2001-359 MS096, PA, New Plymouth.
25 'Recruiting for Taranaki', *Taranaki Herald*, 27 Sept 1881, p. 2.
26 'Native affairs on the West Coast', *Timaru Herald*, 1 Nov 1881, p. 2.

27 Kate Mickelson, *The Clearing: A history of Opunake*, Christchurch, 1999, pp. 102, 111.
28 'Opinions of the press', *Otago Witness*, 29 Oct 1881, p. 21.
29 Thomas Pole Hughson, diary, ARC 2002-851, R4/614, PA, New Plymouth, pp. 20–21.
30 Stuart Newall, 3 Nov 1881, diary, MS-Copy-Micro-0740, ATL, Wellington.
31 Ibid., 5 Nov 1881.
32 I am grateful to Maata Wharehoka for helping to identify the most likely spot.
33 Newall, 5 Nov 1881.
34 Tony Sole, *Ngāti Ruanui: A history*, Wellington, 2005, p. 387.
35 'The demolished whares', *NZH*, 21 Nov 1881, p. 5.
36 James Cowan, *The New Zealand Wars and the Pioneering Period*, vol. 2, Wellington, 1983 (reprint), pp. 517–18.
37 *New Zealand Times*, 8 Nov 1881, p. 2.
38 'Night visit to Parihaka', *NZH*, 21 Nov 1881, p. 5.

CHAPTER 13: IN MEMORIAM

1 *Taranaki Herald*, 6 Jan 1881, p. 2.
2 *Evening Post*, 7 Jan 1881, p. 2.
3 'Round the mountain', *Taranaki Herald*, 24 Mar 1908, p. 3.
4 William Skinner, 21 Oct 1881, diaries 1880–82 (transcribed by Tania Pirini), ARC 2001-165, PA, New Plymouth.
5 'Mrs Ellis Rowan's visit to Taranaki', *Taranaki Herald*, 3 April 1894, p. 2; 'From Wanganui to New Plymouth', *Wanganui Herald*, 15 Dec 1883, p. 2; 'A trip to Opunake', *Taranaki Herald*, 11 Jan 1892, p. 2.
6 'From Wanganui to New Plymouth', *Wanganui Herald*, 15 Dec 1883, p. 2.
7 'A trip to Opunake', *Taranaki Herald*, 11 Jan 1892, p. 2.
8 Thomas Pole Hughson, 'Historical sketch re early settlement of the West Coast with special reference to Rahotu', Hughson family papers, folder 1, ARC 2002-851, PA, New Plymouth; Len Stimpson, interview with the author, 16 Aug 2014.
9 Dudley Dyne, *Famous New Zealand Murders*, Auckland, 1969, p. 47.
10 Iolanthe Small to John McCraw, 19 Oct 2003, in J. D. McCraw, Correspondence, NZMS 1889, AL.
11 Ibid.
12 'Our hearts are sad', *NZH*, 14 June 1911, p. 8.
13 'Old tragedy recalled', Auckland *Star*, 1 Dec 1925, p. 9.
14 Hall, 'Further papers', p. 4.
15 'Report of Constable John Shearman re part taken [by] him in reference to the detection of Tuhi the murderer of Miss Dobie', in 'Murder of Mary Dobie by Tuhi', P1 (Box 281) 1892/222, ANZ, Wellington.
16 C. A. L. Treadwell, 'The Trial of Tuhiata', *The New Zealand Railways Magazine*, vol. 8, no. 7, 1 Nov 1933, p. 32.
17 Bee Dawson, *Lady Travellers: The tourists of early New Zealand*, Auckland, 2001, pp. 87–97.

18 Lydia Wevers, *Country of Writing: Travel writing and New Zealand 1809–1900*, Auckland, 2002, pp. 192–94.
19 I am grateful to Len Stimpson and Darrell Hickey for identifying the spot.
20 'Miss Dobie waylaid while sketching', Auckland *Star*, 26 Nov 1880, p. 3; 'Confession by a Maori', Auckland *Star*, 30 Nov 1880, p. 2.
21 J. Murray Gibbes, coroner, to Minister of Justice, Wellington, 12.20 p.m. 30 Nov 1880, urgent telegram, 'Notes of evidence and other documents re conviction of Tuhi for wilful murder', in inward letters, C490 149, J1 Box 283, 1881/5-50, ANZ, Wellington; 'The murderer's confession', *Taranaki Herald*, 1 Dec 1880, p. 2; 'Confession of the murderer', *New Zealand Times*, 30 Nov 1880, p. 2.
22 Dyne, *Famous New Zealand Murders*, p. 51; 'Death of Te Whiti', *Taranaki Daily News*, 19 Nov 1907, p. 2.
23 Kate Mickelson, *The Clearing: A history of Opunake*, Christchurch, 1999, p. 110.
24 W. K. Howitt to editor, *NZH*, 7 Feb 1928, p. 12; 'Days of Te Whiti', *NZH*, 7 Feb 1938, p. 12.
25 J. D. McCraw, 'Life of H. B. Dobbie', MSX 2730, ATL, Wellington, p. 2; Richard J. Hall, 'Further papers re H. B. Dobbie and family', MS-Papers-6602, ATL, Wellington, pp. 5–6.
26 Bertha V. Goring, 'Orange Leaves and the Simple Life', unpublished manuscript, 1905, pp. 6–7, 39.
27 Ibid., pp. 52–53.
28 Ibid., p. 115.
29 Ibid., p. 179.
30 Alfred Lord Tennyson, 'In Memoriam', VII, XXVII, XXIX, LXXXVII, XCVIII, C, CI, CVII, CXVIII, in *Tennyson's Poetical Works*, London, undated.
31 Goring, 'Orange Leaves', p. 130.
32 Ibid., p. 143.
33 Tennyson, 'In Memoriam', XCV, CXII; Melvyn Bragg, *In Our Time*, BBC Radio 4, 30 June 2011; Alfred Gatty, *A Key to Tennyson's 'In Memoriam'*, London, 1900, pp. 25, 124, 131.
34 Frederick Locker, *Poems*, London, 1868, p. 60.

BIBLIOGRAPHY

ABBREVIATIONS

AL Auckland Libraries
ATL Alexander Turnbull Library
AWMML Auckland War Memorial Museum Library
ANZ Archives New Zealand
NZETC, New Zealand Electronic Text Collection
NZH New Zealand Herald
ODT Otago Daily Times
PRO Public Records Office, UK
PA Puke Ariki

FAMILY PAPERS

Dobbie/Dobie Family Album, courtesy Peter Dobbie and Anne McCarthy, NZMS 1889, AL.
Dobbie/Dobie, Herbert Main, last will and testament, catalogue ref: prob 11/2213 image ref: 371, PRO, UK.
Dobie, Bertha and Mary, 'Diary of a Trip to the Hot Lakes', courtesy Babette Tregent, NZMS 1889, AL.
Dobie, Bertha and Mary, *The Voyage of the May Queen*, Margaret Drake Brockman (ed.), Braunton, 1992.
Drake Brockman, Hugh, 'Descendants of Robert Dobbie', courtesy Hugh Drake Brockman, NZMS 1889, AL.
Goring, Bertha V. and Mary Dobie, 'A Trip to the South Seas', in *New Zealand Graphic and Ladies Journal,* 11-part series, 13 Feb–23 Apr 1892.
Goring, Bertha V., 'Orange Leaves and the Simple Life', unpublished manuscript, 1905, courtesy Peter Dobbie and Anne McCarthy, NZMS 1889, AL.
Hall, Richard J., papers relating to the Dobbie family, MS-Group-0836, ATL, Wellington.
——, 'Further papers re H. B. Dobbie and family', MS-Papers-6602, ATL, Wellington.
McCraw, J. D., 'Life of H. B. Dobbie', unpublished manuscript, MSX 2730, ATL, Wellington.
——, correspondence, NZMS 1889, AL.

ARCHIVES

Alpers, O. T. J., papers, correspondence re Parihaka incident newspaper controversy, MS-Papers-0086, ATL, Wellington.
Anderson, Henry, research notes, 89-249-9/05, ATL, Wellington.

Armed Constabulary Papers, 1880/237, 1880/1227, 1880/1241, 1880/1261, 1880/1264, 1880/3469, ANZ, Wellington.
Blanchett, Thomas Baker, 'Colonial Experiences', diary, ARC 2001-465, PA, New Plymouth.
Buckley, Eugene Charles, scrapbook, ARC 2011-090, PA, New Plymouth.
Fromm, Anton, diary (M. Neuman, trans.), ARC 2002-721, PA, New Plymouth.
Gordon, Sir Arthur Hamilton, papers 1855–1912, Micro-MS-Coll-20-1628-1637, ATL, Wellington.
Gudgeon, Walter, autobiography, fMS-079, ATL, Wellington.
Hall, Sir John, papers 1880–1882, MS-Papers-106171-1, ATL, Wellington.
——, correspondence Oct–Dec 1880, MS-Copy-Micro-0694-29, ATL, Wellington.
Hammond, Thomas Godfrey, Taranaki material, fMS-Papers-4456-01, ATL, Wellington.
Hughson, Thomas Pole, diary, ARC 2002-851, R4/614, PA, New Plymouth.
——, 'Historical sketch re early settlement of the West Coast with special reference to Rahotu', Hughson family papers, folder 1, ARC 2002-851, PA, New Plymouth.
——, 'The History of the Hughson Family', ARC 2002-851, PA, New Plymouth.
Hursthouse, Charles Wilson, diaries and notebooks, E26.10, E26.16, ARC 2001-153, E26.17, ARC 2001-157, PA, New Plymouth.
——, Te Whiti's speech extracts from Hursthouse diary (transcripts), ARC 2001-153, MS 040.
——, telegraph book, Aug–Dec 1880, ARC 2003-213.
Justice ministry correspondence on the Dobie inquest in inward letters, C490 148, J1 Box 282, 1880/5602-5770, ANZ, Wellington.
Lush family papers, MS 780, AWMML, Auckland.
Lush, Vicesimus, journal and diaries, MS 2008/9, AWMML, Auckland.
Mair, Gilbert, diary 1880–1881, MSX-4224, ATL, Wellington.
Messenger, W. B., Military Reminiscences, Messenger family [094] ARC 2002-482, PA, New Plymouth.
'Murder of Mary Dobie by Tuhi', P1 (Box 281) 1892/222, ANZ, Wellington.
New Zealand Press Association records, (MS-Group-1143), ATL, Wellington.
Newall, Stuart, diary, MS-Copy-Micro-0740, ATL, Wellington.
'Notes of evidence and other documents re conviction of Tuhi for wilful murder', in inward letters, C490 149, J1 Box 283, 1881/5-50, ANZ, Wellington.
Outhwaite, William, 'A trip to Manupirua, a journal kept by William Outhwaite, May–Aug 1876', NZMS 1243, AL, Auckland.
Parker, William, diary, MS-Copy-Micro-0510, ATL, Wellington.
Richmond Atkinson papers, inward & outward correspondence 1870–1899, MSY-2776, ATL, Wellington.
Rolleston, William, 1831–1903: papers (77–248), ATL, Wellington.
——, letter book, 77-248 Q0683, ATL, Wellington.
——, correspondence, 77-248-03/2, 77-248-5/6, 77-248-09/3, ATL, Wellington.
——, diary Sept–Oct 1881, qMS-1716, ATL, Wellington.
Rusden, George William, letters to W. B. D. Mantell and others, MS265, AWMML, Auckland.

Salmon, Herbert W., papers relating to the history of the New Zealand Armed Constabulary, MS 92/82, AWMML, Auckland.
Skinner, William, diaries 1880–82 (transcribed by Tania Pirini), ARC 2001-165, PA, New Plymouth.
Taranaki Militia and Volunteers, letter book, Militia and Volunteers Office, New Plymouth, May 1880–Nov 1881, ARC 2001-359 MS096, PA, New Plymouth.
Tauranga City Library, Tauranga Mission Cemetery, also known as the Military Cemetery, formerly Otamataha Pā, register of headstones and plaques and copy of inscriptions, 929.5TAU.
Taylor, Charles, diary, MSX-8142, MSX-8143, ATL, Wellington.
Tennyson family, libraries, letters, manuscripts and papers, Tennyson Research Centre, Lincolnshire, UK.
United Press Association, letter books 1878–1896, 75-213-077, ATL, Wellington.
——, UPA minute book 1879-1880, MSY6830, ATL, Wellington.
Ward, Joseph, diary 1 Jan–31 Dec 1880, MS2293, ATL, Wellington.
Yarborough, Gertrud Flora Cooke, 'Scrapbook of watercolours, prints and photographs', E-881-f, ATL, Wellington.

SELECT BIBLIOGRAPHY

Ahu, Tai, Rachel Hoare and Māmari Stephens, 'Utu: finding a balance for the legal Māori dictionary', in The New Zealand Association for Comparative Law, Te Roopu Whakaritenga O Nga Ture, yearbook 16, 2010, Victoria University, pp. 22–25.
Bassett, Judith, *Sir Harry Atkinson*, Auckland, 1975.
Belich, James, *Making Peoples: A History of the New Zealanders*, Auckland, 1996.
——, *The New Zealand Wars and the Victorian Interpretation of Racial Conflict*, Auckland, 1998.
Bilcliffe, John, *Well Done the 68th: The Durhams in the Crimea and New Zealand 1854–1866*, Chippenham, 1995.
Binney, Judith, *Redemption Songs: A Life of Te Kooti Arikirangi Te Turuki*, Auckland, 1995.
Bohan, Edmund, *Climates of War: New Zealand in conflict 1859–69*, Christchurch, 2005.
Bragg, Melvyn, *In Our Time*, BBC Radio 4, 30 June 2011, http://www.bbc.co.uk/programmes/b0124pnq.
Byrnes, Giselle (ed.), *The New Oxford History of New Zealand*, Auckland, 2009.
Campbell, Caroline Anne, 'In the Realm of the Imagined: Representation and identity in Australasian illustrated junior fiction 1890–1920', PhD, Victoria University, Wellington. Also available at http://hdl.handle.net/10063/969.
Chapman, J. K., *The Career of Arthur Hamilton Gordon, First Lord Stanmore*, Toronto, 1964.
Church, Ian, 'Te Rei Hanataua, Hone Pihama', *Dictionary of New Zealand Biography*, Te Ara – the Encyclopedia of New Zealand, http://www.TeAra.govt.

nz/en/biographies/2t28/te-rei-hanataua-hone-pihama, updated 30 October 2012.
Collins Quotation Finder, Glasgow, 2001.
Cowan, James, *The New Zealand Wars and the Pioneering Period*, vol. 2, Wellington, 1983 (reprint).
Cumming, Constance Gordon, *At Home in Fiji*, New York, 1883, pp. 303-4. Also available at Open Library, https://archive.org/stream/athomeinfiji00cummgoog#page/n10/mode/1up.
Dalton, B. J., *War and Politics in New Zealand 1855–1870*, Sydney, 1967.
Dawson, Bee, *Lady Travellers: The tourists of early New Zealand*, Auckland, 2001.
Dobson, Austin, rev. Katharine Chubbuck, 'Lampson, Frederick Locker (1821–1895)', *Oxford Dictionary of National Biography*, Oxford University Press, 2004. Also available at http://0-www.oxforddnb.com.www.elgar.govt.nz/view/article/16896, accessed 5 Oct 2014.
Dyne, Dudley G., *Famous New Zealand Murders*, Auckland, 1969.
Ehrenreich, Barbara and Dierdre English, *For Her Own Good*, New York, 2nd edition, 2005.
Fieldhouse, D. K., 'Sir Arthur Gordon and the Parihaka Crisis, 1880–1882', *Historical Studies: Australia and New Zealand* 10, no. 37 (1961): 30–49.
Garner, Jean, *By His Own Merits: Sir John Hall – pioneer, pastoralist and premier*, Christchurch, 1995.
Garnett, Richard, 'Locker, Arthur (1828–1893)', rev. Joseph Coohill, *Oxford Dictionary of National Biography*, Oxford University Press, 2004. Also available at http://0-www.oxforddnb.com.www.elgar.govt.nz/view/article/16892, accessed 5 Oct 2014.
Gasgoyne, F. J. W., *Soldiering in New Zealand, Being Reminiscences of a Veteran*, London, 1916, NZETC, http://nzetc.victoria.ac.nz/tm/scholarly/tei-GasSold.html.
Gatty, Alfred, *A Key to Tennyson's* In Memoriam, London, 1900. Also available at http://www.gutenberg.org/files/36637/36637-h/36637-h.htm.
Green, David, 'Gudgeon, Walter Edward', *Dictionary of New Zealand Biography*, Te Ara – the Encyclopedia of New Zealand, http://www.TeAra.govt.nz/en/biographies/2g23/gudgeon-walter-edward, updated 2 October 2013.
Gudgeon, T. W., *Defenders of New Zealand*, Auckland, 1887, pp. 359–60. Also available at Early New Zealand Books, University of Auckland, http://www.enzb.auckland.ac.nz/document?wid=2188&action=null.
Hastings, David, '150 Years of Great New Zealanders', *New Zealand Herald*, 13 Nov 2013.
——, *Over the Mountains of the Sea*, Auckland, 2006.
Hill, Richard S., *The Colonial Frontier Tamed: New Zealand policing in transition, 1867–1886, The History of Policing in New Zealand*, vol. 2, Wellington, 1989.
Houghton, Walter E., *The Victorian Frame of Mind*, Yale, 1985.
Jackson, Keith and Alan McRobie (eds), *Historical and Political Dictionary of New Zealand*, Rangiora, 2008.
Kelly Keane, 'Ngā manu – birds – Symbols of status', Te Ara – the Encyclopedia of New Zealand, http://www.TeAra.govt.nz/en/nga-manu-birds/page-1, updated 22 September 2012.

Keenan, Danny, *Wars Without End: The Land Wars in nineteenth-century New Zealand*, Auckland, 2009.

——, 'Te Whiti-o-Rongomai III, Erueti', *Dictionary of New Zealand Biography*, Te Ara – the Encyclopedia of New Zealand, http://www.teara.govt.nz/en/biographies/2t34/te-whiti-o-rongomai-iii-erueti, updated 30 October 2012.

King, Michael, *The Penguin History of New Zealand*, Auckland, 2003.

Locker, Frederick, *Poems*, London, 1868.

Locker-Lampson, Frederick, *My Confidences. An autobiographical sketch addressed to my descendants*, London, 1896. Also available at Open Library, https://archive.org/stream/myconfidencesan00lamgoog#page/n10/mode/2upp.

McCraw, J. D., 'H. B. Dobbie – Fern Enthusiast', *New Zealand Journal of Botany*, 1988, vol. 26: 171–78.

——, 'Dobbie, Herbert Boucher', *Dictionary of New Zealand Biography*, Te Ara – the Encyclopedia of New Zealand, http://www.TeAra.govt.nz/en/biographies/3d9/dobbie-herbert-boucher, updated 30 October 2012.

Mickelson, Kate, *The Clearing: A history of Opunake*, Christchurch, 1999.

Ministry of Justice, 'Utu', Māori Perspectives on Justice, http://www.justice.govt.nz/publications/publications-archived/2001/he-hinatore-ki-te-ao-maori-a-glimpse-into-the-maori-world/part-1-traditional-maori-concepts/utu.

Munro, Jessie, *The Story of Suzanne Aubert*, Auckland, 1996.

Newbury, Colin, *Patronage and Politics in the Victorian Empire: The personal governance of Sir Arthur Hamilton Gordon (Lord Stanmore)*, New York, 2010.

Orange, Claudia, *The Treaty of Waitangi*, Wellington, 1988.

Platts, Una, *Nineteenth Century New Zealand Artists: A guide and handbook*, Christchurch, 1980.

Porter, Frances, *Born to New Zealand: A biography of Jane Maria Atkinson*, Wellington, 1989.

Quarm, Roger, 'Locker, Edward Hawke (1777–1849)', *Oxford Dictionary of National Biography*, Oxford University Press, 2004. Also available at http://0-www.oxforddnb.com.www.elgar.govt.nz/view/article/16893, accessed 5 October 2014.

Rice, Geoffrey W. (ed.), *The Oxford History of New Zealand*, 2nd edition, Auckland, 1992.

Riseborough, Hazel, *Days of Darkness, the Government and Parihaka 1878–1884*, revised edition, Auckland, 2002.

——, 'Bryce, John', *Dictionary of New Zealand Biography*, Te Ara – the Encyclopedia of New Zealand, http://www.TeAra.govt.nz/en/biographies/2b44/bryce-john, updated 1 September 2010.

Ross, Walter Hugh, 'Matakātea, Wiremu Kingi or Moki', in *An Encyclopaedia of New Zealand*, A. H. McLintock (ed.), Wellington, 1966. Also available at http://www.teara.govt.nz/en/1966/matakatea-wiremu-kingi-or-moki.

Ryan, P. M., *The Raupō Dictionary of Modern Māori*, Auckland, 2012.

Scholefield, Guy H., *The Richmond Atkinson Papers*, vol. 2, Wellington, 1960.

Scott, Dick, *Ask that Mountain: The story of Parihaka*, Auckland, 2006.

Sheridan, Richard Brinsley, *The Rivals*, DVD, Bristol Old Vic, 2004.

Sinclair, Keith, *A History of New Zealand*, Auckland, 1980.
——, *Kinds of Peace: Maori people after the wars, 1870–85*, Auckland, 1991.
Skinner, W. H., *Reminiscences of a Taranaki Surveyor*, New Plymouth, 1946 (Christchurch, 1984, reprint).
Sole, Tony, *Ngāti Ruanui: A history*, Wellington, 2005.
Sorrenson, M. P. K., *Ko Te Whenua Te Utu, the Price is the Land*, Auckland, 2014.
Stokes, Evelyn, 'Völkner, Carl Sylvius', *Dictionary of New Zealand Biography*, Te Ara – the Encyclopedia of New Zealand, http://www.TeAra.govt.nz/en/biographies/1v5/volkner-carl-sylvius, updated 30 October 2012.
Tennyson, Alfred Lord, *Tennyson's Poetical Works*, London, undated.
Treadwell, C. A. L., 'The Trial of Tuhiata', *The New Zealand Railways Magazine*, vol. 8, no. 7, 1 Nov 1933, p. 32.
Tyler, W. P. N., 'Gordon, Arthur Hamilton', *Dictionary of New Zealand Biography*, Te Ara – the Encyclopaedia of New Zealand, http://www.teara.govt.nz/en/biographies/2g13/gordon-arthur-hamilton, updated 1 September 2010.
Ward, Alan, *A Show of Justice: Racial 'amalgamation' in nineteenth century New Zealand*, Auckland, 1995.
Wells, B., *The History of Taranaki*, New Plymouth, 1878 (Christchurch, 1976, reprint).
Wells, Peter, *Journey to a Hanging*, Auckland, 2014.
Wevers, Lydia, *Country of Writing: Travel writing and New Zealand 1809–1900*, Auckland, 2002.
Whangarei Art Museum, 'Portraits of Place: Creating identity in early Whangarei. Works by Beatrix (1887–1945) & Herbert Dobbie (1852–1940)', media release, 7 October–1 December 2002.
Williams, Herbert W., *A Dictionary of the Maori Language*, Wellington, 1975.
Williamson, Jill, 'Outhwaite of Eden Hill, the Life and Times of an Auckland settler 1841–1879', BA (Hons) thesis, University of Auckland, 1999, NZMS1243.

NEWSPAPERS AND MAGAZINES

Bay of Plenty Times
The Budget
Colonist
Evening Post
Free Lance
The Graphic
Grey River Argus
Hawera and Normanby Star
Hawke's Bay Herald
Illustrated London News
Manawatu Herald
Manawatu Times
Nelson Evening Mail
New Zealand Graphic and Ladies' Home Journal
New Zealand Herald

New Zealand Times
Observer, Auckland
Otago Daily Times
Otago Witness
Press
Star, Auckland
Star, Christchurch
Taranaki Herald
Taranaki News
Thames Advertiser
Thames Star
Timaru Herald
The Times
Wairarapa Daily Times
Wanganui Chronicle
Wanganui Herald
West Coast Times

WEBSITES

AtoJsOnline, Appendices to the Journal of the House of Representatives, http://atojs.natlib.govt.nz/cgi-bin/atojs
British Newspapers 1600-1950, http://0-find.galegroup.com.www.elgar.govt.nz/bncn/start.do?prodId=BNWS&userGroupName=auclib
Dictionary of New Zealand Biography, http://www.mch.govt.nz/what-we-do/websites-we-run/dictionary-new-zealand-biography
Early New Zealand Books, Auckland University, http://www.enzb.auckland.ac.nz/
Female School of Art, UCL Bloomsbury Project, http://www.ucl.ac.uk/bloomsbury-project/institutions/female_school_of_art.htm
Ministry of Justice, http://www.justice.govt.nz/
New Zealand Electronic Text Collection, Victoria University, Wellington, http://nzetc.victoria.ac.nz/
Opunake Cottage, http://shaw.org.nz/house.html
Oxford Dictionary of National Biography, http://0-www.oxforddnb.com.www.elgar.govt.nz/
New Zealand Association for Comparative Law, Te Roopu Whakaritenga O Nga Ture, http://www.victoria.ac.nz/law/nzacl/Yearbook%2016-2010.aspx
Open Library, https://openlibrary.org/
Project Gutenberg, http://www.gutenberg.org/
Papers Past, http://paperspast.natlib.govt.nz/cgi-bin/paperspast
Te Ara, the Encyclopaedia of New Zealand, http://www.teara.govt.nz/en
Times Digital Archive, http://0-find.galegroup.com.www.elgar.govt.nz/ttda/start.do?prodId=TTDA&userGroupName=auclib

ACKNOWLEDGEMENTS

Neither Mary nor Bertha had any children but fortunately the descendants of Herbert preserved some of their writings and illustrations. I am grateful to various members of the extended family for their generosity in giving me access to these rich but previously unpublished sources about life in New Zealand more than a century ago. Chief among them are Peter Dobbie and Anne McCarthy who allowed me to borrow and copy the Dobbie/Dobie family album and Bertha's unpublished memoir, 'Orange Leaves and the Simple Life'. Babette Tregent was equally generous in providing a copy of the 'Diary of a Trip to the Hot Lakes' which reveals so much about the Dobie sisters on their trip to the Pink and White Terraces.

Tim Dobbie in Auckland and Richard Hall in Brisbane were of great help in tracking down the people who held the material as was Professor John McCraw, who researched and wrote articles acknowledging Herbert Dobbie's place as a pioneer in New Zealand botany. I am also grateful to Professor McCraw for access to the correspondence and pictures of Iolanthe Small – a plantswoman who worked for many years in the fernery at Pukekura Park in New Plymouth – who was helping him with his research when she visited Mary's grave in 2003.

Hugh Drake Brockman in Britain is the great authority on the Dobbie/Dobie family tree and I thank him for giving me the benefit of his extensive research. Among other things it explained what might otherwise have been a puzzle, the different spellings of the family name at different points in history. I am grateful to Hugh, also, for permission to reproduce some of Mary's sketches from *The Voyage of the May Queen*.

Bertha's memoir, the family photo album and a copy of the Hot Lakes diary are now in the Sir George Grey Special Collections at Auckland Libraries, thanks to Peter Dobbie and Barbara Tregent. Also deposited with the Grey Collections are a copy of the family tree compiled by Hugh Drake Brockman and the correspondence between Professor McCraw and Iolanthe Small.

As part of the research, I retraced Mary's steps in the last few days of her life and was fortunate to be welcomed with some good, old-fashioned Taranaki hospitality, first from Steve Anker at Inglewood. At Parihaka – where Mary drew Te Whiti-o-Rongomai a few days before her death – special thanks go to Te Akau Wharehoka and Maata Wharehoka. Maata was a knowledgeable and insightful guide. As well as imparting a sense of the place and what it still means, she helped to identify the likely spot where Mary drew her famous sketch of Parihaka in November 1880.

Similarly, the people of Ōpunake were both hospitable and knowledgeable. I am grateful to Trish Stevenson (whose husband is descended from the man who hired Stannard to catch a horse) for her guidance and help with contacts. Among them was Len Stimpson who was a deep well of knowledge about the history and geography of the area and how stories like the Dobie murder are preserved in popular memory. He and Darrell Hickey showed me the scene of the crime, exactly where it was marked on a newspaper map in 1880.

I also retraced the Dobie sisters' trip to the Bay of Plenty where the staff at Tauranga City Library – Debbie McCauley, Lee Switzer and Stephanie Smith – were of great help in clarifying references to the Mission Cemetery in the Dobie sisters' diary.

They were among many professional librarians and archivists who have helped with the research, digging out old files and offering suggestions. At the Alexander Turnbull Library in Wellington they included Marion Minson, Graham Langton, Shaun McGuire and Helen Smith. At Auckland Libraries they included David Verran and staff at the central library's Auckland Research Centre and Kate de Courcy and staff at the Sir George Grey Special Collections.

At the National Archives in Wellington, special thanks to Sonya Behrnes for tracking down the summary of evidence given in Tuhi's trial, Jonathan Newport for the valuable file of John Shearman's attempt to win recognition for his part in the investigation and also to Karamdeep Sahota. Lucy Macfarlane, Mike Gooch, Bill Howard and Chanelle Carrick were of great assistance at Puke Ariki. Thanks also to Martin Collett and the archives staff at the Auckland War Memorial Museum Library and to Maree Saunders, collection co-ordinator at the Whangarei Art Museum.

Grace Timmins at Tennyson Research Centre, Lincoln, UK, was of great help in tracking down references to Mary's murder in the correspondence of Lionel Tennyson. And Robert Woodley clarified a point about the picture of Tuhi held at the Mitchell Library, State Library of New South Wales.

I am grateful to Lydia Wevers, director of the Stout Research Centre in Wellington, for reading a draft of the manuscript and making a number of helpful suggestions. At Auckland University Press, thanks go to director Sam Elworthy who was an enthusiastic supporter of this project from the moment it was suggested. And also to editor Anna Hodge, designer Katrina Duncan, cover designer Kalee Jackson, copy editor Rebecca Lal, proofreader Mike Wagg, and Margaret Samuels.

Thanks also to artist Micaela Lowis for drawing the map of the measured ground of Taranaki about the time of the Dobie murder and the Parihaka crisis.

And, finally, thanks to Clarissa Hastings who, with patience and good humour, listened to the agonies of the research, the weighing of the evidence and the writing. And who also made the definitive link between the epitaph recorded by Mary in the Hot Lakes diary and the tomb of Laurence Manion. Was it all worth it? I certainly hope so.

INDEX

About Town column 9–10, 80
Allan, Alexander 161, 163
Anderson, Henry 161
Aotea 115
Aotearoa 115
Apanui 34
Armed Constabulary 1, 3; road building 48–9, 120; Māori dislike of 62; and Parihaka invasion 53, 175–80
Armed Constabulary cemetery 6–7, 95, 184, 188, 190
Atkinson, Harry: pressures Grey 47; exploits settler fear for political purposes 47, 174
Auckland *Star* 4, 27; and Bertha 22–3; reviews *The Rivals* 28; doubts Stannard is the killer 86; on motive 82, 90, 98, 100–1, 109, 110; Māori attitude to Dobie murder 124; links Parihaka and Te Whiti to murder 170, 188; and Parihaka invasion 175

Baker, Ebenezer: likely source of Tuhi's seventh confession 140
Bayley, Emanuel 64, 67, 75
Bayley's farm 45
Bay of Plenty 29, 38, 42, 186, 191
Bay of Plenty Times 123
Belich, James 54
Bell Block 48
Bell, Harry 148, 149
Blanchett, Thomas: friendly relations with Māori 61–2
British Empire 10, 48, 117–18, 140, 142
Browne, James Oakley: describes Terrace Gaol 44–5; describes hanging of Tuhi 161–6
Browning, Robert 12
Bryce, John 148, 178, 182, Fig. 66; regards Te Whiti a dangerous fanatic 58; advocates invasion of Parihaka 102, 121, 169; invades Parihaka 170, 175, 177
Buckley, Eugene Charles: painting of Tuhi and crime scene 135, 172, 186, 187, Fig. 56

Cameron, General Duncan 118
Carey, Dr Langer: post-mortem examination 76, 87–90; rejects rape as motive 89, 93, 139; and stains on moleskins 116; demonstrates Mary's injuries 105, 124, 130; and threepenny piece 103, 108, 133–4
Carlisle 13, 14
Carlyle 48
Christchurch *Star*: speculates on killer 98; on Tuhi's first confession 107; revenge 171, 178
Chute, General Trevor 118, 119, Fig. 64
class: on *May Queen* 8–9; and ideal of womanhood 10, 14; Dobie sisters' attitude to 16, 21–3
Coffey, Martin: storekeeper 64, refuses credit to Tuhi 68, 71; sells Mary a pencil 68; and threepenny piece 103–4, 108, 133–4; and Tuhi's drinking 152–3
The Colonist 159, 161
Connor, Dennis: sees Mary walking towards Te Namu 68, 69; guards Tuhi 124–5
Cowan, James 178
Cowie, Bishop William 26, 42
crime scene: morning after the murder 79; searched 90–1; measured 99; in twenty-first century 186–7; pictured Figs 49, 52, 56, 83
Cumming, Constance Gordon: refuses to pay fee for painting at Pink and White Terraces 29; precedes Dobie sisters to Fiji 41; as artist and hero 186

Defenders of New Zealand 170
Deveril's photo shop 113–14
Disraeli, Benjamin 12
Dixon, Henry 17, 30
Dixon, Mary 14, 30
Dixon, Thomas 30, 31
Dobbie family *see* Dobie family
Dobbie, Herbert Boucher 25, 27, 28, Fig. 11; training 14–15; migrates to NZ 15; multiple talents 15; name change 15; betrothal to Charlotte Gilfillan 15; marriage 42; *New Zealand Ferns* 15, 43, 65; in Samoa and Fiji 37; memoir 188–9
Dobie, Bertha: on last day of Mary's life 1, 3, 66, 72; character of 10, 15; memoirs 10, 12, 189–90; and Disraeli and Gladstone 12; and Tennyson 12, 26, 96, 190–2; royalist and imperialist 12, 191–2; education 14; and *May Queen* diary 14, 16, 17–18, 27; and class 21–3, 27; and poetry 26, 42–3, 96, 190; and Māori 27, 33, 34; and 'Diary of a Trip to the Hot Lakes' 30, 33; and White Terraces 32–3, 37; and Forster Goring 36–7, 42–3; and gossips 42; wedding 42–3; dines with Te Whiti and Tohu 52–3; at Mary's funeral 96; possible author of 'In Memoriam' 96; and Mary's tombstone 188–92; pictured Figs 2, 5, 10, 34, 84
Dobie, Ellen 8, 27, 37, Fig. 57; and drunken captain 10, 13; as story teller 14; children 13–14, Fig. 10; told Mary gored by bull 77; worries about Mary 62; returns to England 181–2
Dobie, Ellen Goodrich (Mary and Bertha's sister) 14
Dobie family: genealogy 10–16; name change 15; reaction to Mary's death 77
Dobie, Herbert Main 13, 24
Dobie, Mary: on day she was murdered 1–4, 63, 65, 68–70, 72–6; sketches in the *Graphic* 1, 11; search for 3–4, 72–4; character 3, 9–10, 20, 39–40; gravestone 5–6, 181–2, 183–4, 190, Figs 4, 80, 81, 82; and *May Queen* diary 9, 16, 17–18; and *May Queen* sailors 8–9, 19–21; education 14; sense of humour 16–17, 18; contrast with Bertha 18–19; love of animals 19; and class 21–3, 26; as Lydia Languish in *The Rivals* 27–8, 42; and Māori 27, 33, 34, 50; and 'Diary of a Trip to the Hot Lakes' 30–3; Whakatāne studies 34; and *New Zealand Ferns* 42, 65; describes Parihaka 52; describes Te Whiti 52; sketches Parihaka 53–4, Fig. 41; draws Te Whiti 53–4, Figs 42, 43; contradictions in Parihaka account 54–6; opinion of Te Whiti 58; criticised after death 110; funeral 95–6; pictured Figs 1, 5, 10, 12, 20, 47, 48
Dobie sisters: social life 16, 25–6, 27; and te reo Māori 27; and racism 34; as pioneers 34, 38, 52; and horror stories 35–6; tramping outfit 39; in Samoa and Fiji 37–42, 48; praised and criticised over South Pacific trip 41–2; at Cape Egmont 49–50; visit Parihaka 50–62; pictured Figs 5, 10, 31
Durham Light Infantry 30
Dyne, Dudley 187

Ebbett, Mary Ann 75, 88
Ebbett, William 75
Egmont, Camp 76, 95
Egmont, Cape 49, 97, 174, Fig. 38
Egmont, Mount *see* Taranaki, Mount
Empire Hotel, Ōpunake 64
Empire Hotel, Wellington 155
epitaphs 5–7, 30, 181, 190–2
Erueti *see* Te Whiti-o-Rongomai
Evening Post: news of murder 4; and revenge 83–4; and death penalty 83–4; criticises *New Zealand Times*

83–4; and Ned Kelly 84; motive 111; covers Tuhi's arrival in Wellington 150–1; covers Tuhi's execution 161–6; mocks Parihaka meetings 168, 172

Evening Star 182

Eyes, William: Tuhi's friend and neighbour 67; sees Mary walking towards Te Namu 68–9; sees Tuhi riding up the Te Namu road 103; receives visit from Tuhi on night of the murder 104–5; delivers verdict at inquest 106–7

Famous New Zealand Murders 187

fear: Pākehā fear 3, 5, 61, 84–5, 100, 172–3, 179; in June 1879 44–6; exploited for political purposes 59, 174; fades 61; Māori fear 118–23, 179; and Dobie murder 139–40, 141–2, 185; and tragedy 191

Female School of Art 14

Fiji 37–42, 185, 186, 191, Figs 31, 32, 33

Forwood, Charles, Tuhi's defence counsel: tactics 132, 149–50, 151–2, 154; background 146–7; delays trial 147–8; seeks help from government 148–9; closing arguments 155–6; attends execution 161

Fromm, Anton 173

'Funeral March in Saul' 95

Gate Pā, Battle of 6, 30

Gilfillan, Charlotte (Tottie): and Herbert Dobie 15–16; and Dobie sisters 26; marriage 40, 42; pictured Fig. 19

Gladstone, William 12

Gordon, Sir Arthur Hamilton: and the Dobie sisters 40, 41; reaction to murder 80–1; and Tuhi's letter 159–60; absence during Parihaka crisis 174

Goring, Bertha *see* Dobie, Bertha

Goring, Forster Yelverton: on fatal day 3, 66, 72, 73; describes Mary's body 3, 74; family background 31;

military career 31–2, 60; and Māori 33–4; and Bertha Dobie 36–7, 42–3; Transferred to Taranaki 44; ordered to arrest ploughmen 48; road building 48–9; at Cape Egmont 49; and foundation of Ōpunake 64–5; orders arrest of Tuhi 92; and Parihaka invasion 175–6; pictured Figs 21, 23, 35, 50, 84

Gorton, Lieutenant Colonel 119

Grand Sightascope 113–14

The Graphic: renowned for illustrations 1, 11; on Mary's character 9; edited by Arthur Locker 11; and Thomas Hardy 11; and the Dobie sisters in Fiji 41; publishes Mary's sketches of Te Whiti and Parihaka 53–4

Grey, Sir George: meets settler deputation 46–7; sceptical of settler fears 59

Guard, Betty 2, 182

Gudgeon, Walter: Dobie murder affects troops at Parihaka invasion 170–1, 175; argues government in the right over Parihaka 171; time-shifting error 171, 180, 187–8

Hadfield, Octavius 128, 130, 158, 161, Fig. 72

Hallam, Arthur 190, 191

Hall, Sir John 174

Handed, Constable 72

Hardy, Thomas 11

Harris, John Chantry: describes Tuhi's execution 161–6

Hawera Star: Tuhi's demeanour at inquest 112; businessman bailed up on Pungarehu road 138; Māori react to Dobie murder 122–3

Hickey, Francis 99, 129

Hickey, John 90

Hikurangi 124

Hinemoa: takes Tuhi to Wellington 142–3, 147; takes witnesses to Wellington 149–51 *passim*; takes Mary's tombstone to Ōpunake 167

Hiroki: kills surveyor 60; Mary comments on 61; sanctuary at Parihaka 60, 93; arrest urged 101–2, 109, 121; arrested 177; pictured Fig. 79

Hot Lakes: and Constance Gordon Cumming 29, 186; Dobie sisters visit 32–7; pictured Figs 22, 23, 24, 25, 26, 27, 28, 29, 30

Hughson, Thomas: challenges Catholic priest 46; plays tennis with Mary 50; tension with Māori 62; guard duty 64; describes unloading steamer 66; and murder suspects 76–7; follows Dobie murder story 82, 97; and road building 120; and Parihaka invasion 175–6

Humphries, George 161

Hursthouse, Charles: questions Tuhi 105–6; publishes Tuhi's letters 125; and Tuhi's second confession 127, 129; abilities and motives questioned 131; first confession ruled inadmissible 132–3; comments on Tuhi's demeanour 143; pictured Fig. 67

Illustrated London News: sketch of people travelling to Parihaka 51; links Parihaka crisis to Dobie murder 70, 171, Fig. 75

Inglewood 48

inquest on Mary Dobie: held in billiard room 93–4; evidence at 102–8; Tuhi's appearance and conduct 112–13

inquest on Tuhi 166

Irthington 12, 13, 43

interpreters and translators: abilities and motives questioned 59

Izard, Charles 151, Fig. 70

James, Superintendent William: leads investigation 81; measures crime scene 99, 187; telegraphs Tuhi's first confession 106

Jeremiah 125

Journey to a Hanging 114

Kawino, Tamati 104

Kelly, Ned 84, 114

Kereopa Te Rau 113, 114

Ketemarae 115

King Country 124

Knollys, Captain Louis 131, 169

Knowles, Thomas: arrests Tuhi 92–3; searches Tuhi's whare 99–100

Ladies' Benevolent Society 27

Locker, Arthur 11, 14, 53, Fig. 6

Locker family 10–12, 14

Locker, Edward Hawke 11

Locker, Eleanor 12, Fig. 8

Locker-Lampson, Frederick 12, 192, Fig. 7

Locker, William 10–11

Lord Worsley 2, 55, 69, 182

looting: at Parihaka 178, 179

Lush, Martin: in *The Rivals* with Mary 27–8

Lush, the Reverend Vicesimus: shock at Mary's death 81

Lyttelton Times: opposes Parihaka invasion 175

McGrath, constable: sees Mary on road 69–70; on Stannard's bloodstains 102

McKeon, Sergeant Arthur: leads search for Mary 72–3; holds Stannard on suspicion of murder 76; convinced of Stannard's guilt 87, 91–2

Mahaena 115

Manion, Private Laurence 30, 190, 192

Manawatu Herald: on motive 82

Manawatu Times 125

Marshall, David 163, 164–5, Fig. 73

Matakātea, Wiremu Kingi: hero of Te Namu 2, 115, 182; and *Harriet* 2; and *Lord Worsley* 2, 55, 69; moves to Parihaka 55–6, 69; arrested 56; allows trading post at Ōpunake

64–5; views Mary's body 98–9; pictured Fig. 44

Matiu, Rona: and alcohol 67; with Tuhi on evening of murder 104; on Tuhi's drinking 117; angry with Tuhi 124

Maungatapu murders 113

May Cottage 25, 26, 27, Fig. 18

May Queen 15–23 *passim*

May Queen diary: 27, 33, 50, 185, Figs 15, 16, 17

Middleton brothers' hotel *see* Telegraph Hotel

Middleton, Harry: on duty on day of Dobie murder 67; described Tuhi on day of murder 71–2; on Tuhi's drinking habits 117, 153–4

Miha 104

Mission Cemetery 6, 30, 31, 184

Moturoa, Battle of 32, 60, 115

Napier Prison 113, 114

Napoleon 11, 34, 138

Napoleonic Wars 11

Nelson Jail 113

Nelson, Lord Horatio 11

Newall, Captain Stuart: hears of Mary's death 76–7; records story of Mary gored by a bull 77, 96; follows Dobie murder story 82; records rumour about Te Whiti's aggressive intentions 100; disdain for Te Whiti 120; officers' shooting parties 121; and Parihaka invasion 176; arrest of Te Whiti 177

New Plymouth: Premier Grey visits in June 1879 46–7, 59

New Zealand Ferns 15, 43, 65, 184

New Zealand Graphic 37

New Zealand Herald: and Ellen Dobie 27; reviews *The Rivals* 28; sceptical of settler fears 59; reaction to murder 80, 124; motive 85, 100–2, 108–9, 110, 111; and Tuhi's mother 114; support for action against Parihaka 121; destruction of Parihaka 179; rape at Parihaka 179

New Zealand Times: women vulnerable 110; calls for vengeance 82–3; motive 108; looting of Parihaka 178–9

Ngā Rauru 60, 118

Ngā Ruahine 32, 60

Ngāti Ruanui 55, 114, 118, 119

Observer: and Mary's character 9; reaction to Dobie murder 80; publishes 'In Memoriam' 96, 189, 190, Fig. 58; publishes letter criticising Mary 110

Ōeo 66, 70–3 *passim*, 123

Ōhinemutu 29, 33

Ōkato 48

Ōpōtiki 29, 31, 37

Ōpunake: description of 50, 63–5; as social melting pot 67; during Parihaka crisis 175; changing face of 182–4

Ōpunake redoubt: description of 3, 50, 63–4; dismantled 182–3; pictured Fig. 46

'Orange Leaves and the Simple Life' 189

Otago Daily Times: women vulnerable 110; doubts possibility of fully understanding Dobie murder 111; reports Tuhi's seventh confession 140–1; reports Tuhi's remorse 160

Ōtahi Stream 69, 74, 129, 182, 186

Ovalau 37, 38

Paki, Caroline 103

Parihaka 51–61 *passim*; campaign against surveyors 44–5, 49; monthly hui 49, 51, 65, Figs 40, 75; population of 50–1, 54; description of 51–2; Mary's description of 52–6, Fig. 41; contrasted with Ōpunake 64, 67; land sales 121, 169; people distance themselves from Tuhi 122–3; wary of Pākehā reaction to Dobie murder 123; linked to Dobie murder 109–10, 169–72, 187–9; invasion of 48, 53, 175–9, Figs 77, 78

Parnell 25, 42
Parris, Robert: overcrowding at Parihaka 55; dispute with Te Whiti 56
Pīhama, Hone: chooses coexistence with Pākehā 55; land grant 55; tensions in his family 55 ; Te Whiti's attitude to 55; sells produce 65; tribal affiliations 114–5; on fatal day 70–1, 75, 153; on fear 118–19, 121, 169, 179; says Tuhi not quarrelsome 117; pictured Fig. 45
Pink Terraces *see* Pink and White Terraces
Pink and White Terraces 28–33 *passim*, 36–7, 138, 185
Poneke 144
population 51, 54, 59
Poverty Bay massacre 60
Prendergast, Chief Justice James: declares Treaty of Waitangi 'nullity' 57; rules Tuhi's first confession inadmissible 132, 151; rejects drunkenness defence 152; sums up 156; sentences Tuhi to death 156–7; role in Parihaka invasion 174
Press Association 87, 161
Pūnehu 65–8 *passim*, 92, 115, Fig. 59
Pungarehu: and news of Mary's death 76–7; base of AC 120; pictured Fig. 65

racism / racial prejudice 34, 98, 97, 107
Rāhotu 176, 183, Fig. 76
Rangitoto 25
rape: motive 5, euphemisms for 82, 179; Carey rejects rape as motive 89–90; cannot be ruled out 139; Prendergast rejects rape as motive 156
raupatu / confiscation: as Māori custom 57; history of 168–7; *Lyttelton Times* questions legitimacy of 175
Reader, Colonel Henry 105, 143, 149
Reed, Micaiah 147, 161, 163, 166
Reilly, Thomas 70, 71

revenge, vengeance: calls for 77–8, 80, 83–4; volunteers seek revenge at Parihaka invasion 171, 178; as possible motive for murder 97, 101; and utu 142
Richmond, Henry 45
Riseborough, Hazel 59
The Rivals 27–8, 42, 81
Riverhead 27
Roberts, Lieutenant Colonel John 76, 77, 95, 175, Fig. 51
robbery: as possible motive 5, 88, 108–9, 138–9, 141–2
Rolleston, William 148, 171, 177
Rotomahana, Lake 28
Rotorua, Lake 29
rumour: about Bayley's farm murders 45; about gun-running ship 45; about Stannard 86; stimulated by fear 45, 123, 172; rapid spread 82; pathological power of 109; about Te Whiti's people preparing for war 100; about Ōpunake closed to Māori 123; about Māori muster army 172–3

Samoa 28, 37, 39, 42, 50
St Mary's Church, Parnell 42
St Peter's Church, Wellington 158
Seffern, William 60
Shearman, Constable John: identifies Tuhi as prime suspect 91–2; campaigns for promotion 185
Sheridan, Richard Brinsley 27
Skinner, William: observes ploughmen arrested 48; buys supplies from Pīhama 65; reaction to murder 80; follows murder case in diary 82, 100; on motive 107; reacts to Te Whiti's speech of Sept 1880 173; records rumour of Māori attack 173; visits Mary's grave 172, 182; pictured Fig. 61
Small, Iolanthe 184
Snipe 32, 68
Sole, Tony: on Hone Pīhama 55; Te Whiti asserts tino rangatiratanga

56; Chute's campaign 119
Stannard, Walter: background 69–70; sees Mary on road to Te Namu 70; at Telegraph Hotel 71; reaction to news of murder 75, 83; bloodstains 72, 75, 87, 91; arrested 75–6, 85; character 85–7, 97–8; support for 87, 90, 97–8; evidence against weak 102, 105; acquitted 105
Stapp, Major Charles: recruits volunteers in 1879 crisis 47–8; men resign 51; recruits volunteers in 1881 crisis 173, 174; pictured Fig. 37
Stevenson, John 71, 75, 105, 152
Stratford 174
Stock, Archdeacon Arthur: arranges prison visitor for Tuhi 140; visits Tuhi 158; with Tuhi at execution 160–6 *passim*; pictured Fig. 74
Stony River 57, 188
suspects 97, 99
Swindley, Captain 34–6

Tahiti 115
Tamaitoha, Erueti 35, 36
Taranaki Herald: reaction to murder 4, 79–80, 122–4; recalls massacres 60; on Te Namu's beauty 68–9, 186–7; and Stannard 85–6; reports three Māori arrested over murder 98; and first confession 106; motive 108, 110–11; describes Tuhi's mother 114; and Tuhi 116, 144; and second confession 130; and prospective executioners 154–5; Taranaki, Mount 1, 44, 52, 186
Tarawera, Lake 29
Tarawera, Mount 28
Tattersall, John 21
Tauranga 6, 30, 184, 190
Taylor, Charles 45, 61
Taylor, George: records Tuhi's dream 126; writes letter for Tuhi 135; records Tuhi's third confession 135–40, 151, 156, 172, 183, 185
Te Arawa, tribe 29
Te Aro 146, 147, 148

Te Huripoto 114
Te Karea *see* Tuhi
Te Kooti Arikirangi 35, 60
Telegraph Hotel 64, 66–7, 75, 93, 182, 183, Fig. 60
telegraph office 70, 75, 99, 129
Te Namu Pā 1–3 *passim*, 65, 68–9, 99, Fig. 3
Te Ngutu-o-te-manu, Battle of 32, 60, 115
Tennyson, Alfred Lord: and Dobie sisters 12, 26, 96, 190; and *In Memoriam* 190–2
Tennyson, Lionel: marries Eleanor Locker 12; reaction to murder 81; pictured Fig. 9
Terrace Gaol, The: description of 113, 140, 144–5, 160
Te Ranga, Battle of 6, 30
te reo Māori 135
terrorism 5, 59, 101
Tess of the d'Urbervilles 11
Te Teko 32, 34
Te Wairoa 29
Te Whakatōhea 35
Te Wharengaro 115, 116
Te Whiti-o-Rongomai: and *Lord Worsley* wreck 2, 69; campaign against land confiscation 44–5, Fig. 36; settler fear of 44–5; and Dobie sisters 45, 50, 52–4, 62; hui 50–1; poses for Mary Dobie 53–5, 58, 177; and Parris 56; and tino rangatiratanga 56–7; and Māori custom 57; and raupatu / confiscation 57, 168–9; and pacifism 57–8, 61, 118, 123, 179; translation problems 58, 59; portrayed as fanatic 58, 61; discourages drinking 67; blamed for Dobie murder 97, 100, 101, 109, 110, 170; and land being 'inundated' 121; condemns Tuhi 122, 167; and land sales 168–9; Sept 1880 speech 172–3; arrested 177
Thames Star 168–9
Tītahi 114

Tītokowaru 60, 173, Fig. 63; 1868 uprising 32, 60, 115, 118, 119
Tohu Kākahi 44, 52–3, 168, 177; speech about 'measured ground' 49, 57, 58
Tosland, Joseph: searches for Mary 72; describes body 90; searches crime scene 90
Trafalgar, Battle of 11
translators *see* interpreters and translators
Tuhi: and ploughmen 65; character and background 65, 71, 114–18; and debts 67; moleskin trousers 67–8, 71, 75, 91, 102–3; on fatal day 67–8, 71, 70, 71–2, 76, 104–5; and alcohol 71–2, 152–4; arrest of 92–3; at inquest 102–7, 124; first confession 105–6, second 127–33, third 125; fourth 135–42, 183; fifth 127–8, 143; sixth 128; seventh 140–1; demeanour 105, 112, 143, 159; description of 112–14; pictures of 113–14, 135, 172, 187, Figs 56, 62; fight with father 116; portentous dream 126; letters to family 125–6; trial 147–57; letter to governor 159–60; execution of 160–6
Tuhiata *see* Tuhi
Tūhourangi tribe 29

United Press Association *see* Press Association
Urenui 47, 48, 59, 174
utu 142

Vanua Levu 37
Viti Levu 37, 40
Völkner, Carl 35, 60, 98, 113

volunteers: recruited in 1879 crisis 47–8; resign and disband following year 61; and 1881 crisis 176, 179; influenced by Dobie murder 170–1, 174–5; pictured Fig. 77

Waikato 2, 31, 51
Waikato tribe 60, 115
Wairarapa 51
Waimate Plains 60, 118, 168
Waitara 48, 174
Waitangi, Treaty of 56–7, 174
Waitematā Harbour 24
Waimate Plains 60
Waingongoro River 50, 57, 60, 119, 120
Waioeka River 31
Waitotara River 118, 119
Warihi, Hitakara 158
Wellington 143
Wellington *Chronicle* 161
Wells, Peter 114
Wevers, Lydia 29, 186
Whanganui 81, 99, 115, 118
Whangārei 22, 189
Whakatāne 32, 34, 35
White Cliffs massacre 60
Whiteley, the Reverend John 60
White Terraces *see* Pink and White Terraces
Wilson, T. of Urenui 47, 48, 59
Wilson, William: searches for Mary 72; finds body 73–4; arrests Stannard 76; describes body 89–90; searches crime scene 90
Written Stone of Gelt 12

Yasawa Islands 37, 38